COMMITTED

CONFESSIONS OF A FANTASY FOOTBALL JUNKIE

Mark St. Amant

SCRIBNER
New York   London   Toronto   Sydney

SCRIBNER
1230 Avenue of the Americas
New York, NY 10020

Copyright © 2004 by Mark St. Amant

First Scribner trade paperback edition 2005

SCRIBNER and design are trademarks of Macmillan Library Reference USA, Inc.,
used under license by Simon & Schuster, the publisher of this work.

For information regarding special discounts for bulk purchases,
please contact Simon & Schuster Special Sales:
1-800-456-6798 or business@simonandschuster.com

DESIGNED BY ERICH HOBBING

Text set in Electra

Manufactured in the United States of America

10 9 8 7 6 5 4 3 2 1

Library of Congress Control Number: 2004052114

ISBN-13: 978-0-7432-6756-4
ISBN-10: 0-7432-6756-7
ISBN-13: 978-0-7432-6757-1 (Pbk)
ISBN-10: 0-7432-6757-5 (Pbk)

For Celia,
for more reasons
than I could possibly list here.

Contents

1

Last Season

"Dude, I get more f***ing e-mails from you than from the girl I'm seeing!"

This was the exasperated, fourteen-word e-mail that told me once and for all, like a bucket of freezing-cold water to the face, that I had officially become a fantasy football junkie.

It was December 2002 and I was desperately trying to make a deal before the trade deadline cut me off. My target was my friend, former coworker, and Felon Fantasy League–mate, Mark "Big Dog" Moll, co-owner of the eponymous Big Dogs. You see, my team—Acme Fantasy Football, Inc., named in honor of the perpetually frustrated cartoon character Wile E. Coyote—was 6-4 and tied with three other squads for the last of four coveted FFL playoff slots. But I was way behind in total points, our league's first tiebreaker. I knew I couldn't pull ahead and make the playoffs without acquiring a total stud and having an absolutely huge final four weeks. Enter Mr. Total Stud, Kansas City Chiefs running back Priest Holmes. I sent Big Dog approximately sixteen e-mails within the span of, oh, three minutes, frantically trying to get him to trade me Priest for near-stud Buffalo Bills running back Travis Henry—whom I didn't really need now that Saints RB Deuce McAllister had emerged into a weekly stud—and Quincy Morgan, the Cleveland Browns receiver who had just had a not-a-chance-in-hell-will-he-do-it-again 118-yard, 2-TD game against Jacksonville. Sell high.

Henry and Morgan for Priest was a very fair deal. And by *very fair*, I mean that I was trying to rob my friend blind. Undeterred by being compared to his latest love interest, I sent Big Dog e-mail number seventeen, the cloak of cyberspace allowing me to grin like Beelzebub himself while typing. "You need a stud receiver," I reasoned, "and I need a stud running back. Henry's almost as good as Priest this year, and Morgan steps right into your starting lineup at wide receiver." Then I added every savvy owner's favorite trade-talk phrase: "This deal helps both teams."

But Big Dog was one of the more obstinate traders in our league, and, dammit, he just wasn't biting. His reply came swiftly and cracked me across the cheek like a mean-ass bitch-slap. "Lucky me," his e-mail read, dripping with sarcasm. "You've got some serious free time on your hands, my friend."

I hated it when they said that! I knew I spent more time on fantasy football than most of the other owners in my league combined. I knew that visiting fantasy football message boards and chatting with total strangers about strategy, trades, and lineups officially made me the league's lone *total* fantasy geek. My devotion to the game was all too evident.

But the truth was I *didn't* have much free time on my hands at all. I was way behind schedule on a couple of print ads I was supposed to be writing for behemoth tax/audit consultant Deloitte & Touche, a client of the Connecticut ad agency for whom I was working at the time. Not that writing ads was splitting the atom—visual of earnest-looking Deloitte employee; cheesy headline touting said earnestness; and earnest corporate tagline "The answer is the people of Deloitte & Touche," which would be a logical response to "Which giant accounting firm do I really *not* want to write ads for anymore?"—but it nevertheless required *some* effort. Still, that didn't stop me from pouring all of my valuable time into my fantasy football team.

There was simply nothing more important in the world than acquiring Priest Holmes from Big Dog. Not the health of my wife or family. Not the growing nuclear threat in North Korea, or al Qaeda. Not Martha Stewart's legal troubles, SARS, or the disturbing number of Ashton Kutcher–related news stories dominating supermarket checkout lanes. And sure as hell not the Deloitte ad I *wasn't* writing at the moment.

No, my only lucid thought on that December day was trying to beat Big Dog into submission until he finally caved and said, *OK, for the love of God, I'll give you Priest for a couple pieces of string . . . a sack of used jock-straps . . . anything! Just stop e-mailing me!*

After I presented the deal from thirty-four different angles, he finally e-mailed me the words I had been dreading from the very start: "I have to talk to Erik." This is fantasy football code for "I'll say anything right now to get you to stop harassing me, you fucking psycho, and I'll even pretend to bring it up with my co-owner. But I can tell you right now there is no way in hell we're making this trade."

Priest Holmes was the missing link to something that, over the preceding five seasons, had become my personal Holy Grail: winning the Felon Fantasy League Super Bowl. Not that we had a trophy or anything Grail-ish—the winner just got $600 in cash, which I'd gladly accept, but always considered pretty unimaginative. Countless leagues across the country had trophies the winner could proudly set on his desk at work or on his mantel at home or, to *really* rub it in on his vanquished leaguemates, have surgically attached to his head.

That said, it wasn't a trophy or a big pile of money that mattered: it was what a league championship would have represented to me—vindication. It was the reward I wanted for five years of being the most devoted, hands-on GM in the league. (Note: we fantasy football players like to call ourselves GMs, short for "general managers," possibly because having a lofty imaginary title makes us feel less guilty for blowing off the work required by the titles on our real-life business cards.) Yes, in the last half decade I'd reeled in one third-place finish, two sixth-place finishes, and, in the utterly forgettable, injury-plagued 2000 season, a dismal ninth. And if I didn't do something to change my fortunes for the 2002 season, I—well, I didn't know what would happen. But it would no doubt involve lots of sulking, followed by lots of swearing, followed, inevitably, by my cranium exploding.

Even worse, another failed season and I might have to come to terms with my identity as a loser. For once in my life, I was actually giving a 100 percent effort, and I didn't know if I could take *still* coming up short. Let me explain by giving you a brief history of one Mark St. Amant, *competitor*:

Grade school—I was the kid who just wanted to make friends with everyone, hated confrontation, and always made sure everyone was included in the kickball games—from the shy, bookish girls with a mortal fear of flying red, rubber balls, to the weird, pale, unathletic boys who typically wandered alone near the woods eating bugs, studying their own hands, or staring up at nimbus cloud formations. And if it took sitting out my turn at "bat" so someone else could have a chance to play, so be it.

High school—I was the kid who was satisfied with C-plus/B-minus grades, i.e., good enough to get by, but not so great that they were a result of actually trying. I got the occasional A in things that piqued my interest: creative writing, English, and other courses. But my GPA was always anchored down by two-ton D-pluses in physics and calculus. I knew damn well my future did not hinge on knowing why an atom does whatever the hell an atom does, or what function of X is a subset of B. Of course, I also fell short of being a three-sport varsity athlete—the Mt. Olympus of high school sports achievement—when my coach, the very serious Mr. Briggs, who never really liked me anyway, informed me that I hadn't played/won enough matches to earn a tennis letter to go with my hockey and soccer letters. I just shrugged and said, "Sure, Mr. Briggs. Whatever." At least I think that's how it all went down; I was still wildly hungover from an all-night graduation party.

At a good-but-certainly-not-great college—I settled right into my familiar roller coaster ride of scholastic apathy mixed with occasional bouts of manic, Herculean achievement . . . for every A-minus in British literature, I'd counter with an F in psychology. I played soccer well enough to be a decent player on a fair Division III team, but not so well that I didn't eventually quit out of sheer boredom with five games to go my senior year.

Out in the real world—I did enough to get by, make a decent living, and win the occasional award that no one (except other advertising pinheads like me) gave a shit about, but I was never going to be the star copywriter whose drive and talent would make his boss whisper reverently to the other agency bigwigs, "That kid, my friends, is the future of advertising."

What I'm saying is, I'd always been utterly nonconfrontational. I'd been in exactly *one* fight in my entire life, and that was only because my sadistic older brother and his delinquent friends set up a ring in our backyard and used me and *my* friends as human cockfighters, transforming a peaceful Boston suburb into a blood-soaked Tijuana cantina. (And to Ricky Rath, sorry I punched you in the ear.) I'd always been average in just about every way—good enough to be considered a *potentially* great find by a coach, a boss, or a girlfriend, but average enough to be quickly forgotten and returned to my rightful place in Vanilla-ville.

But then, five years ago, at the advanced age of thirty, I started playing fantasy football, and all that changed.

I found I couldn't just say "whatever" about fantasy football. Vanilla-ville *wasn't* good enough anymore. This stuff actually mattered to me. But why? Why was I suddenly an achievement-obsessed, competitive, stomp-all-competition, take-no-prisoners holy football terror? Why was fantasy football the lightning rod that conducted 30 million volts of effort into my flatlined apathy and got my juices flowing? And maybe just as impor-tant—why does the game do the same thing to so many millions of other people?

I often thought to myself, good Lord, is this the kind of thing a married, thirty-five-year-old guy should concern himself with? I mean, should a guy like me be wasting time on a little hobby that, from the outside world, looks as frivolous as, say, Dungeons & Dragons or Pokémon cards? I had no idea, but I loved it, and it consumed me.

I remember a few years back, talking to a friend of a friend at a wed-ding reception, Rob, a copier salesman from Dallas whose "testimony" about how he got addicted to FF was eerily familiar. One Sunday back in college (University of Texas), he came home to find his two roommates arguing and hovering over piles of spreadsheets just before a Cowboys-'Skins game. "They looked like a coupla hyenas picking at a deer carcass," he chuckled, sipping his Bud Light. At that moment, he and I (not to mention every other able-bodied man under the age of ninety-three) had escaped to a hidden, golf-plaque-covered, downstairs bar/bunker, while upstairs in the main ballroom our slow-dance-crazy wives/girlfriends frantically searched for us as the band stumbled through "Unchained Melody."

Rob had asked what his roommates were doing, and they explained that they were playing something called fantasy football and went into all the details about their draft, their scoring system, how they had to choose their lineups every single Sunday, the whole bit—and they also informed him that today was their league Super Bowl. "And it was like *bing!*—a light went off in my head," Rob confessed. "From that point on I was hooked." And his instant excitement about fantasy football only gathered more steam when he saw his roommate's reaction at the end of the game, when a late Aikman-to-Irvin 53-yard touchdown won him a league title and five hundred bucks. The kid went absolutely ballistic—jumping on the furniture, screaming, talking smack to Rob's other roommate (the poor sap whom he'd just beaten in their league championship). "It was madness," Rob said. "I've never seen someone get that excited about one touchdown. But what really got me was that he was even *more* excited to win the crappy little league trophy. The thing cost like two bucks. He didn't even care about the five hundred. That's when I knew it [fantasy football] was something I wanted to get into."

We laughed and shrugged in that man-I've-been-there kind of way, picking peanuts out of a little wooden bowl and glancing up at the NHL Stanley Cup Finals playing on a TV suspended behind the bar (the controversial "Brett Hull's-skate-in-the-crease" Stars-Sabres game, if memory serves). We both just . . . knew—we knew how quickly FF can seize you in its clutches and just *own* you, take over your life.

I got the bartender's attention for another round of Bud Lights, and that's when it happened—the door burst open and a gaggle of angry, Ann Taylor–clad females came storming in on high heels like undercover DEA agents raiding a crack house, the butchered sounds of the Righteous Brothers wafting in right behind them like their own estrogen-laced *Cops* sound track. In seconds, we were all upstairs once again, shuffling in depressing little circles to "As Time Goes By." It wasn't pretty.

Anyway, Rob's tale is one that's familiar to a *lot* of FF players—they just happened upon a friend or relative or coworker playing one day, casually asked what was up, and that was that, they were reeled in. And like Rob's victorious roommate, I'd found that my enjoyment and (obsessive, sick, twisted) desire to win my Felon Fantasy League was far less about the money and far *more* about the banter and smack talk, the league camaraderie, the pride, the accomplishment, the hard work and hours of dedication to a "craft," and, of course, showing up my friends in a very public forum.

Ask my poor, beleaguered, confused wife, Celia, about it. Celia's a devout nonsports fan; she can't understand my fixation with the NFL and she doesn't want to. Despite all the evidence to the contrary, she still doesn't believe that I can sit inside on a sunny, beautiful Boston Sunday for approximately fourteen straight hours watching ESPN's *Edge NFL Matchup* (hosted by my football dream girl, Suzy Kolber), *Sunday NFL Countdown*, the early-afternoon game, the late-afternoon game, all the way through ESPN's Sunday-night game, one that often doesn't end until after midnight. She can't understand how I can spend that entire time clicking, ducking, feinting, and jabbing on the remote with the dexterity of Roy Jones Jr., only moving from my pillowy Jabba the Hut–esque throne for food, beverage, and calls of nature.

And she flat out refuses to understand why, when we return from a late dinner or movie on a random Tuesday night, I must immediately sprint across the living room, hurdle the coffee table, grab on to the ceiling fan, and with the perky precision of a young Mary Lou Retton, stick my landing ass-first into the swivel chair in front of the iMac that I've somehow managed to flick on with my toe. All of this to check on any important fantasy football developments that may have occurred in the two hours I was out wincing and squirming through *Chicago*.

And when I find out that—phew!—some totally insignificant player like, say, Aaron Stecker or Ricky Proehl *didn't* break his ankle (only sprained it), I lean back and breathe a sigh of relief while my beloved wife stands in the doorway, arms held tightly crossed, wondering how in God's name she'll survive another football season. On one hand, I pity her because she has to live with me; on the other hand, I pity her because she doesn't play fantasy football. After all, aside from enduring the nonsensical ramblings of Michael Irvin on *Countdown*—dude makes Eric Dickerson sound like Alistair freaking Cooke—I can think of few other fourteen-hour stretches I enjoy more than a full day of NFL-watching.

While sitting there in my office trying to steal Priest from Big Dog that day in December, I couldn't help but wonder how I could go on like this, constantly angling and maneuvering for fantasy football success, especially if I didn't *finally* receive some vindication from the cruel, fickle fantasy football gods that I was in fact worthy to play their game—vindication in the form of a Felon League Super Bowl title. Something had to give, and it *had to* begin with completing that Henry-and-Morgan-for-Priest trade.

And then Big Dog shot me a final trade-killing e-mail saying, "Dude, sorry, I wanted to do it, but Erik negged it. We'll pass." I should have known! That was *always* Big Dog's MO: string me along, pretend that he's the sole negotiator, get my hopes up, say things like "Dude, we can make this work" and "We're getting close," and then blame it on the other guy when it all comes crashing down. Reading his final communiqué that day, my eyes bugged, my brain hurt, and I wondered whether my blood pressure was going to blow the top of my head clean off. Freaking no-good two-owner teams! I hate two-owner teams! Goddamn Erik! I'd only met this "Erik" person maybe once or twice, and yet here he was, single-handedly ruining my season . . . and my life for that matter!

In full panic mode now, I did exactly the wrong thing—I made a knee-jerk "revenge" trade with a different team, a meat-loving squad known as All-American Angus: Travis Henry and my superstud WR Marvin Harrison for Steelers WR Hines Ward (then the #4 overall WR in fantasy football) and the injured—but with high upside—former überstud RB Marshall Faulk of the St. Louis Rams.

"Okay, so I don't get Priest, but if Faulk returns to form, I'll cruise to a Super Bowl," I told myself. "This was the best trade you could make. Screw Priest. You don't need Priest." Yes, I was a freaking genius! Ward and Faulk were mine! Might as well send me the first-place check right then and there, boys!

And how did all that *really* work out? The guys I traded stayed hot; the guys I got were not. Harrison kept blowing up with 140-yard, 2-TD games, and Henry stayed consistent as the Bills' number one rushing/goal-line option. Meanwhile, my newly acquired, gimpy Faulk—the alleged jewel of the trade—played a total of about, oh, three downs for the rest of the season. Bottom line? Using *my players*, All-American Angus cruised to the championship game (where they lost to Priest and the Big Dogs) and I missed the playoffs. Again. I flew too close to the fantasy football sun and blew it. Again. And I was sick of it. But what to do?

The answer came one night in May 2003, months after that painful season had ended with me in a tie for sixth place (right in the middle, average, Vanilla-ville as usual). Unable to sleep despite the best efforts of the *Blind Date* marathon I was half-watching, I grabbed a notebook and wrote the following fantasy football to-do list in big, black, all-cap letters, my course of action more clear than ever before:

Step 1: Quit Job!

Yes, in the midst of one of the worst recessions since the Hoover administration, I would kick my salary and health benefits to the curb, a risky proposition that would surely have both mental and financial ramifications. After all, Celia was a freelance producer, which paid her pretty well, but, as the yang to that yin, wasn't steady and had no health benefits whatsoever. God help us if we accidentally got pregnant or if one of us fell into a manhole somewhere in the Big Dig construction and broke a leg. Then you factor in other things that cost money—mortgage, car insurance, minor survival staples like food and heat. And, self-esteem-wise, having a job to go to every day is always better than sitting home all day watching *A Dating Story* on TLC. Nevertheless, if I was going to finally make a real run at my league title, I would have to flat-out quit. And I'm not talking any wishy-washy sabbatical; I'm talking a final, definitive, sky-diving-without-a-parachute, *Take this job and shove it!* resignation. It might even feel kind of liberating, now that I thought about it. I mean, c'mon, all this nine-to-five, conference-call, status-meeting, birthday-party-in-the-break-room, client-ass-kissing nonsense was beginning to cramp my fantasy football style, taking up valuable space on my mental hard drive that would be better suited for storing running back rankings or performance splits on grass vs. turf. And little luxuries like a steady paycheck and free dental checkups? We'd just worry about those later. So, yes, folks, before the start of the 2003–4 NFL season, I decided that I would make fantasy football—not advertising—my full-time job.

Step 2: Drain the Brain of Every Fantasy Football Player Alive!

After cutting the employment cord, I'd have to make it my sworn mission to get inside the heads of other fantasy football players. I'd meet as many fellow players as possible—twenty-year "vets"; first-year "newbies"; middle-of-the-pack-experienced folks like myself; guys and gals who play in free, local leagues with their friends; people who play in leagues with complete strangers and have a little cash riding on it; total fanatics who play Vegas-based leagues with mammoth entrance fees and six-figure championship purses; anyone. Maybe by interviewing other players and following their leagues, I would learn more about how to finally dominate my own league? Maybe I'd learn more about myself as a player (and maybe even as a person, though I sincerely hoped there would be no Richard Simmons–esque "Deal-a-Meal" infomercial hugging or crying involved). And if all that failed? Well, I'd at least be able to watch and talk a ton of football for six straight months and call it "work."

Step 3: Hunt Down the Experts!

Absorbing fantasy football into every pore of my body wouldn't only be about gathering funny league stories, player rankings, and Joe Schmoe's draft strategies. No, I would also have to learn as much as humanly possible about fantasy football itself. I'd delve into the business side of the game and interview the men and women who have been there from the hobby's infancy, those visionaries who jumped on the early wave of a fledgling technology called the Internet and, in a few short years, rode fantasy football from a mom-and-pop cottage industry to a multi-million-dollar worldwide phenomenon. I'd learn about the history of fantasy football—who started it? When? Why? How? And maybe out of all these industry "experts" there'd be one Yoda-like Jedi Master in some far corner of the universe who could tell me that the fantasy football Force was strong in me, or, if it wasn't, how I could crank it up to a respectable, Luke Skywalker–esque league-winning level.

Step 4: Give Project a Cool Name!

I realized I couldn't just call my newfound mission "Mark Kinda, Sorta, Tries to Win His League." I had to come up with something memorable, something that would imply a shock-and-awe assault upon my league . . . or something really idiotic and childish. Hence, after much soul-searching and thesaurus consulting, I decided on "Project Kick My League's Ass."

Step 5: Get Permission from Celia!

Yes, I love my football, but I'm not a total caveman, and I'm not ashamed to admit that my wife, and not Bruce Springsteen, is The Boss. And though she's always encouraged my "creative efforts," having a steady salary and health benefits have also been important to us. So, quitting a job to play/learn about fantasy football would be a dicey proposition no matter what. I'd have to convince her that this wasn't just a clever ruse to slack off, get fat, and eat, sleep, talk, breathe, and watch football for six straight months. I'd have to convince her that this quest of mine would be a fulfilling endeavor both personally, artistically, and perhaps someday even financially—I'd tell her that I was doing research . . . *for a book!*

Eight weeks after making my list, I presented it to my wife on a cool, midsummer day while sitting on the deck of Farnham's Fried Clams, overlooking a picturesque New England salt marsh and enjoying two of their famous clam-belly plates. More nervous than in any advertising new-business pitch I could remember, I was armed with one PowerPoint slide set, eleven rational arguments, two wild-eyed emotional speeches, a marketing plan (complete with pretty pie charts), a budget planogram, and, if all else failed, a washcloth doused in chloroform, some bungee cords, a burlap sack, and a shovel. But her immediate response to the idea—just the *idea*, nothing more—was simply "Do it." What? It couldn't have been that easy, could it? I didn't even get to show the graph demonstrating that my self-esteem and happiness would increase exponentially the closer I got to a league championship.

"It's a great idea . . . do it," she said again, with even more conviction than before, dipping a belly into her tartar sauce and grinning. She was clearly as enthused by the whole book idea as I was. "Yeah, it's risky," she continued, "and people will think we're nuts if you quit your job—our families already think we're insane because we're not pregnant yet—but sometimes you have to take a risk, right? I mean, especially if you want to do something unique, something great." God I loved when she made complete sense like that!

While she was actually as nervous as I was about this, she was supportive and even downright excited about the plan, far more than most wives whose husband had just suggested quitting his job to play fantasy football would be, anyway. I was a lucky man. But like any sane woman, she had her limits. Case in point, her reaction when I suggested that part of my "book research" could include visiting every NFL stadium and interviewing FF fanatics during tailgates. "So you want to use this 'book' thing as an excuse to go to a bunch of football games and tailgate for six months?" she quizzed me, eyebrows slightly raised. "Did you inherit some money I don't know about?" If you're worried about my spending money on motels, I argued, I'll sleep in the car! I'll eat nothing but McDonald's! Hell, I'll mooch off people's tailgates and eat nothing but beer and sausages donated by kind, shirtless, face-painted strangers! "So what you're basically saying," she replied, "is that when you return from Jobless Football Stadium Tour '03, you'll be a four-hundred-pound, raging alcoholic with a fatal heart condition. Yeah—that's not going to work for me."

Shit. I got greedy. Flew too close to the sun again. My taking Celia on in a battle of reason was like Urkel climbing into the ring with Tyson. So I retreated, which was fine—I'd sold her the main idea, and that's what counted.

A few weeks after that clam-belly feeding frenzy, I gave my notice at work. I didn't break into "Take This Job and Shove It," but they got the idea. I was now officially, 100 percent unemployed. And with that, my friends, my insane, jobless fantasy football quest—Project Kick My League's Ass—was born.

2

Fantasy Football 101

Experts and veterans who have no need for a quick refresher on the basic principles, rules, and regulations of FF, feel free to skip ahead. But I warn you . . . you might miss something funny, insightful, and exquisitely composed.

For starters, let's break down the two F's—*fantasy* and *football*—examining the second word first because, well, I'm backward like that.

> Foot•ball, (foot'bôl) n. *A game played by two teams of eleven players each on a rectangular, hundred-yard-long field with goal lines and goalposts at either end, the object being to gain possession of the ball and advance it in running or passing plays across the opponent's goal line or kick it through the air between the opponent's goalposts; An inflated oval ball used in this game.*

Okay, so that was pretty remedial. And here's another simple fact, but one that some of you might actually try to deny: when it comes to American sports, as of the 2003, the NFL kicks other pro sports' collective asses, both in terms of dollars and cents, and in pure entertainment for the fan/viewer. When it comes to revenue from national television contracts, each NBA team averages $26.4 million; Major League Baseball teams haul in an average of $13 million; NHL teams, about $5.7 million each season. And the NFL? Each of the thirty-two NFL teams sees a whopping $77 million. And comparing typical Super Bowl television ratings to those of the Stanley Cup Finals/NBA Finals/World Series is like comparing the final episode of *M*A*S*H* to the final episode of *B.J. and the Bear*.

Even if most NBA stars *didn't* have their mouths surgically attached to bongs and Michael Jordan *hadn't* retired and unretired seven times, the sport would be facing some trouble, mostly because (a) there are now approximately eighty-five teams in the league scattered in backwater dog-patch towns like Memphis (which, believe it or not, is an exposure upgrade from the team's original home, Vancouver), (b) the Eastern Conference is basically the junior varsity to the Western's varsity, and (c) there are only so many missed three-pointers, circus dunks, and ten-step nontraveling calls the average viewer can stomach. Maybe LeBron and Carmelo can pull a Bird and Magic and rescue the league from its dull, flatlined abyss, but as legit as these two clearly are, the jury's still out, and the NBA—in my opinion anyway—blows. I'll take March Madness in a heartbeat over the dull-ass game played at the proverbial Next Level.

Where do I even begin with the NHL? Aside from the fact that the league's tagline should be either *The NHL: It's Neutral Zone Trap-tastic!* or *The NHL: God We Hope Our Rent Checks Don't Bounce!*, they also have teams in such media-market hotbeds as Nashville and Columbus, none of which will be squaring off in Bruins-vs.-Canadiens-type rivalries any-time soon. Add in (a) the league's crumbling collective bargaining agree-ment, which makes a Haitian dictatorship look stable, (b) the impending lockout/lost season that would result from the CBA's collapse, and (c) that scoring is way down due to the aforementioned neutral zone trapping, thus making the sport virtually unwatchable on TV—this despite Fox's pathetic attempt to add visual/sound effects stolen from Intellivision and/or a Pink Floyd laser-light show. Net result, you've got a sport that's doomed to semi-oblivion.

And what of Major League Baseball? Our "national pastime" (insert seventies sitcom laugh track here) is plagued by steroid scandals and drunken-sailor spending sprees by non-salary-capped large-market own-ers and is more or less dragging its bloated, wheezing Edsel ass into the twenty-first century while the sleek, streamlined powerhouse that *is* football rockets past them in a Ferrari, flipping them the bird out the dri-ver's side window.

And in case there's any confusion, I'm not talking about the kind of football the rest of the world plays—aka *fútbol*, or what we Americans have brazenly renamed *soccer*. No, my friends, I'm talking about *American* football. The one with helmets and shoulder pads. The *pigskin*, the *trenches*, and the *gridiron*. Jim Brown. Lombardi. Broadway Joe. The '72

Dolphins. Cosell and Dandy Don. The Steel Curtain. Walter "Sweetness" Payton. The Monsters of the Midway. "The Catch." Montana to Rice. Aikman-Emmitt-Irvin. Elway. Favre. The $75 million salary cap that teams *actually adhere to.* And, of course, my beloved 2001/2003 Super Bowl Champion Patriots. Yes, I'm talking about *that* football, *real* football, the wonderful sport to which Kobe, the Columbus Blue Jackets, A-Rod, and David Beckham need not apply.

Okay, end of rant number one. Now, let's look at that other word . . . *fantasy.*

Fan•ta•sy (fan'te'se) n. The creative imagination; unrestrained fancy; Something, such as an invention, that is a creation of the fancy; A capricious or fantastic idea; a conceit; Fiction characterized by highly fanciful or supernatural elements; An imagined event or sequence of mental images, such as a daydream, usually fulfilling a wish or psychological need; An unrealistic or improbable supposition.

Fantasy sports are simply everywhere. Baseball, basketball, soccer, hockey, PGA, LPGA, NASCAR . . . any sport there is, there are corresponding fantasy leagues. Hell, while browsing the Web the other day, I learned that there's actually—I kid you not—fantasy bull riding. "Understanding a few bull riding basics is all you need to be a regular contender in Pro Bull Riding Fantasy!" the Internet pop-up ad read. The *basics?* How complex can fantasy bull riding actually be? The guy either stays on the bull or falls off the bull. That's it. The only thing that might make me play is if you get bonus points for either broken pelvises or fatal rodeo-clown gorings. But while fantasy bull riding may or may not catch on as a nationwide phenomenon, the undisputed king is fantasy football.

The "fantasy," I suppose, is the "job" that each "owner"—i.e., the person who pays to own a team and play in a league—gets to do. I mean, every real sports fan has fantasized about owning his or her own team, and then drafting, trading, and starting or benching players at will. Trust me, I'd much rather be Patriots Owner Robert Kraft, Player Personnel Director Scott Pioli, or Head Coach Bill Belichick than Bored Advertising Copywriter Mark St. Amant. And playing fantasy football *is* like being an owner/general manager/coach of your very own NFL team.

First, as an "owner," assuming it's a money league, you buy your way into a league, whether it's made up of work friends, relatives, other convicted killers on the cell block, whomever. Next, as "general manager," you draft a team of players at various positions—anywhere from fifteen to twenty offensive "skill" players, starters and reserves, per roster, depending on league rules. On the defensive side of the ball, you choose either a full team defense, where you get points for sacks, interceptions, fumble recoveries, touchdowns by *anyone* on, say, the Carolina Panthers, or, if the league plays IDP (individual defensive players), you will draft individual linebackers, defensive ends, cornerbacks, what have you. And speaking of skill positions, let's get one thing straight right now—kicker *isn't* a skill position, it's an afterthought at best for most FF players, and typically even the best kickers are late-round picks. Basically, just like in the real NFL, fantasy kickers get about as much respect as Jayson Blair at a journalism convention.

Once you've drafted your players, as your team's "coach," you must choose a starting lineup for each weekly game—quarterback (QB), running back (RB), wide receiver (WR), tight end (TE), kicker (K), and defense/special teams (D/ST). Oh, one more thing: please don't let the presence of a defense fool you. Unlike the real NFL, where the adage is "defense wins championships," fantasy football is mostly about offensive performance. In my opinion, leagues where defense plays *too* large a role in the scoring—how do I put this delicately?—suck ass. Why? I just think that a glue-sniffing chimpanzee throwing its own feces at a corkboard could choose a relatively potent defense . . . but it takes skill, knowledge, strategy, and preparation to draft and maintain a powerful offensive team over seventeen weeks.

More than that, it's a challenge to decide each and every week which of your offensive players (aside from your obvious studs, who play regardless of their real-life NFL matchup) are going to start. The weekly lineup can be one of the more agonizing decisions an FF player is faced with, often sweating bullets right up until game time, the decision between two players sometimes going right down to 12:59:59 P.M. before he/she closes his/her eyes and rolls the dice just nanoseconds before the weekly deadline. Being a good "coach" and choosing the best possible players to start every single week is vital to success, needless to say. And keeping FF players away from such necessities as a computer (or at least a phone) on the day they must submit their weekly lineups is a dangerous, dangerous proposition. I mean, just hop onto any of the nationwide fantasy football message boards whenever the CBS SportsLine server goes down on a Sunday morning, and you'll witness panic, anger, confusion, and swearing. Oh, the swearing.

For each of the regular season's seventeen weeks, fantasy owners start a lineup of NFL players—typically one QB, two RBs, two or three WRs, a TE, a kicker, and a defense—and, based on how they perform in any given game, gain or lose points versus a single opponent from his or her league, if it's a "head-to-head" league. There's also "rotisserie style," where the winner is determined not by weekly head-to-head matchups, but by total points throughout the season.

Scoring is different for every league, but typically, rushing and receiving touchdowns are 6 points (or sometimes higher; e.g., in my league they're 10), passing touchdowns 4 (or in my league, 7). And there are also points given for categories like passing/rushing/receiving yardage, receptions, punt returns for TD, and defensive shutouts. Negative points can come in the form of interceptions, fumbles lost, points given up by a defense, and other ugliness. Unlike the early days, when scoring usually had to be painstakingly compiled by hand using newspaper box scores, today's team/league scores are calculated automatically by a "host" Internet site, from which there are hundreds to choose, both free and pay, such as CBS SportsLine, TQ Stats, Yahoo!, and ESPN League Manager.

Finally, based on how well or poorly your team is doing—putting on your general manager hat once again—you're allowed to trade players within your league and pick up free agents, i.e., players who were not drafted by any team and remain in a free agent pool, just floating there on a big inflatable turtle, working on their tans, sipping piña coladas, and hopefully not getting too fat and out of shape. After all, there's usually a reason why no one drafted them in the first place, but then again, sometimes, a strategic and/or lucky free agent acquisition can be the difference in a championship season. After all, how many FF owners did U.S.-marine-turned-15-TD/1,500-yard Denver Broncos running back Mike Anderson carry to the promised land in 2000? Hundreds of thousands, probably. And which Felon Fantasy League owner did he knock out of playoff contention that year? I'll give you one guess.

The Official Half-Assed Fantasy Football Glossary

What about FF terminology? Are there slang terms that will get you barred from admittance to the club if you don't know them? Hell, yes. Like any good cult/hobby/subculture, fantasy football has its own unique vocabulary. Some terms are real no-brainers. For example, a *QB* is a quarterback, an *RB* is a running back, a *WR* is a wide receiver, a *TD* is a touchdown, and a *football* is—you'll never guess this one—a *football*. (OK, so I dumbed those down a bit, but I thought we'd start out slow in case there are some real newbies here.)

Speaking of *newbie*, some terms like that are cross-cultural enough to not be the sole property of fantasy football but nonetheless appear often. *Newbie*, in most walks of life, means "one who is new to something." In fantasy football, *newbie* is used to describe someone new to a chat room or the game in general, so not much of a stretch there. And then there's *stud*, which in real life means "a man regarded as virile and sexually active and/or attractive," but in fantasy football means "a top player at his position." (Note: *stud* is also commonly used around my house and loosely translates into "anyone but Mark.")

Countless other terms are unique to FF and FF alone. Like, well, *FF*, which is the commonly used (in chat rooms, etc.) acronym for "fantasy football." If you're an FF expert and are busy crafting your own personal, unabridged 30,414-word FF-to-English dictionary (or FF-to-English-to-Klingon), please feel free to skip ahead to page 25. Otherwise, feel free to check out this little glossary. While it's not vital that you commit each and every term to memory for a postbook quiz, it certainly can't hurt.

AUCTION DRAFT: Yes, just like Christie's or Sotheby's—minus tne affected accents and above-average personal hygiene—an auction draft is one in which owners bid on players using a standardized, league-wide salary cap/budget. This is a popular type of draft, especially for more seasoned owners, because it takes the luck of drawing a favorable draft position out of the equation. It also allows owners to strategically "bump up" the price of players they don't want to draft (thus forcing their league-mates to perhaps overspend) and allows all owners to spend like drunk merchant marines in a whorehouse for players they *do* want. Until, that is, they run out of cash after three players and have four bucks left over for the rest of the roster, which then forces them to draft the FF equivalent of the toothless, mustachioed, one-legged hooker.

BASIC SCORING: A dull, unimaginative—in this writer's opinion, anyway—FF league scoring system that only gives points for one lone statistic: touchdowns. No points for torching the Cardinals defense for 178 yards rushing or 453 yards passing. No love for hauling in 13 passes for 207 yards. Just touchdowns, baby. Simple, yes, but so is downing a couple shots of NyQuil.

BUST: (Insert Pamela Anderson joke here.) A bust is any player who—whether due to injury or poor play—doesn't produce statistics commensurate to the high round in which he was drafted.

COMMISH: Short for "commissioner," or the person who heads up a specific FF league, the commish is in charge of (a) enforcing league rules and regulations with an iron fist, (b) moderating and settling all disputes, (c) approving all trades and free agent moves, (d) handling all financial matters (in lieu of a treasurer), such as league dues and weekly transaction fees, and (e) generally keeping all the kiddies in the league happy, interested, and obedient. In short, the commish is part Joseph Stalin, part Judge Judy, part Alan Greenspan, part Dr. Melfi, and part Teletubby.

CONTRACT: (See also "Eternally binding document that Vin Diesel signed with Satan.") Contracts are part of more complicated and, according to some, more skilled/enjoyable FF leagues that require owners to "sign" their players upon drafting, using a set salary cap/budget. For example, a team might be issued $500 to add personnel throughout the season, with minimum player salaries required ($7 for a QB, $6 for a RB or WR, etc.), and is then allowed to retain those players, i.e., "renew their contracts," at a 10 percent increase of the previous year's salary. Clearly, you have to be John *"A Beautiful Mind"* Nash to succeed in these leagues, and they're best avoided unless you want severe migraines and/or you currently hold a doctorate of advanced nonlinear dynamics and chaos theory from MIT.

DUMP TRADE: A trade in which an owner on his/her way to a non-playoff season trades his/her stud players to a contending team in exchange for draft picks, promising rookies (if it's a keeper/dynasty league), or cash to be used the following season. Dump trades are especially fun when the first-place owner is a complete a-hole and you, an owner who's "rebuilding for next season," decide to hand all your good players to the second-place owner on a silver platter just to piss off the first-place owner. Fun stuff, fun stuff. Of course, it's totally illegal, immoral, and will normally be overturned by any Stalinesque commish worth his/her salt.

DYNASTY LEAGUE: Any league in which Joan Collins, Linda Evans, and John Forsythe are the first three draft picks. (Sorry, couldn't resist that one.) A dynasty league allows owners to retain players based on yearly or multiyear contracts, using rules like "All players whose contracts expire to zero on January 10 will become Restricted Free Agents. All players who have multiple contract years remaining on January 10 will be reduced by one contract year, and all teams recover any years encumbered by players waived during the year." In other words, a cheat sheet ain't enough; you'd better have your Harvard Law degree handy. But, many fantasy football nuts love dynasty leagues because they have more control over assembling their teams, and it allows the possibility of building a 1970s Steelers or 1980s 49ers dynasty. Then again, they could also build a 1990s Bengals, so buyer beware.

FLEX (player): While flex is what the Austrian-born governor of California probably does nude in front of the mirror regularly, in FF, leagues sometimes have lineup rules that allow a "flex" player—most often WRs and RBs—to be started. In other words, each week an owner can choose to start a combination of either one RB and three WRs, two RBs and two WRs, or three RBs and one WR, and so on. Oh, and I'm flexing in the mirror right now, and trust me, it's very un-Ahhhhnold-esque.

FREE AGENT: Any NFL player, no matter how low on a team's depth chart, who was not drafted onto an FF team in a particular league and is available to any owner who wishes to add him to his/her roster throughout the season. In fact, just about the only players not commonly picked up as free agents from year to year are "Carruth, Rae" (incarcerated), "Lane, Fred" (deceased), and "McNown, Cade" (now bussing tables at Fuddruckers).

GM: Short for "general manager," GM is what we fantasy players call ourselves, as stated earlier, to make the whole fake-sports-team thing sound more official and, as a result, incite more ridicule from our wives and friends who don't play. *Owner* and *player* are also used throughout the book to describe anyone who joins a league and—duh—plays fantasy football.

HANDCUFF: Beyond the game of Vice Cop and Sexy Perp that you often play with your wife, *handcuff* also has another meaning: to "handcuff" a player, usually a running back, is to draft his backup as insurance against injury. E.g., if you draft Marshall Faulk or Fred Taylor, you should also draft Lamar Gordon or LaBrandon Toefield; if you draft David Lee Roth, you should draft Sammy Hagar (though Gary Cherone has no Fantasy Rock Star value), etc.

HOMER: Scholars point to the end of Western civilization as being the exact moment when Homer, the *Simpsons* character, became more famous than Homer the *Iliad* and *Odyssey* author. (Personally, I prefer Homer the *Simpsons* character.) But in FF chat rooms, a *homer* is that person who is so deeply entrenched in his/her hometown team that it's often the only thing he/she knows about. Warning: the inside information of the homer can be a double-edged sword, dangerous because the homer is often more biased than an O.J. jury and any opinions/advice on players/teams might be severely tainted; but homers are *also* useful because they provide timely, inside local dirt that no one else in your league usually has access to, thus giving you a strategic advantage. It's just up to you to decide whether your chat room homer is a bumbling, four-fingered yellow cartoon character or a sagelike, toga-wearing genius.

KEEPER: Also known as a carry-over league, a keeper is a type of league in which owners are allowed to retain a player(s)—usually one to three—on their roster from season to season without any salary cap or budget restrictions. E.g., "I've kept Michael Westbrook every year in my twelve-team keeper league and, shockingly, have never won a single game in my entire fantasy football career." Opponents say keeper drafts can often be boring because the best players are already safely stashed away on existing rosters. But sometimes, creative rules can offset this problem, e.g., players drafted in the top three rounds in 2002 are returned to the common draft pool in 2003. Except for Westbrook, a guy whose owners have often wanted to hog-tie, wrap in a burlap sack loaded down with bricks, and throw into an actual pool.

LOCAL LEAGUE: A local league is any FF league that is *not* made up entirely/mostly of owners in cyberspace, but rather, consists of friends, coworkers, anyone in your immediate geographic location. E.g., "I play in a twelve-team local league I started with Mort 'Ice Pick' Hoffman, Rick 'the Death Clown' Lynch, and nine other guys here on death row."

LURKER: A lurker is the deranged lunatic hiding in the bushes right outside your window as we speak, holding a meat cleaver, duct tape, and some Hefty bags. Seriously. I'd call 911 if I were you. But before you do, know that in FF, a lurker is someone who frequents FF message boards, reads the content, absorbs the information, but never/rarely posts messages to the boards.

MOCK: While in some circles a mock is a seriously out-of-style turtleneck favored by mafiosi and partied-out college basketball coaches named Larry Eustachy, in FF, a mock is a preseason practice draft that FF players use to gauge the value of potential draft picks.

NEWBIE: As explained earlier, someone new to a forum, chat room, or to the game of fantasy football itself. *Newbie* is usually followed by *tool* on most forum posts, just to add insult to injury and allow the *non*newbie to feel like a big ol' veteran FF tough guy.

PERFORMANCE SCORING: No, this is not a sick sexual perversion where you insist on making love to your spouse/girlfriend/boyfriend in front of a panel of international gymnastic judges. Rather, performance scoring is the "antibasic" scoring, and the most common type of scoring system used by FF leagues. It not only awards points for touchdowns, but also for passing/rushing/receiving yardage; touchdowns over a certain yardage (e.g., in my league a 30-yard-plus TD is worth a 10-point bonus); receptions; completions; field goals; even defensive stats like sacks and interceptions—basically, any relevant

statistic that the NFL counts on Sundays. Although, now that I think about it, I *would* like to see if I could get a good "performance" score from the Russian judge for my dismount.

POST: Both pay and public FF websites often have member forums or chat rooms in which FF players from around the world can "post" something for their fellow FF fanatics to read, whether it's for general NFL discussion or information, to get specific team/trade advice, or to just waste time during a day that should be spent on more important things like work, relationships, bike-a-thons, or blood donation. And, by "more important," I, of course, mean "far less important."

PUBLIC LEAGUE: Public leagues are usually found on sites like Yahoo! and can be joined by anyone in the world who has a computer. In most cases, public leagues consist of precocious ten-year-olds and other newbies who typically draft only players they've heard of on *SportsCenter* and/or the entire Rams roster because they "like the swirly helmets," thus making the whole competition aspect of fantasy football virtually nonexistent. That said, while they're hell on Earth for FF veterans who *don't* get their rocks off beating up on ten-year-olds, public leagues are a great place for a newbie to get his/her feet wet and learn the FF ropes anonymously, without the ridicule that sometimes comes from vets in more established/skilled leagues.

RBBC: Acronym for one of the most diabolical creations ever known to man: the running back by committee. A purely evil game plan that involves giving two, even three running backs carries during a game. RBBC is every fantasy owner's worst nightmare, because it makes it nearly impossible to determine from week to week who will get the most carries and, therefore, have the chance to put up the most points. Nine times out of ten, you will choose the wrong guy while some doofus third-string RB will rack up 100 yards and 2 TDs. Some of the most notorious criminal coaches who should be put to death for RBBC war crimes inflicted upon FF Nation include Dan Reeves, Jon Gruden, Bill Belichick, Tony Dungy, Steve Mariucci, and perhaps the Dr. Joseph Mengele of RBBC, Mike Shanahan. Thinking about RBBC makes my eyes burn and ears bleed, so let's just move on . . .

REDRAFT: A type of draft/league where owners do not "keep" players from year to year, meaning every NFL player is thrown back into the available draft pool after each season. Opponents might argue that redrafts are less challenging because they don't allow you to build a dynasty and/or have to manage

contracts/salary cap, but proponents say that the promise of a new bunch of "toys" to play with only increases draft-day anticipation and excitement.

SERPENTINE DRAFT: (Aka snake draft.) Common round-by-round pattern of FF drafts. E.g., in a twelve-team league, round one begins with, as you might expect, Team 1 making the first selection and ends with Team 12 making the twelfth. Then, round two begins with Team 12 making the first selection and working back to Team 1, which has the final/twelfth selection. This pattern of "snaking" back and forth continues for as many rounds as the draft entails. Get it? Yeah, me neither. To this day I sometimes think it's my pick when it's not, but let's move on.

SLEEPER: A Woody Allen movie? A hold employed by Bruno Sammartino and countless other seventies pro wrestlers? Yes and yes. But in FF, a sleeper is the complete opposite of the aforementioned bust, or any player GMs believe will perform and/or produce numbers far better than expected from the round in which he is drafted.

STUD: As explained earlier, a stud is any top-rated/desirable player at his position, e.g., "Last night I dreamt that I got three stud RBs—Ricky Williams, Clinton Portis, and LaDainian Tomlinson—with my first three picks, and they carried me to an easy league championship . . . and then I woke up and discovered that I'd had, um, an accident."

STUD RUNNING BACK THEORY: A popular draft strategy whose proponents claim that picking top running backs early and often is the key to a successful FF draft. Then again, many say that getting your league-mates stinking drunk is also a fine strategy.

VET: This word has a twofold meaning: (a) it's a common chat room term that's short for "veteran," or someone who—at least in his/her own mind anyway— isn't a newbie and has FF experience, and (b) it is also the nickname of the former home of the Philadelphia Eagles, a bland, cookie-cutter, round cinder block of a stadium with a field that was nothing more than glorified green-spray-painted asphalt and fans that booed Santa Claus and cheered players who received career-threatening spinal injuries. God, I miss the Vet.

VULTURE: You probably know the real-world meaning of *vulture:* (a) a large bird of prey that feeds on carrion, or (b) a person of a rapacious, predatory, or profiteering nature. While I'm sure that players like Stacey Mack and Moe Williams *do* in fact feed on the emaci-

ated carcasses of antelope at team dinners, in FF these guys are better described by definition number two, as they are the primary examples of any player who does not get enough touches to be considered a viable starter, but typically steals or "vultures" touchdowns and valuable fantasy points from players who *are* starters. E.g., any given Sunday you can hear me and millions of other FF players across the nation screaming, yelling, "So lemme get this straight: Fred Taylor rushes eighty-five yards to the one-yard line, gets taken out, and Stacey Mack comes in and vultures the one-yard TD?!—THERE IS NO GOD!"

ADEBISI'ED: I know this is out of alphabetical order, but that's because this is my own personal term to describe an extremely lopsided trade in which one owner is roughly, um, "taken advantage of," by another. E.g., "Wow, I really Adebisi'ed that other owner on that Neil O'Donnell/Skip Hicks for Daunte Culpepper/LaDainian Tomlinson deal." Of course, the "Adebisi" in question refers to the hulking, sexually aggressive *Oz* character who often treats weaker residents of the cellblock to his special brand of "prison lovin'" without the benefit of lubrication and/or a romantic, mood-setting dinner.

3

The Book
of Fantasy Football Genesis

There's some dispute over who created fantasy football, how, and when. Mainly because there's just no official record. Some claim that it started in the seventies, an imitator of rotisserie baseball. Some think it was spawned in the eighties at sports bars thanks to beer companies that would distribute "league rules" and "scoring" sheets to customers on their delivery rounds as a quasi-marketing tool. And most people assume it began in the nineties with the dawn of the Internet/information age, having never heard of FF prior to its cyber-explosion.

But the story with the most testimony and evidence to back it up begins more than forty years ago.

The Oakland Raiders had a bad year in 1962. The two-year-old American Football League franchise opened the season with a 28–17 loss to the New York Titans and enjoyed it so much that they just *kept on* losing, dropping thirteen straight games before finally bringing their record to a stellar 1-13 and—mercifully—ending their season with a 20–0 rout of my Boston Patriots. (Well, not *my* Patriots; I wouldn't be born for another five years, and the Patriots wouldn't become the *New England* Patriots for another nine.)

Anyway, as forgettable as that season was for the Raiders, one memorable event did occur halfway through the dismal campaign. On a bitter cold evening in early November, after making the then-arduous cross-country journey to the East Coast, three men—Raiders limited partner Bill Winkenbach, *Oakland Tribune* writer Scotty Stirling, and Raiders PR executive Bill Tunnell—found themselves holed up in New York City's Manhattan Hotel (now the Milford Plaza) the night before their sorry squad would lose its rematch with the Titans. Looking to kill some time after the room service trays had been cleared, the talk turned to—what else?—sports.

Winkenbach began reminiscing about the "fantasy-esque" games involving golf (using total weekly scores) and baseball (drafting home run hitters and pitchers) he'd played in the 1950s, in which participants or team "owners" would receive points based on the performances of real-life players on "their" teams, allowing them to compete against friends in "leagues." And from there (perhaps after a few imagination-inspiring Harvey Wallbangers), it wasn't long before the three began to adapt this rough concept to their one true sports love—professional football.

On hotel napkins, stray menus, fleshy parts of forearms, anything they could find, they began to scrawl out the rules for a brand-new game. Before the weekend trip was done, they had the basics in place. And when the three returned to the Bay Area, they let *Oakland Tribune* editor George Ross* in on their brainstorm, and soon the four created the first fantasy football league, giving it a fairly clumsy, long-winded name: The Greater Oakland Professional Pigskin Prognosticators League. Okay, try saying that ten times fast. (Hell, try just saying *prognosticators* ten times fast.) Anyway, they soon shortened it to just GOPPPL, rhyming with *topple* (as opposed to *scrapple* or former Detroit Lions quarterback Eric *Hipple*).

In fact, they didn't even call the game itself fantasy football—it, too, was called GOPPPL.

Whatever the name, the original eight-team league, consisting of

---

*In their fact-filled article for 2003 *Fantasy Football Pro Forecast* on the founding of fantasy football—a great piece on FF's early days that's provided me with a lot of the essential, nuts-and-bolts historical info for this chapter—writers Emil Kadlec and Bob Harris report that Ross is often given credit for being one of FF's original founding fathers. "George Ross was simply not present when fantasy football was first developed in that New York City hotel room," Kadlec writes. "In addition to Winkenbach and Stirling, the third person was actually Raider P.R. man Bill Tunnell." This makes Bill Tunnell the Pete Best of fantasy football (the original Beatles drummer who was kicked out after their early days in Hamburg), and Ross, no offense intended, the Ringo Starr—the lucky Liverpudlian bloke who replaced Best and enjoyed the praise and adulation of a zillion adoring fans for the next four decades. Interesting. Aw, hell, let's just give them both credit. I mean, as long as *someone* invented this game, I'm happy.

friends within the Raiders organization and the *Tribune*, set off on its frail little legs hoping to survive in the wilderness. GOPPPL soon spread from the *Tribune*, through the Raiders ranks, and then to a local Oakland bar called the King's X, where, subsequently, thanks to the owner and original GOPPPL league member, Andy Mousalimas, several other leagues formed, making the King's X the first unofficial headquarters of fantasy football. (If there isn't a historical-landmark plaque on the bar, there sure as hell should be.) Soon, mostly through word of mouth— remember, these were the days not only before Internet chat rooms, but before fax machines, voice mail, and even push-button phones—word about this new football-related game spread, just like that old commercial for Wella Balsam shampoo: "You tell two friends, and they tell two friends, and so on, and so on, and so on . . ."

GOPPPL, later known as the fantasy football we all love (and let's be honest, sometimes hate), was on its way to becoming a full-fledged hobby. A small hobby, yes, but a hobby nonetheless. And a growing obsession. It's well documented that for the first couple of weeks of the Raider season, Winkenbach, Stirling, Tunnell, Ross, and the others were more concerned *not* with how their beloved Raiders were doing, but with how their GOPPPL teams were doing. Sound familiar? And to think, the frustrated spouses and bosses of future fantasy-football-obsessed nuts had no idea what was about to hit them.

When fantasy football—err, GOPPPL—was in its infancy, the NFL "establishment," whether out of snobbery or fear, had an unofficial policy of ignoring the upstart AFL. The bad blood eventually forced the AFL to file monopoly and conspiracy charges in areas of expansion, television, and player signings against the NFL, and the two leagues constantly battled to the death to sign top draft picks, especially underclassmen, which had been unheard of before but was now becoming a necessity as the leagues tried to "outdraft and outtalent" each other. However, because GOPPPL was formed in an AFL town (Oakland), the original eight fantasy own- ers—according to the Kadlec/Harris article, the league consisted of Winkenbach, Stirling, Tunnell, Ross, Raiders radio announcer Bob Blum, ticket manager George Glace, and season-ticket sellers Phil Carmona and Ralph Casebolt—gladly included the talented AFL stars right alongside more established NFL studs such as Cleveland Browns RB Jim Brown, Packers RB Jim Taylor, and the Giants QB Y. A. Tittle. These early AFL studs included Buffalo RB Cookie Gilchrist, San Diego QB Tobin Rote, Buffalo QB and future congressman Jack Kemp, and, of course, the *very first* number one overall fantasy football selection, multipositional Houston Oiler QB/K George Blanda.

In fact, that first round of the inaugural draft, held in August of 1963 at Wickenbach's home, went: the unstoppable Brown at #2; the strong-armed Rote at #3; the AFL's first 1,000 rusher, Gilchrist, at #4; Kemp at #5; 1962 MVP Tittle at #6; Chiefs versatile RB Curtis McClinton at #7; and 1,000 rusher Taylor at #8. Also, two additional points of interest: (a) a multipositional player such as Blanda could be drafted by one team as a quarterback and another team as a kicker; and (b) even back then there were two-owner teams, with Mousalimas joining forces to "coach" Stirling's team, and a young whiz kid named Ron Wolf, a former Colts water boy who had just been hired by Al Davis to work in the Oakland front office—yes, the very same Ron Wolf who would later become GM of the midnineties Super Bowl Packers—joining up with Ross. In the *Pro Forecast* article, Mousalimas described the mood at that first draft as "euphoric," something present-day players can certainly relate to, and went on to highlight some of the basics. Like most drafts today, it was a "snake" or "serpentine" draft, where teams drafted one through eight, followed by "the turn," where Team 8 would get two straight picks (eight and nine), and then all the way back to Team 1 (which would get picks sixteen and seventeen at the next "turn," and so on). Owners drafted twenty players from each league—four offensive ends, four halfbacks, two fullbacks, two quarterbacks, two kickoff or punt return men, two field goal kickers, two defensive backs or linebackers, and two defensive lineman. No more than eight "imports" were allowed from NFL teams (again, Oakland was an AFL town, baby).

A commisisoner (Winkenbach, naturally) was appointed to preside at all meetings and settle all disputes, as was a secretary, who kept the league scoring and collected dues. Competition was cutthroat—"Friendships were destroyed, there were some divorces," Stirling says—and as word spread, people wanted in. Problem was, it wasn't like just any schmo off the street could join GOPPPL. Early league rules state that one had to (a) be affiliated with an AFL team in some capacity, (b) be involved in pro football as a journalist, or (c) have bought or sold ten season tickets for the Raiders 1963 season. Mousalimas is widely acknowledged to have been responsible for introducing performance scoring into the mix in the early seventies—points for yardage, receptions, etc.— as an answer to the TD-only boredom that players like Raider RB Pete Banaszak brought on. (Banaszak was one of the first in a long, annoying line of these touchdown "vultures," the forefather of the Leroy Hoards and Stacey Macks, who come into games for the express purpose of poaching easy goal-line carries and causing a collective rise in the blood pressure of FF players worldwide).

You'll be happy to know that GOPPPL suffered the same intraleague issues, conflicts, and smack talk of today's leagues, only with an added twist: due to the absence of technical-genius-turned-vice-president Al Gore and "his" invention—a little ol' thang known as the Internet—it was a helluvalot harder to manage a league. I mean, imagine being a commissioner in 1962 trying to collect dues, run the waiver wire, set lineups, and prevent collusion? Utterly nightmarish. But to encourage all owners to be "hands-on," the GOPPPL rules stated, *Lack of skill or study will also afford the heaviest loser the yearly trophy symbolic of the loser's ineptness in this grueling contest.* Winkenbach even had a trophy made especially for the last-place finisher—a wooden football face wearing a dunce cap— that would be presented to that poor sap at the year-end banquet, an inauspicious award that, by rule, the loser had to keep on display on his mantel in plain view for the entirety of the following season "or there was trouble," Stirling recalled in the *Pro Forecast* article.

Little by little, the game caught on, but the founders, having failed to copyright or patent it, never saw a dime in royalties. "Wink [Winkenbach] asked me once to put together a board game or something like that which followed our rules in GOPPPL, but I never had the time," Ross says. "It probably would have made a few bucks if we could have copyrighted or patented it." And according to Stirling, the last time he spoke to Winkenbach, FF's true founder was more blunt about it: "I ran into Bill and he told me, 'I told you we should have copyrighted the damn thing!'" Yet they were (and are) still amazed by the game's growth. "We had no idea it would explode into the kind of mania that exists today," Stirling says. "Pro football isn't a game. It's a cult. And this stuff [fantasy football] is close to a cult."

Um, did you say "close to" a cult, Mr. Stirling? Fantasy football is more than a hobby, more than an obsession—it's *more* than a cult . . . it's become a phenomenon. A tsunami. A cult on creatine. And thanks mostly to the advent of the Internet, it continues to grow at astronomical rates, sweeping up all in its path. In August of this year, Lycos reported that fantasy football ranked fifth on its top fifty list of most-popular user searches (just a few spots behind the ubiquitous Britney Spears). And according to a recent survey for the Fantasy Sports Trade Association, somewhere between 15 and 20 million people across the United States own at least one fantasy football team, and in 2003 they spent more than $4 billion on their hobby. That means right now, as you read, a group totaling somewhere near the combined populations of New York City, Chicago, Boston, and Atlanta are thinking fantasy football—compiling cheat sheets for a draft, cursing a sleeper-turned-bust wide receiver, suffering postseason depression, or sending wives and kids off to live with relatives up near the arctic circle for six months.

And FF isn't a phenomenon restricted to U.S. borders. Thanks, once again, to the magic of the Internet, it's spread worldwide like a benelovent virus. One of the big international hot spots for fantasy football is on military bases. "We only get one American TV channel that plays two games a week, so not being able to see all the games sucks," says Gary, a Packer fan stationed at Aviano Air Force base in Pordenone, Italy, an hour north of Venice on the foot of the Dolomites mountains. "That's why most shops in my unit have [FF] leagues. It's *big* in the air force. It just keeps us all connected to American football wherever we are in the world." Students and other vagabonds backpacking through Europe stop at Internet cafes to change their lineups or make free agent pickups—and then, maybe, *if* they have time, they'll e-mail their parents to let them know they're alive. When Celia and I lived in Florence in 2001, I can't tell you how many times I hopped onto a computer in Italy, Germany, France, Spain, Ireland, wherever, to check my Felon League and, instead of being taken to *my own* CBS SportsLine league home page, was immediately taken to the home page of *some other dude* who'd forgotten to log out. (Strangest place this happened? At the summit of Zugspitze, Germany's answer to Mt. Everest. They have a single computer kiosk for tourists to send e-postcards, but, based on the fact that CBS SportsLine's FF home page was bookmarked, it was clearly used and abused by gondola-riding FF players in need of a fix. C'mon, people, who actually checks their FF team instead of soaking in the majestic, snowcapped, four-corners view of Germany, Italy, Austria, and Switzerland?! Then again, that's a tad hypocritical of me, considering I was checking *my* team 9,720 feet above sea level, but we'll just let that slide.)

I've also come across an FF player in the distinctly non-football-playing country of Norway. "Last year I was the commish of a twelve-team league with owners from around the globe," says J. M. Henriksen, who's finishing up a degree in human resources management at the college of Stavanger in Sandnes, Norway, while also teaching American football to local high school kids. "Teams were named Holland, Germany, Norway, South Korea, New York, and so on, depending on where the owner was from. Until I started playing fantasy football, it was really frustrating not really having anyone to talk football with, considering everyone here only cares about soccer." That said, J.M., who lives near a NATO base and, luckily, gets to hear NFL games on the Armed Forces Network, hasn't seen FF spread outside the small community of Americans. "I seldom explain it to the locals, but when I do, I usually describe it as a more advanced form of fantasy soccer." But, he *has* seen firsthand how huge it's gotten within American expat communities all over Europe, having frequently chatted with FF players in Sweden, Austria, Germany, Spain, Netherlands, Great Britain, Ireland, and his own Norway. "It's fair to say fantasy football is huge overseas," he concludes.

While Winkenbach played his beloved creation until he passed away in 1993 at the age of eighty-one, to this day Ross and Stirling haven't played the game in decades. They both attribute their nonparticipation to the thing that most often confounds and frustrates FF players: lack of time thanks to other annoying responsibilities like work, family, and—well, life. "It got to the point where I was forgetting to phone in lineups and losing games because of it," Ross said in the *Pro Forecast* article. "I was just too busy." Ross served as the sports editor of the *Tribune* for more than ten years and retired at the age of seventy-seven; and Stirling took interest in another sport entirely: basketball. He is presently director of scouting for the NBA's Sacramento Kings, where he now helps draft real players for a living (although, given the choice, I'd rather draft fake NFL players than real NBA goofballs). So while the two surviving founding fathers may no longer play, thankfully millions still do, intravenously pumping fantasy football into their bloodstreams not just during the NFL season, but year-round.

In other words, GOPPPL, a silly little game created by three bored (and possibly tipsy) men suffering from cabin fever on a snowy night in New York, has survived four decades, nine presidential administrations, three wars, the Pet Rock, bell-bottoms, disco, Rubik's Cube, leg warmers, hair metal, the Berlin Wall, grunge, dot-com stocks, and reality TV. And it's not only survived, it's thrived, its popularity snowballing as the years pass. There's hope for this world yet.

4

Open Tryouts

In the beginning, back when the GOPPPL boys were going at it, and then on into the seventies, eighties, and even the early-to-mid nineties, you could—well, you had to—run your leagues and manage your team the old-fashioned way: with a phone, lots of newspapers, a yellow legal pad, and well-sharpened No. 2 pencils.

But then along came the Internet.

Since I am a child of the "new" fantasy football—the one rooted in the World Wide Web with all its user-friendly FF bells and whistles—the first place I start recruiting my "teammates" for this season, the "ringers" who will hopefully take me to the Felon League promised land, is on the main message board of my favorite FF website, TheHuddle.com. Under my oh-so-covert user name, msaint, I post the following:

```
Wanted—Interviewees for a Fantasy Football Book.
```

Inside the post, I explain a little about my project—what types of "case studies" I'm looking for; that I've quit my job to devote 100 percent of my time to FF and finally win my league, et cetera—and ask them to contact me at my satire sports website, The Sports Rag (www.thesportsrag.com) if interested. As I expect, TheHuddle.com being the epicenter of FF cyberspace as far as I'm concerned, the response is enthusiastic and encouraging, from people of all ages and sexes. Some congratulate me on having the guts to quit a job to play fantasy football, but wonder if my project is a result of being fired or laid off, as so many have been these days. One guy writes, "Dang, msaint, was this [quitting your job] by choice? If so, the glare off of those brass balls of yours must be intense. I'll send you a note with my background and contact info, if you're interested. Best of luck on this effort!" Mike, a retired navy man from the Seattle area writes, "So you're looking for a retired, older type gentleman, who is into FF locally and on the Internet, helps run a league with his kid, and has free time for you to be bugging, uh, interviewing them during the season. Hmmmm . . . I think I might know someone who fits that bill."

Honestly, it's a little odd to be "outing" myself like this. After all, one of the things that people like about cyberspace, especially message boards, is the "anonymity factor." While sometimes people use anonymity for evil—grown men posing as teens and luring young girls to malls, for example—most normal people use it to express opinions they might not otherwise express, to share ideas freely, to bond over common views, and to argue over conflicting ones. So with my interview post, I've now taken the formerly one-dimensional persona (msaint, generic fantasy football fan) and made him more three-dimensional (Mark St. Amant, writer/editor of The Sports Rag, Boston native, crazy fantasy football fan who worked in advertising, but now, with the blessing of his wife, has quit his job to write a book about his quest to win his FF league).

I'm not sure I'm comfortable with being three-dimensional, but I'm going to have to be if these people are going to trust me enough to share some of *their own* personal tales, fantasy football and otherwise, that make them three-dimensional.

Over the next few days I hunker down in the Huddle message boards and start to assemble a master list of interviewees, all of whom expressed sincere enthusiasm for my endeavor. Here are just a few of my helpful volunteers:

- Mike, a sixtyish-year-old former navy man and semipro softball pitcher from the Seattle area.
- Twenty-one-year-old air force senior airman Jake, who works for Armed Forces Radio on a Nebraska base.
- Mark, a big-air dog trainer—you know, those bionic dogs you see hurling themselves off docks at 2 A.M. on ESPN's *Great Outdoor Games*—former pro golfer, and real estate developer from San Diego, who plays in an FF league with his wife, Karla, and their roommate, Max, a native New

Zealander who came to the United States for a wedding twelve years ago and loved it so much he just decided to stay.

- Jay, a Daytona-area restaurant manager/surfer dude.
- Lisa, a hospice social worker from New Hampshire.
- Victor, a reseller of German engineering equipment, from Nyack, New York.
- Trey, a financial adviser from Atlanta who's having one hell of a time getting his frustrated wife to like football.
- Jeremy, a nineteen-year-old Georgetown University student who's been playing FF since he was nine and is dead set on becoming the youngest (real) GM in NFL history.
- John, a USA Today FF columnist, lawyer, and writer/creator of a new website, FantasyFootballFreaks (www.FantasyFootballFreaks.com).
- Patrick, an actual real live NFL player, the long snapper for the Chicago Bears. (Okay, so long snapping isn't exactly a major FF stat category, but, hey, Patrick is closer to NFL players than I'll ever be, and he provides some insight into how the average player feels about FF.)
- And finally, some of the bigger fish I've managed to reel in: Huddle cofounders David Dorey and Whitney Walters, two of the pioneers of the online FF industry; Emil Kadlec, cowriter of the aforementioned GOPPPL article, the president of Fantasy Sports Publications, Inc. (the country's largest publisher of fantasy football magazines), and the cofounder of the Las Vegas-based World Championship of Fantasy Football, the single largest FF league in the world, boasting total prize money of more than $600,000; and Chris Schussman, last year's inaugural WCOFF champion.

I start making my calls. This is the level of "three-dimensionalizing" myself that I never thought I'd reach. I mean, I never imagined I'd actually call someone I'd "met" on a message board. Having personal contact with people from the Internet has a certain sexual-deviant stigma, you know? While I'm clearly nervous at first, I quickly realize that we're all FF fanatics, and these people are talking to me because they want to, not because they *have to*. Bottom line, we have the love of this game/hobby/obsession in common and have already gotten to know each other over the past months (and in many cases, years) on the Huddle boards . . . as much as people on message boards *can* get to know one another.

Fortunately, I've always had a good rapport with my fellow Huddlers and have never gotten into any of those ridiculous cyber-fistfights that sometimes break out. Without patting myself on the back, I've often received a few votes in the "Most Respected" and "People You'd Want to Have a Beer and Talk Football With" categories in the annual member-run Huddle Awards, so I feel that my interviewees already know that I'm not a pantsless psycho. And with most of my subjects being men, the ice-breaking goes faster than usual because, let's face it, it doesn't take human males much more than *You like football? Me like football. We now friends. We bash head with rock. Ugh* to start up a "friendship."

While many of my fellow Huddlers are enthusiastic volunteers, some decline interviews because of the fear of being exposed, especially in front of their bosses. One Huddler explains his reasons for politely blowing me off by writing, "So I'm profiled as a FF addict who spends hours a day reading articles, posting, drafting, etc. My bosses read the book and realize that I'm spending countless hours a day on the Huddle. I lose my job. No thanks, msaint, but good luck with the project."

Can't say I'm surprised. FF's effect upon America's workplace has become a hot topic the more the hobby has grown. America's bosses would probably suffer a collective coronary if they knew just how much time FF players devote to managing their teams. I mean, we're already a fairly powerful country, no doubt, but imagine if we harnessed the time, energy, and pure nose-to-the-grindstone effort that fantasy football players devote to their hobby and channeled it toward, say, improving education, cancer research, or health care reform? For these reasons, some say it's downright detrimental to office productivity.

One Huddler writes of his company, "My employer finds it necessary to block certain websites they think are inappropriate for work. Now I can see them blocking porn sites and stuff like that, but when I try to go to Yahoo's fantasy site it blocks me! Does anyone know of a way around this besides getting a new job?" While a few subsequent anti-FF-at-work responses have a "What's more important: a paycheck or fantasy football?" ring to them, others claim that fantasy football is actually *good* for a company, fostering intra-office relationships that might not otherwise have existed. According to Huddle cofounder David Dorey, while FF players do spend considerable time on their computers managing their teams when they *should* be working, FF "brings employees together. It connects different groups that might not interact otherwise." CEOs play in leagues with interns. IT geniuses chat about the upcoming draft with sales guys. People who wouldn't normally even say hi in the break room now have a common bond. And better employee relations, one can only assume, lead to a more productive business, right?

I do notice, however, that most of my early interviewees choose to talk away from the office on their lunch breaks, in their cars between sales calls, or after hours, leading me to believe that while it might foster good morale and intra-office relationships, FF is still a bit of a dirty little secret. When I ask Jake, our air force Armed Forces Radio voice-over, how much time he spends on FF while on duty, he laughs and, in a deep Sam Elliott *Beef: it's what's for dinner* voice, simply responds, "Can I plead the Fifth?" He then goes on to say that he had a much easier time when he was stationed over in Germany, where there was ample free time on a normal five-or-six-hour shift to do as much FF stuff as he wanted.

"Now," he reports sadly on his situation back stateside, "there's only about a half hour of FF time I can get at work, and I have to wait until I get home to my DSL line." He pauses and sighs before adding, "It's been a rough transition, man."

Along with all the phone interviews, I zero in on another league that I want to monitor from start to finish (aside from my own Felon Fantasy League, of course). Through a friend of a friend, I contact Cenk Uygur, a thirty-three-year-old, LA-based radio talk show host. He plays in a league called the Hershey Highway, mostly made up of guys he grew up with in Freehold, New Jersey, with a few assorted college buddies thrown in. Like many leagues, because the owners are now spread out all over the country (and the world), their draft isn't just a one-day event—it's a seventy-two-hour hoops/touch football/poker/basketball/barbecue/"guy stuff" extravaganza that, of course, centers around the main event: the draft itself.

Every late August for the past ten years, league owners have traveled back to Cenk's parents' house in Freehold from as far as LA, San Francisco, and Cochabamba, Bolivia. I immediately plan on attending this year's draft in person. In our first conversation, Cenk—pronounced *Jenk*—who hosts a teen current-events show on Sirius Satellite Radio called *The Young Turks*—reels off a list of impressive occupations that sounds more like a Harvard Business School class than a fantasy football league: investment bankers, a real estate developer, a high-tech CEO, a management consultant, a lawyer, a doctor, three computer consultants, and a geologist turned radio producer. From his description, these league members are clearly the dedicated (read: obsessed) types I'm looking for. One guy will be postponing his one-year-anniversary trip with his wife. Another guy's wife *just* had a baby . . . we're talking like days ago. Most of them are rearranging business schedules and canceling important board meetings.

While hearing more about his league mates, I can't decide whether Cenk's describing fantasy football players or members of an MIT card-counting blackjack team. The league is a veritable United Nations—two Chinese guys, one Japanese, three regular all-American Joes, and two Pakistanis—the reigning ethnicity is Turkish, with four league members. FF may have its original roots in the white, professional world, and later in the high-tech community of the Internet, but today it truly knows no ethnic boundaries.

As for other "case studies," it goes without saying I'm going to cover my Felon Fantasy League draft and document my own season. How else will you find out whether I did actually kick my league's ass? As I've told you, my own local league is made up of former coworkers at Arnold Worldwide, a Boston ad agency. A few days before the draft, I'm already as giddy as a fourteen-year-old girl at a Justin Timberlake concert. My buddy Shergul, who has the draft slot right after me (I pick fifth, he goes sixth) and I have already been plotting strategies around the players likely to be there when we choose—Marshall Faulk, Shaun Alexander, Clinton Portis, Deuce McAllister, possibly even Priest Holmes. (Ahhh, Priest, my personal white whale, whom I was unable to procure from Big Dog last season. With his hip injury and uncertain contract status, he might just slip my way. Light a prayer candle for me . . .)

Of course, Shergul's probably lying through his teeth about which players he wants, but, hey, I might be applying a little misdirection myself.

After all, while being my closest fantasy confidant, Shergul is also my sworn FF nemesis, a man who would sell his own son to a traveling freak show if it gained him any advantage in the Felon League. A sly, smooth-talking, part-Italian, part-Pakistani marketing guy who was raised on Italian Serie A soccer in Florence, Shergul is perhaps even more addicted to sports—especially (American) football—than I am, judging from the NORAD-like basement FF command center/wifeproof bunker/sports-memorabilia showroom he has in his Lexington, Massa-chusetts, home. (And two years ago, in 2001, when Celia and I lived in Italy and Shergul and his wife, Alison, had come to visit his family, he and I found ourselves high atop a medieval tower overlooking the main piazza in the beautiful city of Siena, Italy, and yet, instead of marveling at the architectural wonders all around us or natural splendors of the lush vineyards spread out below, the two of us were hotly debating the pros and cons of my latest, and in my mind quite strategic, free agent acquisition for my then first-place Acme squad, Ricky Watters. We absentmindedly took digital pictures in the hopes of fooling Celia and Ali into believing we were appreciating our surroundings.) So he's a savvy FF player, and I have to watch what I say to him. He'll probably want to meet before the draft to "compare notes," as he does every year. No way do I let him peek at my cheat sheets.

A third league that I'll be keeping an eye on, though it's just too immense to follow specific teams, is the Vegas-based World Championship of Fantasy Football or WCOFF, now in its second year. Back in the fall of 2001, Emil Kadlec and his cofounder, Lenny Pappano, had an epiphany about how they could succeed where other high-stakes leagues, and even FF conventions, had failed. "All those other events were for people to come and watch the experts draft or watch the experts talk," Kadlec says. "Look, people don't want to come and stand on the sidelines; they want to come and *be part of* an event. Like the World Series of Poker. People don't come to watch *somebody else* play poker, they come to be the champion themselves, and they'll throw down big money for that chance. Once we figured out the concept—having people *be* the show, not watch it—we finally said, "Okay, let's do it.""

With fifty leagues made up of twelve teams apiece, each team paying a $1,500 entrance fee, WCOFF boasts the largest single payout in FF history: two hundred grand to the winner (along with five grand to the individual-league winners). Add in the customized crystal trophies and trips to Houston on the weekend of Super Bowl XXXVIII, and it's no wonder people will be coming from all over the country to participate in the second season. But don't let the fact that the WCOFF draft is held in Sin City fool you into thinking that FF is about gambling for most players. It's not. Most, if not all, of my early interviewees say that the "gambling high" doesn't even enter their mind.

Victor, the engineering-equipment reseller from Nyack, says, "I don't gamble, I don't go to casinos, that's not my thing. Yeah, the money's nice when you win, but it's mostly about the competition—trying to know more than my opponents and, bottom line, be better at fantasy football than them."

David Dorey adds that just because people put money into FF and sometimes get money in return, it's not necessarily gambling, mostly because the time people devote to it (usually more than five months) versus the payout (usually minimal) does not satisfy the typical gambler's insatiable jones for that quick explosion of adrenaline and/or the big cash score. "People who play [FF] for money will eventually stop," he says. "And they sure as hell won't enjoy it as much."

Still, Vegas will have a Capistrano-like allure to thousands of FF players come September. But I will not just be casually observing this fantasy football lunacy from the sidelines; I'll be actually working at the draft as a "facilitator," which means I'll be a combination of Vanna White, Mel Kiper Jr., and a trained chimpanzee. It's not open-heart surgery, trust me. Two facilitators "work" each league, writing down each team's picks and placing them on giant, magnetized draft boards. Basically, the only "skills" required are solid NFL knowledge, a few years of fantasy experience, a central nervous system, and opposable thumbs. Rarely have I felt more qualified.

5

Huddle Up

David Dorey has arguably been The Man in fantasy football—or one of The Men, anyway—ever since he and his now partner, Whitney Walters, both programmers for Silicon Valley's Electronic Data Systems Corporation (EDS), the behemoth IT outsourcing company, met at a local league draft back in 1995 and, two years afterward, founded the first website devoted entirely to fantasy football, the Huddle (TheHuddle.com).

The old-timers speak of FF newsletters printed on—get this—paper. The advent of e-mail quickly took care of this messiness. E-mailed newsletters were common for a while. Then chat rooms. And then the Huddle broke all previous molds. It was the first site that wasn't merely an extension of an online newsletter, something that, at the time, was a pretty revolutionary idea—no one had ever just launched a site without having built up a base of readers or users. Sure, there were some other "underground" efforts from such well-known early industry scribes as Adam Caplan (who started writing articles on defensive players in 1997 for the *Fantasy Football Insider* newsletter and started cohosting a fantasy football radio show that same year) and Bob Harris (editor of the *TFL Report* since 1993, and senior editor for Kadlec's Fantasy Sports Publications), who are still doing their thing today and doing it well, all to help make FF a mainstream business and an enjoyable hobby. But the Huddle was a whole new animal entirely—an all-encompassing, soup-to-nuts fantasy football headquarters. It was FF's "field of dreams." They built it and we came.

For myself and twenty-seven thousand other subscribers like me, prior to each FF season draft preparation begins and ends at the Huddle, the largest FF site in cyberspace. While traffic is consistent throughout the off-season, people come flocking back in the late summer as they brush the sand off their bodies, replace their swimsuits with sweaters, and start to prepare for their upcoming drafts. The Huddle has been voted the number one FF website every year since 1998 and has continued to feed devotees from around the world with some of the best articles, analysis, preseason rankings, and message boards in cyberspace. Long story short, Dorey and Walters are two of the five or six faces that would be on the FF Mt. Rushmore, if such a thing existed. (Can't a guy dream?)

Dorey is the closest thing to a "rock star" you'll find in most fantasy football players' lives. The first time I call him I feel like a giddy Marcia Brady meeting Davey Jones. But when he greets me with an amiable, down-home, Texas-drawled "Hey, buddy, how's it going?" as if we've known each other all our lives, I know I have nothing to fear. I'll come to understand that Dorey is perhaps the nicest guy in the entire FF universe.

Back in 1985, like many postcollege youth looking for a path in life, David Dorey dabbled in many professions: trucking, plumbing technician, dry cleaning, and something vague having to do with warehouses. Then, at age twenty-five, he joined EDS as a programmer. EDS employs sixty-four thousand people in the United States alone, many of them software engineers, programmers, and countless other techy-heads that we commonly refer to as—well, geeks. Every day, these geeks put their main-frame, data-center, help-desk, desktop services, application maintenance, and development skills to use in such industries as energy, health care, communications, government, transportation, finance, manufacturing, retail . . . and, of course, in starting fantasy football leagues. In 1991, a couple of the company's software engineers invited Dorey to join their FF league, which had been thriving since the mideighties. Having been born in East Texas, where football is king—baseball, basketball, and every other sport are mere nuisances whose sole function is to kill time between football seasons—David, a hard-core Cowboys fan for all of his natural life, jumped at the chance.

And it was four years later, in 1995, that Whitney Walters, a fellow EDS programmer, sat down next to Dorey just minutes prior to the draft of the Idiots Fantasy Football League (IFFL), an offshoot league that Dorey had recently started with another EDS coworker, and Walters had himself just joined. Having won the league's Super Bowl the previous season, Dorey was sure the "new guy" now sitting beside him was just trying to peek at his cheat sheets, you know, keep tabs on him.

"You ever go on the Internet?" Walters asked.

"Sometimes," Dorey responded, naturally suspicious of the new guy's sudden interest, as any player would be of such brazen small talk prior to a draft. He figured Walters was sizing him up, like two pit bulls sniffing each other's butt before either becoming pals or fighting to a grisly death in front of a cheering group of drunken, twisted gamblers. But as the tension melted, the two spoke in general terms about the relatively new technology of the Internet, and more specifically, about fantasy football websites containing information on the NFL. Not that there were many to choose from at that fetal stage of cyberspace. And by not many, I mean exactly none. As of 1995, the FF landscape was like a barren, undeveloped stretch of Kansas heartland, the only sign of life being the occasional renegade cyber-gopher popping his head up out of his hole with an FF newsletter and then burrowing back underground. Sure, maybe the occasional one-horse town took an early stab at the "modern" website format, but it, and other attempts like it, for whatever reason—maybe the hobby just wasn't ready to be mined yet?—would always find itself boarded up and overrun with tumbleweed as soon as it was constructed.

"We should open an Internet site," Walters suggested after a while, casually sipping a draft beer.

Who the hell *is* this guy? Dorey found himself thinking. Stop eyeballing my cheat sheets, pal! Despite his paranoia, he couldn't ignore the man's fine idea. Dorey himself had already been dabbling in FF writing, not only for the IFFL—e-mailing elaborate articles on teams, players, matchups, and other weekly information—but also writing game predictions for an early FF website called Fantasy Football '95, one of those "one-horse towns" that would start off strong each season but consistently lose steam around Week 12 and fizzle out due to overall lack of interest. Dorey loved writing the game predictions—to this day his Huddle specialty—and each week they got more in-depth. He'd always had a gut feeling that thorough, reliable (but also entertaining) information could be the backbone of a newer, better FF site.

With the 1995 season about to start, however, it was way too late to launch a site right then. So they decided to give it some more thought after the season.

Dorey went on to win the Super Bowl that year. Walters, his new fantasy nemesis, finished second. And while a friendly rivalry was born—the two would always be in the hunt for the IFFL title—so, too, was the germ of an idea that would eventually set the standard by which all FF websites would be measured for years to come.

After that 1995 season, Whitney called Dorey to ask if he still wanted to do that website they'd talked about at the draft nearly a full year before, which, honestly, took Dorey by surprise.

"I was shocked he'd even remembered," Dorey says, laughing. "But the Internet was still new back then and there were only a couple viable FF sites out there at the time, and a lot of them weren't even 'sites' as we know them today—their online presence was just the tool they used to gather e-mails and send out their newsletters." They sensed a need for a site like the one they had in mind, one where the *site itself* delivered the information rather than simply serving as a way station between a newsletter and its recipients. Hell, even as late as 1997 there were still football "sites" that would *fax* people their articles. But for Dorey, it was about more than just creating and writing a fun FF site; it was about taking advantage of an opportunity that had passed him by once before.

"I lived in Silicon Valley and still somehow missed out on being involved in the evolution of the PC," he says, his voice tinged with genuine regret. "People became millionaires overnight. So when I saw the Internet for the first time, I thought, 'If we don't take advantage of this right now, we'll never have this opportunity again in our lives.'"

So over the next few months the two EDS programmers and league rivals held official meetings at Roundtable Pizza—I can't help but picture the two "Spy vs. Spy" characters from *Mad* magazine writing notes and drawing diagrams over a couple of pepperoni pies—a location chosen less for the garlic bread and more for its being halfway between their houses. It was an equal partnership from the start.

Before talking about content or coming up with a business plan, they had to choose a name. Dorey showed up at the inaugural Roundtable meeting with a list of about fifteen, each, of course, relating to football. "'Blitz' this and 'Touchdown' that," he says, chuckling, with the same amused relief that John Lennon probably felt when reminiscing about the Beatles almost calling themselves Johnny and the Moondogs. But even in 1996, surprisingly, most if not *all* of the names on their list were already registered. They both *really* liked the concept of the Huddle—"It had legs," Dorey says—but unfortunately, *Huddle* was already taken by someone named David Huddle, who owned a financial group somewhere in the Northeast. They were stuck.

But have you ever heard that urban myth where an eighteen-wheeler is accidentally wedged under an overpass and is stuck for hours while experts in science, architecture, physics, and construction are brought in to debate how to free it? After several hours of arguing, they come up with nothing, but then a shy little girl steps out of the crowd and offers the most simple, obvious solution. "Why don't you just let some of the air out of the tires?" she whispers. Well, that's exactly what happened at one of those Roundtable Pizza meetings. After hours of fruitless debate, David and Whitney finally had one of those forehead-slapping, *Why didn't we think of this before?* solutions to their *Huddle* problem: Add a simple article—*The*—in front of *Huddle*. That would work, right? Whitney liked it. Dorey liked it. So they immediately registered *The*Huddle.com, and the heavens cried.

"We didn't really like anything else that was out there," Dorey admits. "Most of them were just football sites with the word *fantasy* slapped onto them, but they weren't fantasy football sites *per se*. Sure, they dealt with NFL teams, but the information wasn't organized very well, and there was nothing on fantasy football strategy."

Of course, they had all the growing pains of any new business. It cost $29.95 per month to host the site, and they took turns paying it each month, often getting into those "It's your month . . . No, it's *your* month" arguments. And that first year wasn't exactly successful. They lost money. But, honestly, they didn't care. "Hey, we opened a business for $29.95 a month," Dorey marvels. "Is this a great country or what?"

Eventually, Whitney sold advertising on the site to offset the $29.95 hosting fee. And what began in 1997 as a word-of-mouth marketing campaign—an e-mail to one hundred or so "movers and shakers in our little miniature industry," as David explains, laughing at the concept of actually having movers and shakers in such a fetal business world—soon grew to target two hundred people, then six hundred, then a thousand, and so on. By 1998 the site was getting 5 or 6 million hits a month, they got a mini-write-up in *Sports Illustrated*, and in short, they were getting noticed. And then in 1999, Fox Sports, one of the big corporations that were just then beginning to sniff the barely noticeable smell of money to be made in this fledgling little cottage industry called fantasy football, contacted David and Whitney about supplying Fox with all of its fantasy football content.

As Dorey recalls their brief fling with Fox, his tone makes it clear that it wasn't exactly a good relationship, in an Ike and Tina Turner kind of way. But, being a nice guy and, more likely, a smart guy who's mindful of any legal implications, he doesn't get into specifics, other than to say that Fox might not have lived up to some promises involving David and Whitney's content. "Hey, live and learn," Dorey says. Nothing seems to faze this easygoing Texan. He works at home. He writes about football—one of his lifelong loves—for sometimes eighteen hours a day. He's forty-two years old and happily married with a ten-year-old son. He runs a successful FF business that finally allowed him to quit his "real" job at EDS a full year ago. As he puts it, he's one of the only guys in the world who can yell to his wife during a football game, "Hold it down out there, I'm trying to work!"

But the Huddle is no longer the only game (site) in town. Since fantasy football moved lock, stock, and statistics onto the Web in 1997, an increasing number of large corporations like Fox have sought the millions of players—and dollars—that David, Whitney, and other early site owners pulled together. ESPN began hosting leagues and even offered some content as early as 1998. And Fox made that semi-aborted attempt to bring the Huddle on board and beef up their content in 1999. But not until 2002 did the official NFL website, NFL.com, finally admit that there was any such thing as fantasy football. Fearing the gambling aspect, the NFL had previously just covered its ears, shaken its head, and screamed *"Na na na na na na!"* whenever anyone even *mentioned* fantasy football. Unlike Major League Baseball, which quickly jumped on the fantasy baseball money bandwagon, offering leagues and information through MLB.com, the NFL took much longer to realize that fantasy football is big business, and that it was getting bigger by the year—hell, by the month—and there was serious coin to be made. Now, it's become a more or less accepted part of the league's infrastructure. "You have players talking about it, broadcasters—it's become a natural part of the NFL," the soft-spoken Walters, the technical guru behind the Huddle operation, says. "It's no longer just this little oddball thing that only geeks and weirdos do. It's a part of the mainstream football world."

When the NFL jumped in, however, problems (and lawyers) soon began to rear their gray and grisly heads. The NFL (which owns team logos) and the NFL Players Association (which owns player images and, essentially, the players themselves) quickly weighed in, and suddenly the FF websites started to look a little bare as logos and photos disappeared. And for a homespun website that was just starting out, this litigious interference seemed like the proverbial greedy, bloated, corporate fat cat pinch. One reason Dorey and Walters have managed to avoid legal action all these years is that they *never* use team logos or player images on any part of their site. "If you're using pictures, they'll come after you, no questions asked," Walters says. "If you're big enough and they think they can get some money out of you, that is."

However, Dorey says an even more important legal issue that the Huddle and every other FF site should be concerned with is the question of who owns the stuff that makes FF possible—statistics. It's truly one of those hazy, multifaceted chicken-or-egg debates that may never be solved. The NFL claims it owns the statistics because it provides the forum in which the stats are created in the first place: the stadiums, the teams, the games, et cetera. Simple, right? Oh, no, says the NFLPA—whom I picture dressed like Little Lord Fauntleroy, licking a giant, swirly lollipop and stomping his little foot while counting his money—*we* own the stats because our players are the ones who do the *actual creating of the stats* on the field. And then you have the the FF sites, sitting there in their basement home offices wearing their Hawaiian shirts and sandals, claiming that stats are nothing more than news, just a bunch of random numbers and symbols floating out there in the public domain for anyone to use any way they see fit. "It's just a big gray area," Dorey sighs. But one of the main problems, as David sees it, is that no one dares challenge the NFLPA. "The NFLPA will come after certain types of businesses—primarily games and contests—saying they own the stats and the players based on 'right of publicity.' And no one's been willing to fight them in court because they're so big and powerful." What it comes down to is that the NFLPA wants money. And while it won't sue a newspaper for using and/or reporting the stats its players create and, therefore, the NFLPA "owns"—after all, newspapers promote its players, which makes said players famous, which, eventually, makes the NFLPA *more* money—it will go after some of the smaller fish who, it believes, are benefiting financially from stats. "They want to stick their hands in that pie. They're a big organization, they've got the lawyers, and do you really want to go to court against them?" And like with newspapers, the NFLPA will also look the other way when it comes to the ESPNs and CBS SportsLines of the world using "its" players and their stats. After all, just like the *Boston Globe* or *Houston Chronicle,* those sites will interview and publicize its players, so that's one hand the NFLPA doesn't want to bite.

Unlike ESPN, Yahoo!, and other big league-hosting sites such as CBSSportsLine, MyFantasyLeague.com, and TQ Stats, the hosting arm of CDM Sports—whose revenues are predominantly derived from FF players paying fees of anywhere between $50 and $120 to have the sites host their private leagues—the Huddle only *reports* stats rather than generating income off stats. In other words, the Huddle makes its money off the proprietary, original content it generates and provides, and its interpretation of those stats. It's a subtle difference, yes, but it's a difference. And luckily, based on conversations Dorey has had with NFLPA people, they consider the Huddle to be more "newspaperlike" than anything else, a site that writes content about players and stats without profiting directly from the NFLPA's "property." As Dorey puts it, "We collect information and offer advice, opinions, and editorial content based on that information, and that's it. So to the NFLPA, it's not like we're a store selling NFL merchandise, so they're cool with us." However, he quickly adds, "But if they thought they could squeeze six figures out of the Huddle, believe me, they would."

While Dorey accepts this corporate invasion as part of the game and just the natural evolution of an industry that started out as a mom-and-pop operation, he's clearly no fan of the big guys and doesn't like how they've begun to butt in. Soon, he suggests, they'll want it all.

"Let's not kid ourselves," he says, "the NFL is a business, period, and they're cashing in on all the fantasy nuts needing DirectTV's NFL Sunday Ticket packages to keep up with all the games. And the NFLPA is a business, too, because players get national recognition faster, and become stars faster, and sell more jerseys faster, and get endorsements faster, all because of people playing fantasy football. Fantasy football is the greatest thing to ever happen to both of them."

He's 100 percent right. After all, why else would some guy in Moose Anus, Maine (not a real town), buy a LaDainian Tomlinson #21 San

Diego Chargers jersey? Because he has LT on his fantasy team, that's why.

That said, despite now recognizing FF more than ever before, the NFL hasn't *completely* embraced it yet. Take game footage, for example. Even though Fox Sports Net is part of the Fox network—which just happens to be a TV partner of the NFL—it is nevertheless legally prohibited to use *any* game footage for its weekly fantasy football show. *The Ultimate Fantasy Football Show.* Why? Because the league specifically prevents fantasy football shows from using NFL game footage. "We haven't licensed footage to fantasy shows," said Dan Masonson, corporate communications manager for the NFL. "I don't think there is anything more to it." While some, like me, might first see this as an ignorant slap in the face of fantasy football, once again, there's a simple, all-too-common explanation for the league's firm stance: cold, hard cash profit. On the league website, NFL.com, fans can choose from three pay packages, including NFL Fantasy Extra, which costs $9.95 a month and offers video highlights of players fantasy footballers might consider drafting or picking up for their teams. In other words, if anyone's going to benefit financially from game footage, it'll be the NFL and *only* the NFL . . . not the offshoot fantasy football industry. Still, Dorey explains, the clumsy, elephantine pouncing of the big boys hasn't been all bad. The ESPNs, CBS SportsLines, and Foxes are able to promote the game/hobby of fantasy football more widely and frequently than the little guys could ever hope to and, therefore, attract brand-new FF players. All the Huddles of the world can do is gather people who, in most cases, are *already into* FF. But he feels that the landscape of the industry has just become . . . different. Used to be, all the fantasy football conventions were mostly made up of all the guys Dorey and Whitney knew from the "Wild West" days, their old compatriots who rolled the dice with that there newfangled big-city Internet technology and built an industry from scratch. But now, conventions are dominated by the big, elaborate trade-show booths of ESPN, CBS, and Fox.

Still, the Huddle has enjoyed steady growth year after year, even after the online advertising industry tanked in 2000. After trying to survive as a free site for another year, it was forced to change to a pay format in July of 2001. Considering the new economic climate, that was its only choice. "In '99 and 2000, we had three times the traffic of the previous year, but only about a tenth of the advertising revenue," David tells me. In other words, it was either start charging or turn into yet another dusty, boarded-up Tumbleweed City. But lo and behold, by August of that same summer of 2001 it became more than apparent that the Huddle was here to stay. They doubled their best-case projections, mostly because while, yes, charging twelve bucks was twelve more than they had been charging their customers *before* July, that fee was still about *half* of what everyone else was charging at the time. "A dollar a month" was their mantra, one that was understood and well-received by the core users, who all stuck around, partly out of loyalty, sure, but mostly because the Huddle was helping them be better, more informed, more successful FF players.

"We were early to market and created our own large, loyal community," Whitney responds when I ask him about the Huddle's staying power. "I honestly think we have better quality [content] than most or many sites out there. And we've always evolved and changed the way we do things, so I think we'll always have a niche. But it would be incredibly hard to start a fantasy football site now. It's expensive just to get your name out there and compete with big boys."

Things have changed so much in the FF landscape, Walters continues, that it'd be virtually impossible for someone to start up a website the way he and Dorey did back in '97, when the Internet was like California circa 1847, just ready and waiting to be mined for riches—after spending virtually nothing on mining supplies, no less. "Like David said, we started the Huddle for twenty-nine bucks a month," he says. "To get noticed on the Internet now is not just a matter of saying, 'Let's start up a website, hope people find it, and try to get link exchanges.' We're way beyond that kind of environment. Now it takes a million-dollar marketing plan, print, TV ads, to even get noticed." Yes, fantasy football has gone from being the Wild West—where everyone knew everyone else and they were all in it together—to being, as Dorey says, "the business district of a big city, where no one knows each other or wants to reveal what's going on in the next building. It's too bad," he sighs, and I can tell there's some honest nostalgia for those Wild West days. "But, hey," he adds, "that's just evolution."

Having grilled two of the founding fathers enough about their website, I ask Dorey, how should I go about launching my Project Kick My League's Ass assault upon my league? Will quitting my job and devoting all my time to FF give me a better shot at the big money of the Felon

League Super Bowl? At first glance, he'd have to say no, free time alone *won't* be a difference-maker because the increasing parity in the NFL is making it harder than ever for FF players to draft a dominant team and figure out the best players to start each week.

"The NFL is big business, with a huge 'win now' mentality," David explains. "Put it this way: Tom Landry's first eight years in Dallas were losing seasons. *Eight* losing years," he repeats with utter disbelief. "That could *never* happen now. A coach has two, maybe three years to win, max." What I gather he's saying is, NFL coaches are under pressure to assemble the best team possible, as quickly as possible, and if every coach pretty much has the same agenda, this leads to parity in the league. "And parity sure as hell makes my job harder, especially the game projections," he continues. "I used to be about seventy-five percent right per week, which—not to beat my own chest, but it's true—was better than anyone out there doing game predictions. Now? I'm at about sixty-five percent and it's because of parity."

As for my upcoming draft, Dorey tells me to remember that I'm drafting this year's team, not *last year's* team.

"Big rookie mistake not to pay attention to off-season player movement, and even coaching changes," he tells me. "A running back can lose his best lead blocker. A quarterback can lose the left tackle that protects his blind side. A fun-and-gun West Coast offense coach can be fired and replaced with a more smashmouth guy. Subtle things can change from year to year. There's lots of information out there these days; you just have to weed through it all and find what works for you."

Last season doesn't matter anymore, I jot down in my superkeen Project Kick My League's Ass spiral notebook, followed by *Weed through the information and find what works,* followed by *Stop writing in a superkeen spiral notebook because you look like a friggin' dork.*

And what of FF skill? I ask him. How can you tell if you're any good at this game? Can I become an expert if I just put enough time into it?

"There's no such thing as an expert," David responds, with not a small trace of disgust in his voice for the people who dare to call themselves FF experts. "And with all the differences in the leagues around this country, all the different rules, skill levels of players in each league, it's virtually impossible to say who, if anyone, is the best fantasy football player out there."

He pauses. Having been trying so hard to listen intently this whole time, it's during this brief moment of silence that I hear music playing in the background of his den down there in Tyler, Texas, aka The Huddle International Headquarters. It's Dylan. "All Along the Watchtower." Ah, Dylan. Oddly appropriate. *There's too much confusion, I can't get no relief.*

Finally, Dorey wraps it all up for me in a neat package, at least for now. "Look, don't try to become an expert." He again says *expert* with disdain; the way most people say *asshole* or *the French.* "Just find out who plays this game and why, and find out what you, yourself, love about it and why you keep coming back. That's what I'd want to know, anyway."

6

Christmas in August

Draft Day Eve, I sleep a total of about forty-five minutes. I'm all over the bed, tossing, turning, muttering incoherently. I kick Celia at one point; she kicks back.

Part of it has to do with my totally creepy dream: I'm in a hard-core, maximum-security prison for—and this makes absolutely no sense—driving with an expired inspection sticker. I spend most of the time fighting (something I'm not good at) and, far more disturbing, fending off the brutal sexual advances of my new "roommates." God knows where *that* whole scenario came from. Might've had something to do with that damn show *The O.C.* Not since *Melrose Place* have I been hooked on such a trashy nighttime soap. After each episode, I feel that I should bathe in a tub full of vinegar and tomato juice, as if I've contracted poison oak. But I just can't explain it; when *The O.C.* comes on, I simply can't look away. It's like when you get those spam e-mails advertising teen sex, and you "accidentally" open them before dragging them into the trash. You know . . . those teen-sex e-mails . . . that you open and then trash . . . right? Right? Am I alone on this one? Hello?

Anyway, I think my dream was spurred on by a scene in that damn O.C. where the slightly more compact Russell Crowe look-alike, "Ryan"—or "Mini-Crowe" as Celia and I call the dude who plays the troubled, sixteen-year-old punk with a heart of gold from Chino, aka the wrong side of the tracks—gets tossed into juv hall and gets in all kinds of scrapes with a stream of thugs. Poor kid. I mean, poor twenty-nine-year-old actor. They're just actors, Mark, I have to keep telling myself . . . they're just actors . . . it's not real . . .

But I awake to Felon League Draft Day!

It's Christmas Day in Boston, and I'm a six-year-old. Excited. Edgy. Jumpy. Mind racing a million miles an hour. Occasionally doing jumping jacks or having conversations with inanimate household objects. I should really eat something. But while I'm completely jazzed up, I'm also tired, having spent most of the night (when not fending off shankings from crudely made shivs in the prison yard) watching a full-color mental slide show of the 324,982 different scenarios that might unfold in the first three or four draft rounds. We drew our draft order a few days back—like many leagues, we like knowing our draft order beforehand so owners can start plotting strategy, perhaps trade picks, et cetera—and I drew fifth overall out of twelve. I like it; comfortably in the middle. Most likely, I'll be looking at a top RB and a good pick on the rebound in rounds two and three. Then again, so is the owner in the fourth spot, and the seventh, and sixth, and eighth, and third, and just about anywhere else. Will I start off with Priest, Eddie George, and Koren Robinson? Will I get Marshall Faulk, Donovan McNabb, and a third-tier RB like the Lions' James Stewart? Will I have a couple too many beers beforehand and draft Wayne Chrebet, Ian Ziering, and Jessica Simpson? Time will tell. But my bet as of 1:30 P.M. EST? Priest in the first, Eddie George in the second, and either Plaxico Burress or Chad Johnson in the third. I'll try to hold off on Jessica till the later rounds.

Shergul e-mails me first thing in the morning, "Eight months of painful waiting is over!"

He and I also discuss the first major preseason blow to FF players worldwide: Michael Vick broke his fibula in the final preseason game and will be out six to eight weeks. Reason #2,253 why leagues should never draft until *after* all the stupid, no-good preseason games are finished and NFL rosters are set. Seriously. Right up there with telemarketers and the script for *Gigli*, the NFL preseason is easily one of God's worst-ever creations. Wait, cancel that, the NFL preseason wasn't created by God at all; it was created by Satan himself and shipped to earth for the express purpose of torturing FF players across the nation by injuring the top FF studs. There's always, *always* a major injury to a fantasy star in preseason. In Vick's case, some blame the turf, some blame his scrambling style. But other more superstitious sorts blame the "Madden Curse." The cover boys for EA Sports' *Madden* video game—Eddie

George in 2002, Marshall Faulk in 2003, and now Mike Vick in 2004—have all either missed an entire season due to injury or just had awful years. Losing a star like Vick is no doubt a collective kick to the crotch of the millions of Vick owners who've unfortunately already drafted, as well as NFL fans in general. I mean, even if you don't have him on your team, who *doesn't* like watching a talent like Mike Vick run around the field, performing incredible acrobatic feats of superhuman skill that you normally only see in Looney Tunes? But therein lies that FF "X-factor" again: luck. Can bad luck and serious injuries be overcome by great drafting and smart weekly team management? All the Vick owners are about to find out; I hope I don't have to.

The excitement leading up to Draft Day for the average FF fanatic is overwhelming. It's Christmas Day, New Year's Eve, your birthday, and a bachelor party all thrown into a blender. Trust me, there's nothing like it, with the (possible) exception of childbirth. For local leagues that hold their annual drafts in person, it usually means lots of beer, pizza, cigars, "guy talk," and even the occasional stripper or two. Not that the Felon League has ever hired a stripper (he writes, knowing that the Felon League wives might possibly be reading this someday). But over the following few months, I hope to learn about the unique draft traditions of various leagues. And, yes, I have heard of Draft Days that involve female nudity. A buddy of mine from high school, now a high-roller financial guy, belongs to a league that recently held a draft in Las Vegas, and, man, they went all out—penthouse suite at the MGM Grand, black tie, catered dinner, and (ahem) "hostesses." Personally, I'd think that getting a lap dance while trying to decide between Warrick Dunn and James Stewart would be a tad distracting. But, hey, to each his own. And who knows, maybe "Bubbles" or "Candi" knows something firsthand about the stud running back theory?

As great as the regular season is, after Draft Day, everything else is a bit of a letdown, adrenaline-wise. It's like any relationship: that "butterflies in your stomach" feeling lasts only so long and is eventually replaced by comfort, routine, and ultimately either long-term joy or heartbreak. I'm hoping it'll be the former, but right now, uncertainty is the rule.

That said, I *do* know one thing for sure heading into this season: there's no way in hell I will ever, *ever* have a draft as god-awful as 1998.

It was my very first season of fantasy football, and I was worse than your average newbie, primarily because most newbies *actually want to play* when they first join a league. Me? For some reason, I had no desire whatsoever. I barely knew what fantasy football was. My fellow league members now laugh—in that semirueful "Oh my God, what kind of monster have we created?" kind of way—about how they had to practically pull my teeth out and bribe me into joining their Felon Fantasy League, which had been formed a few years earlier.

Like so many, I mistakenly believed that fantasy football was just some sort of Dungeons & Dragons–esque knockoff played exclusively by thirty-three-year-old virgins still living in their parents' basements. I mean, whom exactly did owners draft in this stupid game, Brett Favre and Jerry Rice, or Gath the Dwarfen Cleric and the Wild Elf Barbarian?

Look, at the time I was a healthy, OK-looking guy of twenty-nine with a pretty good job, and no prior convictions or visible scars—translation: I was a mildly eligible bachelor—yet I still had enough problems finding myself the right girl. So the last thing I wanted to do was mess up all my chances of happiness with some beautiful lass on a blind date by admitting, over a lovely plate of shrimp shooters or extreme fajitas at Chachkis, that I was into something called fantasy football. She'd either label me (a) a total geek or (b) some kind of creepy perv.

"When fantasy football started," David Dorey says, referring to the geek factor, "it was 99.8 percent white men working in the IT industry. Look at the very first ESPN commercials for fantasy football. They show the FF player as the stereotypical nerd with the pocket protector and taped glasses. There was definitely a stigma of it being a game for computer-geek losers early on."

Naturally, I wanted no part of it. But even more than the geek factor that could possibly nuke all chances of success with the opposite sex, I was also a little wary that these fantasy-football-playing coworkers of mine were just trying to find the single largest sucker within a twenty-block radius who'd be willing to cough up the $100 entrance fee.

But I joined anyway. Hell, how hard can it really be? I thought. I knew football. I had been a longtime Patriots fan—from the semiprosperous midseventies Jim Plunkett/John Hannah/Russ Francis era, through the upstart Steve Grogan–led '85 Super Bowl team that was Fridge-ized by the Ditka/Buddy Ryan Bears juggernaut, through the agonizingly embarrassing Rod Rust/Dick MacPherson/Lisa Olsen/Zeke Mowatt 1-15 laughingstocks, to the midnineties rebirth under Robert Kraft/Bill Parcells/Drew Bledsoe, to the current Belichick/Brady dynasty in the making.

So, naturally, I did what most newbies do in that first draft: I went with my heart and used my first pick, #8 overall, on a beloved Patriot, Drew Bledsoe, completely unaware that the former Washington State star QB was being drafted, on average, at the end of the third round. Translation: I'd taken him approximately twenty-four picks too early.

Good start, Mark, good start. Way to make the most of your $100 entrance fee. And it only got worse. I might as well have gone to the nearest ATM, taken out five crisp $20 bills, doused them with kerosene, and immediately lit them on fire. I had a half-full beer thrown at me when I drafted a tight end (another Patriot, Ben Coates) in the third round. I had a *full* beer thrown at me when I followed up that stellar choice a round later by taking the Chiefs defense/special teams—yes, that's right, a defense in the fourth round. I still remember pleading my case: *But Tamarick Vanover is the best punt returner in the NFL! He'll get me big points! What are you all laughing at?! Is there food on my face?! What's so funny?!* The catcalls rained down, and when I meekly defended that the Chiefs would be a steal in the fourth round, Shergul cracked, "Yeah, good thing you jumped on that defense thirteen rounds before the rest of us."

This was my indoctrination to one of the most alluring aspects of FF: the smack talk. I would get better at it. Really. But at that point, I just sat there and took the abuse like a puppy who'd just piddled on the rug.

Looking back, I remember my first FF draft as an odd, confusing, scary, intimidating, hazy, semidrunken, yet utterly exhilarating experience that didn't last nearly as long as I'd hoped it would, but I knew damn well I wanted to do it over and over and over again. Sort of like the night I lost my virginity, but no one wants to hear about that, trust me. Let's just say that it involved far more apologizing than it should have.

Anyway, into the eleventh round, it was clear that I had drafted the most hideous bunch of deadbeats in fantasy football history. I would later learn that every FF league in the world has That Guy, the one who makes the bonehead draft picks, trades away all his best players in exchange for shitty ones, often forgets to set his lineup from week to week, and even when he *does*, it typically includes players on their bye weeks, on injured reserve, or in one memorable Felon League case (Rae Carruth), a player who was on trial for conspiracy to commit murder.

In late August of 1998, sadly, *I* was That Guy.

"He's paid his hundred bucks, right?" another Felon League member, Blaz, asked Shergul. Clearly, I was nothing more than a human ATM to these guys. Probably had a Cirrus logo stamped on my forehead.

"Yup, he donated . . . um, I mean paid." Shergul grinned, patting the shirt pocket where he had deposited my $100 check just minutes before.

Smiling like a used-car salesman while the customer drives off in a '79 Pinto with no back windshield and a bumper dragging against the pavement causing sparks, Shergul then leaned forward toward the speaker-phone where the disembodied voice of the Texas-based "Big Country," the near-perennial Felon League regular-season and Super Bowl champ, had been living throughout the first four rounds, announcing his picks with a deep, confident Southern drawl. He sounded like the spirit of football itself—an imposing mix of Bear Bryant, Amos Alonzo Stagg, and George Halas, with the wit of Art Donovan thrown in for good measure.

Even though I was a grown man not prone to being afraid of other grown men, I was immediately petrified by Big Country.

"Yo, Country," Shergul asked, "should I just endorse St. Amant's check over to you now?"

Big Country unleashed a booming laugh—you expected a different kind of laugh from someone named Big Country?—and answered, "Sure thing, Sug." And then he addressed me in his deep, drawled baritone, something that I had hoped wouldn't happen that evening, or anytime within the next twenty-five years. "Hey, Mark, buddy, thanks for your donation to the Big Country beer and stripper fund."

The whole room erupted. Smack talk had struck again at my expense. Worse, I was paying a hundred bucks to be ranked on.

Yes, within a few rounds, I had single-handedly turned my first fantasy draft into a fucking Gallagher concert—comedy so bad it's good, flying debris, people cringing and wanting their money back. I was a human fantasy football watermelon smashed under the sledgehammer of poor draft preparation and ridicule. And as I limped through the remaining rounds, I swore that I would never again be so unprepared for a draft.

But as soon as I was ready to curl into the fetal position and soil myself, to my complete surprise the tide began to shift. The FF gods, who had only led me astray until that point, decided to cut me some slack when the eleventh and, later, thirteenth rounds arrived.

Over my first season, even the vets got stung by some picks. After all, 1998 was an odd year for the *real* NFL draft, too. Curtis Enis and Ryan Leaf were stamped by the NFL establishment with the deadly "can't-miss prospect" tag, with Leaf having, in most opinions, "better size and arm strength" than Peyton Manning. Of course, they had some minor concerns about Leaf's maturity and leadership ability. In hindsight, this was like having some "minor concerns" about Jeffrey Dahmer's dining habits. But while Enis and Leaf have since been banished into football oblivion, two other players drafted in 1998 would eventually affect not just my team, but fantasy football itself for years to come: a talented but troubled wide receiver out of Marshall named Randy Moss, whose stock leading up to draft day had plummeted faster than Pets.com's, and Florida running back Fred Taylor, taken in the NFL draft by Jacksonville with the ninth overall pick, giving birth to the single greatest love-hate relationship in my personal fantasy football history, and that of countless other poor souls who have been physically unable *not* to draft the oft-injured Taylor every year since.

Yes, in that eleventh round of the Felon draft, still sitting there in *Street & Smith's* WR rankings—like so many, I mostly used magazines back then—was Moss, the one with the questionable work ethic and heaps of off-field troubles, mostly involving a penchant for allegedly smoking the ol' hippie lettuce. But I figured, *Shit, what harm can it do now? A criminal type will fit right in with the other deadbeats on my team.* So, when my pick rolled around, I slammed down half a beer, boldly wiped my mouth with my sleeve, held my head up high, and proudly announced, "Randy Moss." I then immediately ducked, my Pavlovian response to the inevitable beer-can missile that would no doubt be launched at my skull a few seconds later.

But nothing happened. No aluminum projectiles were hurled. No catcalls rained down. Not even the great Big Country had anything patronizing to say from his lofty throne way down there in ten-gallon, spur-wearing speakerphone land. My fellow Felon Leaguers all just shrugged, wrote in "Randy Moss," and moved on. One guy even said, "Nice risk-reward pick there," albeit reluctantly, as if he didn't want to provide the verbal defibrillation paddles that would jump-start my flatlined fantasy potential. But somewhere deep inside me, in whatever part of the human brain that houses things like confidence and self-esteem, that Randy Moss pick screamed *CLEAR!* followed by the *Zap!* of the paddles.

CLEAR! Zap! CLEAR! Zap! . . . I think we have a heart rate . . . I think he's going to make it!

Did they all but ignore this historic selection because, like the "Nice risk-reward" guy, they didn't want to give me hope? Did they regret not having the balls to take Moss earlier? Had they stopped paying attention to my picks altogether, assuming that I would eventually just start drafting NBA players, people in our office, or members of the traveling cast of *Cats*? Or was it because, deep in their cocky little minds, they knew that a high-risk, high-reward pick like Randy Moss might just be the start of my becoming—dare they even think it—competitive?

And if you think I enjoyed their reaction to that Moss pick, you should have seen their faces two rounds later when I grabbed Fred Taylor—then just the projected backup to James Stewart in Jacksonville. They all thought the flashy, explosive rookie out of Florida might slip until the last round or maybe even be picked up as a free agent once the season began. But I used my Gallagher sledgehammer on those plans. Sure, they tried to pretend it didn't make a difference, considering I had botched my first ten rounds with a slew of backup kickers and practice-squad wide receivers. I think I even drafted a team mascot at one point. But this Taylor pick alerted them that, hey, maybe this guy isn't such a moron after all. Maybe he knows something about picking high-upside sleepers in the late rounds. Was it dumb luck? Perhaps. Did I just close my eyes and throw the dart at the board? Probably. Were the terms *high upside* or *sleeper* even in my lexicon at that point? Hell, no . . . but they didn't need to know that.

I had redeemed myself in the tiniest, almost barely noticeable way, but I had redeemed myself nonetheless. I was a man again. But more than that, I was officially hooked on the endorphin-releasing high of the draft—the head games, the strategy, the plotting, the planning, the rolling of the dice that the guy you want will be there one round later, if you can just hold on one more round . . .

For better or worse, I was in the Felon League to stay.

As the subsequent sixteen weeks unfolded, my team performed just about as expected. Bledsoe threw a bunch of touchdowns and finished as the fourth-rated quarterback, but even his solid production couldn't offset all the Eric Pegrams and O. J. McDuffies on my sorry-ass roster and make a difference when all was said and done. My team, in short, sucked.

But Taylor and Moss? Well, anyone who played FF in 1998 knows what they did:

Taylor: Twelve starts, 1,223 yards, 14 TDs.

Moss: Eleven starts, 1,313 yards, 17 TDs, 14 of them for 40-plus yards (which count for *huge* bonuses in Felon League scoring).

I didn't win that year. Didn't even finish top three (i.e., in the money). But, just like the two wide-eyed, clueless rookies that I drafted almost accidentally, just like the upstart AFL who forced the old-boy NFL to stand up and take notice, just like the Winkenbach crew who formulated an almost cultish fantasy game based on the stats of real-life NFL players, I had started something. Something exciting and fresh and even potentially life-changing. Yes, I may have entered the league a doe-eyed Bambi on rickety legs, but I finished that 1998 rookie season walking on my own, with a small degree of pride, and even a little respect from my league-mates. From then on, I knew I could not merely survive in fantasy football, but, if I started paying more attention and dedicating myself a bit more to learning the intricacies and subtleties of the game, I might even succeed.

This last point was driven home when, at the end of my 1998 season, despite the unnecessary presence of the Chiefs defense on my roster, and thanks mostly to my two huge sleeper picks, I finished a semirespectable sixth place out of twelve—two full spots ahead of the scary, intimidating Big Country, who uncharacteristically finished eighth.

He quit the Felon League a year later. I have no idea whether he still plays.

As I iron my shirt around 4 P.M. (T-minus three hours until the first Felon League 2003 pick is announced), Celia points out with no shortage of amusement that I, a man who is often too lazy to iron clothing for weddings or funerals, am meticulously ironing a shirt for a fantasy football draft.

"It's my lucky draft shirt," I tell her, as if this is a completely rational explanation.

She considers this for a moment, then grins. "How lucky can it be? You've never won the league."

"Well aware, thanks," I semisnap back at her, annoyed that she has the nerve to remind me of my FF futility this close to a draft. She might as well tell me my penis has always been too small while she's at it. "I meant that it's my lucky shirt starting *this* year. I'm winning this year. Did I tell you that?"

"Trust me, I hope you do," she says, and she means it. Not that it's the most important thing in the world to her (as it clearly is to me), but she's the supportive type. Plus, it'd mean I'd finally shut up about *not* winning.

I meet Shergul a half hour before the draft at McCarthy's, one of the many pseudo-Irish pubs on Boylston Street that cater to underage college kids and keep plenty of sawdust around to sprinkle on the floor whenever they start yakking up such traditional Irish fare as jalapeño poppers and boneless buffalo wings. Like David Dorey was with Whitney Walters all those years ago, I am immediately suspicious of Shergul's intentions in wanting to meet here first to "talk draft." He's been after me to make some sort of "arrangement" whereby I let his preferred guy slip to him at number six in round one, in exchange for *him* giving *me* his one-slot-better picks in a few subsequent rounds. Translation: he was blatantly trying to Adebisi me. When you deal with Shergul, you always have to read the fine print; he could end up owning your house, car, and eternal soul, not to mention a few of your prized players.

He's trying to talk me into taking Shaun Alexander, telling me that he met "a guy" at the San Francisco airport who approached him when he saw Shergul reading a fantasy football magazine. "Good Lord," I can't help but think, "fantasy football has become *Fight Club*!" Apparently, as we speak, men all over the country are sidling up to each other at airports, restaurants, real estate conventions, bars, wherever, exchanging some sort of secret handshake or hand signals and saying, "Pssst, hey, you. . . . You play fantasy? . . . Me, too. . . . Hey, I got an inside track on Shaun Alexander." The guy was from Seattle, Shergul explains, and said he had no doubt that Alexander is primed for an *incredible* year and, therefore, should easily be drafted ahead of Faulk or Priest, one of whom will surely slip to me at the fifth pick, assuming the first three are some mix of LaDainian Tomlinson, Ricky Williams, and Clinton Portis.

"So what you're saying is you really want Priest or Faulk?" I ask him, knowing damn well the answer is yes, but just wanting to hear him try to bluff some more.

"No, not necessarily," he says. "I'd take Alexander if he fell to me. I'd take him over Faulk, Priest, Deuce [McAllister], all those guys." If God had a sense of humor, Shergul's nose would grow and smash right through the picture window next to us.

"Even though Walter Jones is holding out again?" I ask, throwing him a curveball to gauge how serious he is about Alexander. Jones is Seattle's best O-lineman and, obviously, a key to Alexander's success.

"Yes," he affirms, though with far less conviction than moments earlier. "Screw Walter Jones. Alexander would be a stud with *me* blocking for him."

"Great then, I'll gladly let him fall to you at number six," I say, smiling, entertaining dreams of my white whale, Priest, gracing the backfield of Acme Fantasy Football, Inc. "I'll take Priest or Faulk."

He swallows a sip of Bud Light and laughs. "Priest? His hip is a mess again, and I hear he might hold out, too, if he doesn't get a new deal. Big-time risk. He won't go until late first round. I'd easily take Alexander, Deuce, Ahman, even Edge, over him." Translation: I want Priest at number six and will therefore say anything to talk you out of taking him.

"Well, then, it's your lucky day—all those guys should be there for you." I grin. "If Priest is there, he's mine."

"Okay." He shrugs. "Your funeral." Oh, Shergul's good. Very good. But I'm onto him, boy. I can play the misdirection game, too.

Before we finish our beers and leave McCarthy's, I run into an old work acquaintance, George, who is meeting some other guys we used to work with. When he finds out that Shergul and I have our draft in a few minutes, he says that he's in a league that drafts next week, and that Kevin and Rick, the two other guys he's meeting, are also in FF leagues. When they arrive—even though I haven't seen them in what feels like decades— thanks to the common male bond of FF, we don't miss a beat, discussing players, draft strategy, our leagues, and all the other secrets that we *Fight Club* members are wont to discuss at the drop of a hat in bars, airports, and anywhere else in the known universe. You know, it's really nice to be a shallow, uncomplicated male. Just makes casual friendships that much easier to manage.

As always, we start the Felon draft about a half hour late at the offices of Arnold Worldwide. There's a myriad of technical problems caused by our need to hook up five guys via phone. While we wait, we make idle (but semiguarded) football banter and general "How are the wives/kids/

jobs/dogs doing?" chat, eat pizza, and crack open beers. As always, I pinkie-sip my Bud Light like a debutante nursing a mint julep while hoping my competition starts shotgunning their cans and crushing them on their foreheads. Drinking and drafting is never a good thing. I can already see a public service announcement, maybe starring Laura Bush or David Schwimmer, imploring FF players to "just say no to drinking and drafting." After all, an owner can get reckless, cocky, downright brazen, with his picks if he's all liquored up. He can draft a wide receiver like Joey Galloway second *overall*, which is precisely what I did in 1999, even though Galloway was poised to hold out to start the season, which is precisely what *he* did for the first eight weeks. Having learned that lesson, my sips are always dainty, at least until the late rounds, when you can slur the words "Mar Tay Jenkins" or "Greg Comella" and not feel the slightest bit of regret.

Finally, after what feels like two weeks, we start, and a curveball is quickly thrown when, after Ricky and Portis go 1-2, Ivan, owner of a team inexplicably named SoCo, takes Marshall Faulk third overall. I knew Faulk was top five, but I never expected him to go number *three*. But this leaves two total studs at RB, one of whom will fall to me. The guy picking at #4, Josh "Blaz" Blasingame, owner of the Rat Bastards, loves Priest, I just know it. And though I've told you ad nauseam that Priest is my white whale, I would gladly sacrifice him for the chance to get the guy who's been going number one overall in most drafts I've seen thus far: LaDainian Tomlinson. Take Priest, I urge Blaz with all the ESP I can muster up, take Priest take Priest take Priest. LaDainian should put up the same numbers, but without the injury/hold-out risk. But Blaz, calling in from below the Mason-Dixon line in Chattanooga, ruins those plans when—after thirty seconds of deliberation that seems like five minutes and almost makes me scream *Oh, just fucking choose already!*—snatches up Tomlinson.

That's OK. At least my decision is now a no-brainer, and before the last two syllables -*linson* are even out of Blaz's mouth, I'm proudly announcing, "I'll go with Priest," which, I find, is quite exhilarating. Really, trust me, I'm *more than* OK with Priest at number five. After almost a full year's wait, I've finally harpooned my elusive white whale, the leading scorer in all of fantasy football not only last year, but the year before that!

Captain Ahab, Big Dog, you can both bite my ass! *I have Priest!*

Over the next three hours or so, still riding the high of the Priest selection, I make some good picks (Stephen Davis is a steal in the second round, especially since I had been planning on settling for Eddie George; I see a big year for Davis), and I make some questionable picks (James Stewart in the fifth? Ehhhhh . . . he might be OK with Steve Mariucci in Detroit, but, then again, he might suck). Thankfully, however, from where I'm sitting, no downright shaky picks. Bottom line, my team looks as strong as any other, with maybe an extra advantage at TE (Todd Heap) and defense (Bucs), two areas I've virtually ignored in the past but jumped on early this year just to mix things up.

Some other highlights: Shergul's less-than-enthusiastic, conciliatory selection of Shaun Alexander at number six, which prompted me to make several Walter Jones wisecracks; Edge climbing to number eight overall after idling at the end of the first/beginning of second round for the weeks leading up to the draft; Big Dog and his faceless partner, Erik, taking approximately seventeen days between picks; the guy (Karl) who drafted Peyton in the first round inexplicably taking Tom Brady in the fourth, followed by the useless Todd Pinkston in the fifth and Duce Staley in the sixth, thus ruining any chance of winning even one game this year; debating who's more likely to be suspended this season between Moss and Shockey (Moss, by a nose) and for what (either not having his jersey tucked in or double homicide); Fred Taylor being drafted one slot ahead of my second round pick (Davis)—by Shergul, no less, which I find hugely comical—thus sparing me the agony of once again having to draft that fragile son of a bitch out of sheer habit; Shergul then immediately offering me Alexander and Taylor in exchange for Priest and Davis mere seconds after picking Taylor; people predicting that while I won't dominate in actual league play, I will easily dominate in the sheer number of annoying league e-mails; Shergul admitting that he also couldn't sleep last night, mostly due to a raging "Tiki Barber vs. Jamal Lewis" internal debate; and, finally, people giving me endless crap for wasting a pick on a player none of them knew—Priest backup Derrick Blaylock—when his bigger-name backup, Larry Johnson, was available.

I try to calmly explain that Blaylock is the *real* backup and Johnson is the third-stringer, but they won't hear of such blasphemy. "Johnson was KC's number one draft pick!" they cry. "You could have had Blaylock as a free agent!" they wail. "You fucked up your entire draft!" they guffaw.

"Who do you think you are with your inside information, Chris Mortensen?" they howl.

Hey, if all they can give me shit for is Derrick Blaylock versus Larry Johnson in the fifteenth friggin' round, then I had a pretty good draft. At least I didn't take Todd Pinkston in the fifth, for chrissakes (or the Chiefs defense in the fourth, for that matter).

Anyway, at long last, after fifteen rounds and three and a half hours, I present to you the 2003 Acme Fantasy Football, Inc., squad . . . the one that, I hope, will finally take me to the FF promised land and help me launch the successful first campaign of Project Kick My League's Ass (backups in parentheses):

QBs: Trent Green (Jay Fiedler)
RBs: Priest Holmes, Stephen Davis (James Stewart, Michael Pittman, Derrick Blaylock)
WRs: Plaxico Burress, Darrell Jackson (Travis Taylor, Reggie Wayne, Javon Walker)
TE: Todd Heap
K: Jeff Wilkins
D/ST: Tampa Bay Bucs

I like it. I like it a lot. Then again, I say that every year, even the "I got drunk and drafted Joey 'Holdout' Galloway second overall" year (which was also the year, '99, when Aeneas Williams blindsided my *first*-round draft pick, Steve Young, and ended his career. Good season, good season). But seriously, look at this Acme team—every one of these guys has Pro Bowl potential. Well, maybe that's pushing it. Maybe I'm a little too jazzed up from the postdraft high, the FF endorphins doing somersaults in my head. Still, I think Green will end up being one of the top QBs not only in the AFC, but in the league; that KC offense is going to be explosive. Darrell Jackson is a great sleeper WR. And people forget how *freaking* good Stephen Davis was two years ago when he was in Washington and used in the right offense. OK, Felon League . . . bring it on!

But now, it's time to head down to my first *non*-Felon League live draft ever for an experiment in total FF immersion.

7

Road Game

Six A.M. I love the smell of Jersey in the morning.

Actually, if you didn't know you were traveling through the northern swamplands of the Garden State, you'd think it's a pretty beautiful area. Ahead of me on the two-lane highway, a stunning, bloodred sun hangs low on the horizon, and I aim straight for it. Unless I get drastically lost, however, I assume I'll first reach the town of Freehold, where I'll meet Cenk Uygur, who'll be hosting the annual Hershey Highway League draft at his parents' home.

Considering I've only "known" Cenk via e-mail correspondence after a mutual friend hooked us up a few weeks back, to pass the time, I think of a few things I could do to freak them out when I arrive. I could show up in drag or, better yet, in a complete football uniform—shoulder pads, helmet, eye-black—and pretend to be shocked when they tell me it's not *that* kind of football. Now that would be good fun. Clearly, I'm bored.

As local sports radio drones on about shit I couldn't care less about—Royals vs. Indians, Andy Roddick at the U.S. Open, oh, just bring on the NFL already!—I pass an exit sign for Asbury Park and suddenly realize that I am deep into Springsteen country. *Thunder Road. Greetings from Asbury Park. Darkness on the Edge of Town.* All the greats. I flip through my CD holder and am saddened to discover that the only Springsteen CD I have is *The Ghost of Tom Joad.* Dammit! This is clearly a *Born to Run* moment. Even *Nebraska,* far away as the actual state is from here, would be more appropriate, with its seminal ballad of failed Jersey pipe dreams, "Atlantic City." *Tom Joad* will have to do, and as Bruce launches into the title track, even though it's way too early to belt out a deep, baritone "Bruuuuuuuuuuuuuuuuuce!,," overcome by my surroundings, I do so anyway, alone in my car, all hopped up on Dunkin' Donuts coffee. It's a semipathetic moment.

I arrive at Cenk's house around 8:30 A.M. or so, high on The Boss and enough caffeine to wake your average corpse. After a push of the door-bell—or ten—Cenk greets me at the door and apologizes for not hearing the bell sooner, but with twelve guys inside all yapping away about the upcoming draft, it's understandable.

Inside, the foyer is filled with about three hundred pairs of dirty cleats and running shoes, jackets, the odd knee brace or ankle support, sweat-shirts, and baseball caps—all remnants from the various sporting events that play a large part of their draft weekend. In the back of my mind I hope that I don't make an ass out of myself on the athletic field later on.

We head through the kitchen where an older couple—his parents, I can only imagine, as the gentleman looks like a late-fiftysomething Cenk—are busy cracking eggs, flipping bacon, and slicing bagels and dropping them into the toaster. Being those kind of people who, I can tell right away, would welcome a homeless drifter into their house, bathe him, feed him, give him some pocket money, and expect nothing in return, his father, Dogan, and mother, Nukhet, smile and greet me warmly, as if I, too, had gone to high school with their son. "Oh, yes, welcome, please come in, have you eaten breakfast?" Nukhet asks, motioning toward the sump-tuous buffet on the marble island in the middle of kitchen. I politely decline, telling her that I stopped at Dunkin' Donuts and, as proof, hold up the box containing a dozen chocolate, glazed, jelly, and cream-filled artery-cloggers that I've brought as a sort of offering, an entry fee, a thanks for their letting me invade their home. After all, the quickest way to a fan-tasy football player's trust is through his ever-expanding stomach. "Oh, how nice, here, let me," Nukhet says, smiling, and takes the box from me and places it in the middle of the four thousand other, healthier, tastier food items she and her husband have prepared.

I then head into the next room to meet Cenk's *other* family.

Tired, rumpled-looking young men lay scattered haphazardly on the floor in sleeping bags and messy piles of pillows and blankets, their hair sticking up at various angles, eyes ringed and bloodshot, wearily stretch-ing, yawning. It's a slumber party gone horribly, horribly wrong.

Turkish artwork decorates most of the room: Ottoman and dervish paintings, ceramic plates, porcelain panels, meerschaum pipes, and other ornate but classy pieces that you'd picture gracing the walls and mantels of some sultan's palace in Constantinople a thousand years ago. All of these lovely antiques make the TV, which is roughly the size of Iowa, stick out like a sore thumb. It sits on the floor and takes up nearly the entire right wall, blocking the view of the pool out back as well as most of the sunlight trying to slip in. MTV, on mute, plays a Snoop Dogg video showing Snoop sippin' on gin 'n' juice, smokin' some bubonic chronic, and generally gettin' laid-back with his mind on his money and his money on his mind . . . all while wearing—get this—a #31 Priest Holmes Chiefs jersey! A sign from the fantasy football gods that I made the right draft choice, perhaps? Hey, if Priest's good enough for the Snoop D-Oh-Double-G, he's good enough for me, beeyotch.

This is the official war room—and not just because of the steel, curved Turkish saber shamshir that hangs on one wall. This is where, in a matter of minutes, the 2003 rotiss (as they call FF) draft will take place and their fantasy season will officially begin.

Each of the slumber partyers is surrounded by thick piles of papers, notebooks, accordion folders, manila folders, and, with the exception of one or two of them, an open laptop. These guys spent the previous night boozing and playing poker until 5 A.M. after a full day of playing basketball and soccer. I can feel the excitement in the room. It's a tired excitement, just a buzzing undercurrent at this point, but it's there nonetheless, waking itself up with each flip of a fantasy magazine, click of the mouse, each reranking of sleeper running backs.

It's August 30. Seventy-seven degrees and already sauna humid at 8:45 A.M. Christmas Day in Freehold.

I make the rounds and introduce myself, knowing damn well it's going to take me hours to remember who is Samip, who is Sujay, who is Shailesh, which one is Paul Wong and which is Phil Kwan, and who is Kaan and who is T.K. I grab a hopefully inconspicuous spot on the carpet in the far corner and take out my tape recorder, laptop, pad and paper—all the writerly accoutrements that make me look as if I know what the hell I'm doing—and settle in for what should be several hours of draft day antics.

"We had an interior designer at our house yesterday, and when he asked why I was flying out East, and I told him it was for a fantasy football draft, he rolled his eyes and said, 'That's *so* sophomoric,'" says Steve Oh, inducing a good deal of laughter from all present. "He just kept saying, 'So you guys *pretend* you own an NFL team and fly out to the East Coast every year for your *pretend* draft? I just don't get it.'"

Everyone present relates to how the outside world sometimes views FF, as if we're all either Star Trek convention–going geeks or frat boys spanking each other with giant paddles. Steve Oh—not to be confused with Steve-O of *Jackass* fame, though Steve Oh also has a playful, I'm-up-for-anything glint in his eye that tells me he might not be a stranger to wrecking a golf cart or lighting himself on fire—is a two-time HH League champion, and a former lawyer (like Cenk) who's now CEO of an import-export company in LA. As Cenk wrote in an e-mail describing his league-mates a week or so ago, "Steve is the father of rotiss, he brought us rotiss, and as cocky and unbearable as he can be, this is a gift that is hard to ignore."

The predraft banter heats up. They make fun of Shailesh for his inevitable upcoming draft pick of Kyle Brady. Why he picks Brady every year, no one knows, but he just . . . does. They make fun of the brittle-but-talented Fred Taylor for always having "an injured uterus." They try to talk each other into drafting Terry Allen, Webster Slaughter, Errict Rhett, Andre Rison, Fred Lane, Rae Carruth, Frank "the Colonel" Sanders, and other retired/incarcerated/deceased players. They pass around my own recent Felon League draft sheet to get an idea of where players were drafted, prompting Samip, upon seeing the picks made by *my* league's That Guy (you know, the guy who makes every conceivable bad move), to exclaim in utter disbelief, "Wait, wait, wait—this guy took Tom Brady in the fourth after already having Peyton! And then he took Pinkston in the fifth? Before Duce in the sixth? What the *fuck*?! This guy's an *ass*hole!" He then apologizes to me in case the "asshole" was the best man in my wedding or something.

"Is Hakim hurt," Sujay asks, trying to get a handle on Lions WR Az-Zahir Hakim.

"You mean Olajuwon?" the ever-helpful Cenk answers. "He's fine. So is Patrick Ewing. Take them early."

They make jokes about being so pathetically addicted to anything fantasy that they should form a fantasy *Lord of the Rings* league. "I'd draft Legolas first overall," Steve Oh says, although there are some votes for Viggo Mortensen's Aragorn.

It's at this point that I see Greg—bespectacled, studious-looking, midthirtysomething, black wavy hair, slightly graying temples, the kind of guy you'd trust with your tax return—quietly watching the TV, which is now showing one of those Sally Struthers "For just ten cents a day you can support a starving child" infomercials. He points at the screen and shakes his head. "Guys," he says, chuckling slightly, "we're drafting football players, and these people are living in raw sewage."

Cenk and Samip riff off Greg's comment with some Sally-Struthers-could-save-a-few-kids-by-sharing-a-few-candy-bars jokes, and soon the room is exploding with laughter. While they're clearly joking, and they aren't actually happy about the children swimming around in their own filth, they also seem—how do I put this without making them seem like insensitive jerks?—almost proud of being so uninterested in the outside world right now. Not proud because they or anyone else in this room is callous enough to actually wish starvation and pain upon another human being, but rather, proud because they're so dedicated to this hobby, this draft, this league, and, indirectly, to their friendship. This is just one more example of how obsessed with FF people can get, and how, on draft day, even the world's most horrific problems are reduced to mere specs on the radar. It's just the way it is for FF players nationwide. That's what this addiction does to people.

After some aborted trade attempts that, for some reason, lead to a round of wife-swapping jokes and to Steve oversharing that he's finally getting "some action" again after a few long months (his wife just gave birth to their second child), the tenth annual Hershey Highway D-day begins at exactly 8:52 A.M., fifty-two minutes late because of a lone straggler, Phil Kwan, who sheepishly apologizes and settles in right next to me on the floor, back against the couch. We shake hands, though he doesn't seem to understand who I am or what I'm doing here.

Cenk bangs a little pewter gavel onto a little pewter palate (yes, they have an official draft gavel). "Order . . . order. . . . The 2003 Hershey Highway draft begins *now*. Kaan you're on the board." From my early observations, Cenk is the alpha male of the group, perhaps because it's his house, perhaps because of his deep, baritone radio voice, and perhaps because he's clearly, as he would tell you himself, the most competitive human within a hundred-mile radius of Freehold. He wants the title this year. Badly. But even Cenk's borderline insane dedication to rotiss—

not to mention wielding a brain big enough to receive a Wharton business degree *and* a Columbia University law degree before following his broadcasting dream—doesn't guarantee success. There are just too many unforseen variables in FF. The smartest/loudest/most competitive don't always win. Just the way it is.

Kaan Erenler, the thin, bookish league commissioner for life and onetime champion (1995), has randomly drawn the #1 overall pick from names they crumpled up and picked out of a wool ski hat, which looks oddly out of place set against the August day heating up outside draft central. Within the Hershey Highway, Kaan's nickname is Computer, based both on his occupation (software developer) and his unbending adherence to computer rankings rather than gut feeling during drafts. And today, Kaan, also clearly a disciple of the stud running back theory, makes LaDainian Tomlinson the first overall pick in the 2003 Hershey Highway draft.

We have Cenk picking second. "I've developed a reputation in the league as the man you most want to cheer against. I'm the originator of the Injustice on Top of Injustice theory, which holds that one injustice done to my team is not enough and is usually followed by another injustice on top." He then provides an example, citing an *extremely* infamous play (in FF circles anyway) from 1996: Brad Johnson's throw and catch to himself for a touchdown. It gave his opponent, a Johnson owner, double rotiss points, just enough to make Cenk lose his game that week. "It's easy to root against me because I have a reputation of whining about injustices," he says. "I'll offer outlandish trades and act cocky, which is a deadly combination." Cenk, a onetime champion (1997), quickly follows Kaan with an extremely confident pick. "I very enthusiastically take the best player this year, Mr. Clinton Portis." As the choices continue, I realize that this league, personality-wise, is a carbon copy of my own league and, I can only assume, the innumerable others across the country.

Kaan, with his Bill Gates–like approach to rotiss, is the Analytical Guy.

Cenk, by his own admission, is the Weasel Guy, whom nobody trusts.

Paul Wong is the league's Lucky Guy. Cenk explains, "Players will perform for Wong that would never lift a finger on any other team. He's considered among the two luckiest players in the league, but how much of that is due to jealousy over his two trophies is unclear. Paul does some sort of graphics for a living, no one really knows what it is, not even Paul. Wong is also nicknamed Applehead, odd considering, outside of Yao Ming, Chinese guys don't tend to have large heads." Now that I look at Wong, he *does* have a pretty large melon. I can't also help but notice that Cenk reveals Paul's nickname with a refreshing, unapologetic lack of political correctness, being that, while some of the HH League members met at the University of Pennsylvania, most of them have been best friends since elementary school and are like brothers. And naturally, brothers make fun of each other without fear of societal ramifications.

Shailesh, aka Sly, is the league's Swindler Guy and, according to Cenk, the least trustworthy guy in the league besides himself. "After trading with him you want to take a bath, and perhaps you already have," Cenk tells me. "Sly is passionate but lazy." There is apparently still disagreement over whether he was asked to leave or quit in a fury a few years ago over lineup disputes. Sly has never won the championship, but he proves himself sly, in my mind anyway, when he picks Ricky Williams, a player who has been going #1 overall in most drafts, with the #4 pick—a steal if you ask me. But Priest is still there, too . . . hmmmm . . .

Sujay, aka the Dark Monkey (like I said, political correctness is simply a foreign concept to these guys, no pun intended), has the fifth pick. While Wong is lucky, Sujay is the *Really* Lucky Guy. "This man's luck is legendary and puts Applehead's luck to shame," Cenk explains. "At least Wong does some scouting. The Dark Monkey only relies on his mysterious dark powers. Sujay is a two-time champion, 1996 and 2001. In 2001, the players he won with were so preposterous and outside the bounds of reason that we're not sure any of them even play in the league anymore. This guy *invented* luck." That said, Cenk does grant his buddy Sujay some skill props. "In fairness to him," Cenk concludes, "he *did* lose Edgerrin James the year Edge blew out his knee and *still* managed to win. People less bitter would call that a tremendous job of coaching." Sujay happily takes my boy, Priest. Naturally, I think this will be the steal of the draft—Priest himself said in a recent interview that if he played fantasy football, he'd draft himself first overall and cruise to a championship—though, trying to remain impartial, I simply say, "Nice pick."

Our late arrival, the tall, lean Phil Kwan, is the Trader Guy. "He's the kind of guy who can wreak havoc on a league. He's never won a championship, but he often finishes close to the top and can never be counted out." Kwan, a solid contender, takes the equally solid Deuce McAllister.

T.K.'s close-cropped black hair, *negative* percent body fat, gifted athleticism, and intense near-black eyes hide that he's a friendly, laid-back, good-natured (if only semi-organized) competitor. Too friendly and semi-organized, in fact, which is why he is the league's That Guy, as in That Guy who *always* makes the worst picks, trades, and free agent moves year in, year out. As I've said, every league's got one. The proto-typical That Guy absolutely loves the camaraderie, is just happy to be hanging out with the guys, and always enjoys draft day more than anyone else, yet is always by far the least prepared, usually due to outside life nui-sances like family or employment. "He's among the two people in the league never actually considered a threat to win," Cenk admits. As such, after they all joke about his accidentally drafting Troy Aikman, T.K. selects Edgerrin James seventh overall. That's a leap in my book; Edge's surgically repaired knee is still no sure thing.

Greg Russo, aka The White Monkey (no race is spared when it comes to the nicknames in this group), is the reigning rotiss champion, and the league's Quietly Confident Guy, earning him a second nickname in the league, Cocksure, a name he received in last year's draft when he averaged five seconds per selection. "No hesitation, obvious preparation, and by the end, complete annihilation," Cenk says, describing Russo's simple for-mula for destroying his league-mates. While Greg is a successful real estate developer—if you go out at night in Hoboken and have a good time instead of getting mugged, you have him to thank—and a gifted athlete, he is humble enough that his league-mates don't loathe him for winning. Russo, with trademark confidence, waits only about ten seconds after T.K.'s Edge pick and selects Shaun Alexander, good value as the #8 overall pick, in my opinion.

Dave Koller, is the Reckless Guy. He's the all-time winner of the HH long-distance award, having once flown in from Cochabamba, Bolivia, for a rotiss draft. Just prior to making his pick, Dave, a former geologist, was telling a story about a time in Brazil when three women he met at a bar tried to rob him in his hotel room. When he caught them and confronted them, two of the women turned on the third like jackals and held her down until she produced his money and credit cards from—well, let's just call it a secret hiding place. And here I am thinking that visiting New Jer-sey for an FF draft is an adventure.

True to form, Dave, already looking a bit edgy and riled up, takes the most time so far to make his first-round selection and breaks away from the pack of running backs and chooses the first wide receiver. "Marvin Harrison," he says, his deep voice rivaling Cenk's baritone, sounding a bit odd coming from a guy who's about five feet seven inches and wiry. Dave is clearly a wild card.

Providence, Rhode Island–based ob-gyn Tolga Kokturk's nickname is the none-too-surprising Doctor. From what I've seen so far, Tolga is probably the mellowest of the group, just lying in the middle of the plush carpet on a pile of blankets, crossing off picks as they go, and, other than making the occasional farting noise when he doesn't like a selection, seems to be the most soft-spoken, even-keeled of the bunch. He's the league's Nice Guy and with surgical calm and precision takes Ahman Green, after saying he was hoping Edge would drop to him. I think to myself that he needn't worry—I have this feeling that Ahman will have a better year than all RBs *not* named Priest, LaDainian, or Ricky, and certainly better than Edge.

Steve Oh, the aforementioned father of rotiss, is the league's Veteran Guy, and Cenk hints that, sometimes, this veteran status goes to his head. "He will be the first to tell you that he is a two-time champion—1994 and 1999—but his '94 championship has an infamous asterisk next to it because it was our first year, and unlike the rest of us, Steve had played in a league before." But Cenk adds that they can only complain so much because Oh did bring them rotiss, after all. With his pick, Steve nabs Bills running back Travis Henry.

At age twenty-six, Samip Parikh, who sits at "the turn" with the #12 and #13 picks of this snake draft, is the youngest of the group. He perpetually wears a wry grin while observing the action—does he know something the rest of his league-mates don't?—and even early on, as he sits cross-legged in a fully reclined La-Z-Boy, he's been lobbing a barrage of sarcastic insults down onto his buddies after their picks. While his Hershey Highway buddies call him Teddy KGB after John Malkovich's Russian-mobster character in *Rounders*, Samip earns the FF title of Jokester Guy. Samip, also a poker fanatic, gambles on the first round's other recent knee-surgery outpatient, Jamal Lewis, followed by William Green at the turn. Two solid backs, especially Lewis. If Green doesn't prove to be a one-half-year wonder after his great final eight games with Cleveland last season, Samip's backfield might immediately be the best in the league. Good start for the Jokester.

The draft goes deep into the bowels of NFL rosters (they draft eighteen rounds, as opposed to my league's fourteen), with most of the guys picking quickly. The chances are awfully slim that the Nate Burlesons, Neil O'Donnells, and Rod "He Hate Me" Smarts of the world will have any effect on a fantasy team. Finally, five hours or so later, the 2003 Hershey Highway League draft ends with Kaan making the immortal Kris Brown, kicker, Houston Texans, the 216th and final pick.

Bleary-eyed, worn-out, stretching stiff necks and backs, and yet jabbering on left and right about whose teams suck and whose don't, who made shitty picks and who stole what sleepers out from under whose noses, this amusing pack straggles out into the front hall, where all their athletic gear is piled. It's time for the next stage of D-day: the Hershey Highway tradition of hard-nosed, no-holds-barred athletic competition known simply as "sports." Luckily, Cenk had prepared me for the touch football and hoops portions of the program beforehand, so I, too, have the appropriate footware in the form of Nike high-top softball cleats. With only a small bit of trepidation I lace them up. These guys are mostly younger than I am and extremely competitive, while I rolled not one *but both* of my ankles the last time I stepped foot on an athletic field. After a quick lunch of turkey subs provided by the ever-attentive Dogan and Nukhet, we pile into various cars and head over to a barren, airless high school practice field for some touch football in what's roughly 187-degree heat.

I learn quickly that they take this shit seriously. Before we've stepped on the field, Phil Kwan has provided a chart that compares each league member to an NFL player based on his speed, skills, position, body type, attitude, et cetera. As we stretch our sore bodies in preparation for the game, Kwan explains his choices.

"Cenk is definitely Jim Kleinsasser. He plays fullback, tight end, and can catch passes. Russo has Amani Toomer–size speed, and vertical leap, and like Toomer could get Randy Moss–like numbers if not for being so unselfish. Sujay is Brian Mitchell 'cause he plays all positions well, but not great. Dave is Wayne Chrebet—hardworking, shifty, and would clash with any egomaniacal Keyshawn-like player. Steve is Torry Holt—runs all routes at full speed, can't block if his life depended on it. Kaan is clearly Easy Ed McCaffrey—beats anyone on a slant, very reliable hands. Sly is a great Vinny Testaverde 'cause the guy's been around, throws a damn good deep ball, and will play backup to help the team. Tolga makes a great Brad Johnson, who has led both Super Bowl teams and teams in the gutter. He has great touch and can pick apart defenses like a piranha. T.K. is Bledsoe—came out of college as a prodigy, can gun a ball in any tiny crack. Samip is Bettis—wouldn't be picked as a starter, but plays with experience, and flat out pounds the ball. And Applehead is Larry Centers—reliable receiver out of the backfield, runs nice short routes."

I'm certainly impressed: Kwan knows his NFL players. I just hope that when the game's over, Kwan will not retroactively add me to his list as either Jim Marshall ("often runs the wrong way, scores touchdowns for other team"), Leon Lett ("starts touchdown celebrations way too early, gets ball knocked out of hands from behind"), or George Blanda ("plays like seventy-three-year-old man, appears lost, frightened").

For the next two hours, under the scorching, late-August sun, I run and fall and wheeze and trip all over the parched field, trying to keep up with the likes of T.K., who brushes off my blocking attempts as if he were swatting at a gnat; with Kwan, whom I accidentally slam into and commit pass interference against no fewer than seven times; with Tolga, whose passes drill me in the chest like Brett Favre bullets and bounce away after leaving a *Spalding* imprint on my sternum; and with Greg "White Monkey" Russo, whose nickname is evident every time he leaps twenty feet above my head to catch a touchdown pass that most humans have no business catching. I do manage to make a couple of nice catches myself, however, and a few sliding defensive plays that break up key passes (note to self: don't slide on dirt and rocks because it hurts real, real bad later on). But, basically, my twenty-year-old brain starts writing checks that my thirty-five-year-old body simply can't cash, and at the end of the three games—I'm on the losing team twice, something I prefer to think is merely a coincidence—I literally crawl off the field and into my Jeep for the long drive home.

Trying not to fall asleep as I cruise past the swamps/Genovese crime family burial grounds that line the Jersey Turnpike, I'm aching in places I never knew a human being could ache—under my eyelids, behind my left pinkie toe, and in my spleen, wherever that is. Maybe the seventy-three-year-old Blanda is a *generous* comparison.

8

Vegas, Baby . . . Vegas!

I've always thought my first trip to Sin City would be for a bachelor party. Or a business trip. Or maybe a golf outing. Hell, even a shotgun wedding or a quickie divorce would have made sense. But a *fantasy football draft*? Never in my wildest dreams would I have believed that in 2003 I would be flying to Las Vegas to attend the draft of something called the World Championship of Fantasy Football, or WCOFF.

I don't even have to leave the plane to meet my first card-carrying fantasy football junkie, coincidentally sitting right next to me in Row 34, up against the bathroom wall, bathing in that lovely antiseptic-meets-urine stench—the Worst Seats in the House.

His name is Joe. He's a backward-hat-wearing, unshaven, twenty-three-year-old trainee for a large investment bank who's flying out to Vegas for—you guessed it—a high-stakes fantasy football league draft. Joe knocks back anywhere between two and fifty-seven Skyy-vodka-and-tonics during the flight (ah, the good ol' days when I was young enough to inhale that much booze before lunch), and he's very open about his life and glad to chat about FF, work, football in general, anything at all to pass the time between Newark and Vegas.

"Sorry to look over your shoulder," he says about fifteen minutes after takeoff, just after I've set up my iBook on the handy little tray table. "Are you writing something about football?"

His good manners surprise me. I just always assume that unshaven, backward-baseball-hat-wearing dudes are going to be complete a-holes, the kind of punks you'd see walking around in a perpetual state of waxed shirtlessness on the *Real World–Road Rules Challenge*, and not polite, smart, well-spoken human beings.

"Yeah," I answer, "well, fantasy football actually."

Hearing that, Joe is off and running, knowing he's found a kindred spirit. I mean, here's a guy—me—who is not only into FF, but is writing a book about it. Once again, the *Fight Club* theory makes a cameo appearance, proving yet again that men need little in the way of common bonds to form some kind of connection, no matter how small or brief. *You like football? Me like football. We be friends. We now go kill saber-toothed tiger. Ugh.*

Within minutes, I realize that Joe is the most addicted FF player I've encountered so far. As of the moment, he's playing in nine—*nine!*—FF leagues, because he "simply can't say no when someone asks me to join." Joe and his buddies are heading out to an FF draft at the Venetian, one that, while not quite as large or popular as WCOFF, is still one of the big ones.

Joe's been playing FF since seventh grade (which, for him, is like ten minutes ago, my bitter thirty-five-year-old bruised ego chimes in). He took a break for a few years toward the end of high school, but started back up again in college. He's also no stranger to putting a little cash on games every Sunday, you know, through an actual bookie.

"I only have two hobbies: fantasy football and gambling," he admits with only a trace of embarrassment. "My parents think I'm a complete asshole for skipping work to come out here for a fantasy football draft. God knows what they'd say if they knew I started a fantasy WWF league just to kill time between football seasons."

OK, hold it right there . . . did he say fantasy WWF? I've heard of FF players—myself included—reluctantly joining baseball leagues, basketball leagues, even fantasy NHL leagues for God's sake, *anything* at all to endure that painfully interminable dead zone between February and September. But fantasy *wrestling*? Then again, considering there's such a thing as fantasy bull riding, this shouldn't come as much of a shock.

"You'd get points if your guy won, negative points if your guy lost," he explained, laughing and shaking his head. "You got points if your guy was introduced first, or if he made some crazy speech and the crowd booed him, or if he came into the ring with a couple of hot chicks, if he hit someone over the head with a chair. It was fucking idiotic."

He orders another Skyy-and-tonic from the flight attendant, who, by this point, has clearly filed Joe into the Potentially Unruly Guys Who Might Get Tanked and Try to Defecate on the Drink Cart category. But she has nothing to worry about. He's obviously living that "work hard, play hard" postcollege rite of passage by which all young investment bank trainees in New York live or else be excommunicated from the profession, but he seems like a good-natured kid.

A good-natured kid who has an odd vendetta against Daunte Culpepper, that is.

"I'll never draft Culpepper again," he jokes, yet dead serious at the same time. "He screwed me last year with all his fumbles. I hate that fucker. He's so overrated. I'll never draft his ass again. Ever."

Fearing a sideways elbow to the head, I admit that I actually have Culpepper rated higher than McNabb this season, but he only shrugs. "That's what's great about this game, everyone has different values for different players. What fun would it be if everyone went after the same players? Take Culpepper, be my guest. You just won't catch his ass on my team."

Like many FF junkies, Joe loves fantasy football because it's kept him in contact with his friends, two of whom are sitting toward the front of the plane and chatting with, I would soon discover, about eight or nine other people heading out to Vegas for WCOFF or some other giant, high-stakes FF draft. One older gentleman, easily sixtysomething, even has a polo shirt sporting the WCOFF logo on the front left pocket.

That does it. This is no longer Continental Airlines—it's the FF Junkie Express.

Inside the terminal, I write down the URL of my Sports Rag website, wish Joe luck in his draft, and tell him to contact me anytime about FF, let me know how his nineteen thousand teams are doing, whatever. We give each other the secret *Fight Club* handshake— which looks and feels like a regular old handshake to the untrained eye, but we FF players know better—and go our separate ways. He and his two fellow backward-baseball-cap-wearing buddies head off to potentially do the terrible stripper-, drug-, and gambling-related activities that I would do if I were twenty-three years old and unleashed upon Las Vegas for a weekend, while I drag my old, nearly forty-year-old ass off to meet my own buddies—Craig, an FF rookie from Manhattan, and Adam, another college buddy who drove up from LA and a six-year FF vet—at which point we'll probably just shuffle over to a $5.99 early-bird-special buffet dinner, then settle in for a nice, quiet evening of chilled prune juice and *Golden Girls* reruns before falling asleep around 8 P.M.

I hop a shuttle bus. For what feels like the next four weeks, we stop at every single hotel in the city—the Bellagio, the Venetian, Mandalay Bay, Barbary Coast, the Luxor, the Flamingo, Tropicana, New York New York, the Hard Rock, Caesars, a Motel 6, a Dumpster behind the Motel 6, every conceivable stop within a twenty-block radius—before the driver finally pulls up to my home for the next two nights, Bally's, and mercifully releases me.

Despite the butt-numbing shuttle ride, I still feel that little electric undercurrent of excitement because—well, I *am* in Vegas for God's sake, and if you're not excited to be in Vegas, you might want to stick a mirror under your nose to see if you're still breathing.

Vegas, baby!

Opting out of the *Golden Girls* marathon, I spend a few minutes watching Craig and Adam lose about $100 apiece playing blackjack at the Palms before I head over to the Rio Hotel Pavilion for the WCOFF draft facilitator orientation at 8 P.M.

This is less a "room" and more of an airplane hangar: an absolutely gargantuan, sixty-thousand-square-foot ballroom (up from last year's thirty-five thousand square feet, a testimony to the hobby's instant growth) with hundreds of white-cloth-covered banquet tables—three tables to each "draft section"—arranged into a U or horseshoe shape, and each facing a giant board onto which, tomorrow, I will be sticking the draft picks for each team à la Vanna White.

I wish I could claim that being chosen to be a draft facilitator required a grueling, NASA-esque battery of psychological tests and feats of strength, after which only the most perfect human specimens were selected (and the weak given lethal injections and dumped into a nearby swamp). But, honestly, the process wasn't nearly so scientific; all I did was (a) notice on the WCOFF home page that cofounders Lenny Pappano and Emil Kadlec were looking for facilitators with solid NFL and/or FF knowledge and, to boot, would pay a hundred bucks for each draft "facilitated" and (b) send an e-mail to say that I was interested in helping out and sported a higher NFL/fantasy-football IQ than your average garden tool.

I pick up my facilitator information packet, my two free-drink tickets (with which I gladly procure my free Bud Light), and make my way over to one of the draft sections where about twenty guys and one woman sit at the tables facing the draft board. The draft hasn't even started, but already a small crowd of curious onlookers stands behind them, watching intently, almost reverentially, quietly whispering to each other like spectators at a chess match or medical students about to watch one of their professors perform open-heart surgery in an amphitheater.

This is the fantasy "experts," or Draft Masters, draft, a league of twelve teams made up of FF writers and/or the owners of various FF websites from around the country. It's sort of an "exhibition draft" that pits some of the big names against each other for bragging rights and, quite possibly, will give us facilitators a glimpse into how some of the drafts might go when the masses arrive tomorrow for the real thing.

I eavesdrop on a few conversations and learn that one of these FanEx teams is last year's $200,000 WCOFF champ, Chris Schussman, and his wife, Melissa. Even though Chris no doubt has a big target on his back heading into tomorrow's draft, with six hundred FF rebels waiting to stage a bloody coup and storm his cushy pigskin palace on high—I will learn tomorrow that, for this reason, he is actually quite paranoid about disclosing his draft strategies to the film crews who interview him—tonight anyway, he and Melissa seem to be enjoying themselves as they joke and make small talk with their competitors at the experts table.

The draft begins, and my fellow gawkers and I soon realize that, as David Dorey told me, there truly is no such thing as an "expert." Even though these are *supposed to be* some of the most insightful FF minds in the country—David and Whitney of TheHuddle.com fame; Dave Dodds and Joe Bryant (founders of another well-known FF site, Footballguys.com); owners/operators of other sites like FantasyAsylum.com, DraftSharks.com, and many more—all of whom have been specially invited to participate in this exhibition game of sorts, it's not long before I hear rumblings in reaction to some of their shaky picks. The two owners of one team, who started out fine, if slightly injury-risky, with Priest Holmes as the first overall pick, are the main target of the crowd's wrath. They choose Redskins RB Trung "Soon to Be Backing Up Ladell Betts If Last Night's Season Opener Is Any Indication" Canidate in the second round, which causes some audible wincing and skeptical murmuring. But this pales in comparison to the reaction to their fourth-round selection—Ike Hilliard, WR, New York Giants. Ike Hilliard . . . *in the fourth?!* And this despite the availability of monumentally better WRs such as Derrick Mason, Jerry Porter, Peerless Price, and—for the love of God—Hines Ward, who's only been one of the best WRs in fantasy football over the past few years!

Upon seeing the Hilliard pick, the rumblings turn to outright gasps of horror.

"Holy shit, that's awful!" exclaims a flabby mountain of a guy who looks like a former high school offensive lineman who's let himself go. He's wearing a Brett Favre jersey and those swirly, multicolored, elastic-waistband, pajama-like sweatpants (Packer green and yellow, appropriately), not even trying to control his volume and conceal his contempt for the Team 1 owners, who sit not three feet away from him. And he's relentless. "Jesus, did they not see the game last night? Canidate sucks!" he chuckles (speaking for all of us, honestly, but we're all too polite/wimp-like to speak up), and spits some dip juice into his empty Coors Light bottle. "I mean, shit, Canidate probably isn't even starting anymore. That was a fucking horrible pick, just *horrrrrrible.*" They pretend not to hear him now doing his Bill Walton impression and sit there with frozen smiles on their faces. The whole crowd is staring at them. They *have to be* dying here. I don't even want to say which website they're from, as business will surely take a dip if word ever gets out that they took Ike freaking Hilliard in the fourth round.

But Brett Favre's fat, Skoal-chewing brother isn't letting them off the hook. "Seriously, how do you guys make a living at this stuff?" he asks, loud enough for all to hear. "Fuck, guys, Ike Hilliard in the *fourth*? What, Alvin Harper wasn't available?"

One of the Team 1 guys finally turns around, smiling, but I can almost hear his teeth grinding. "All right, take it easy, we get it."

"I'm not saying," Fat Favre says, innocently holding up his hands, "I'm just saying."

Obnoxious? Yes. But he's got a point. Seeing their last two picks, I find myself doubting their skill. Did these two jokers chloroform the team that was *supposed to be* drafting, drag them into a nearby janitor's closet, switch clothes, and take their place at the "experts" table? I quietly mention to the guy standing next to me that Price, Ward, and Mason were still on the board when they took Hilliard.

"Those guys are idiots," he whispers. I study his profile out of the corner of my eye, not wanting to stare at him too long. There's something familiar about this guy. Where do I know him from? I quickly scan through my mental hard drive, downloading mental PDF files and JPEGs of my recent past.

He wasn't on the airplane.

He wasn't on the shuttle bus from the airport.

He's not Craig or Adam.

He's not my dad.

He's not . . . wait, I got it! He's Green Monster guy! Way back in May, Big Dog, Shergul, and I went to a Sox-Angels game at Fenway—managed to snag Green Monster seats, no less—and were talking about my impending trip to the WCOFF. All of a sudden, the guy next to us, there with his teenage son, leans in and says that he, too, would be heading out to WCOFF. I was blown away. Just another unexpected *Fight Club* moment in the Green Monster seats.

I tap him on the shoulder. "Hey, you're the guy from the Sox game . . . the Monster seats."

He faces me, takes a second to figure out just who the hell *I* am, and then smiles. "Hey! Mark, right?"

I shake his hand, marveling that he remembers my name. "Yeah, we met at the Sox game a couple months ago."

"Sure, sure. I'm Jeff," he reminds me, perhaps sensing that I wouldn't remember his name if it were tattooed on his forehead. "Hey, I checked out your website. Funny stuff." (Like the shameless promotional whore that I am, I had written down my Sports Rag URL on a Fenway frank napkin sometime and given it to him around the seventh inning.)

Jeff Mowery, forty-five, is a CPA from Chicago. He looks every bit the accountant—round glasses, a little on the pale side, a constantly quizzical expression; he sort of resembles a slightly smaller version of former Clinton prosecutor Kenneth Starr—all of which is deceiving, because underneath that unassuming, not-exactly-athletic demeanor is a sharp wit and a competitive marathon runner. Jeff is married with two daughters (a twenty-year-old at the University of Illinois; a ten-year-old) and two sons (a seventeen-year-old applying to Harvard early decision; the fourteen-year-old whom I met briefly at Fenway). The latter, he tells me, is the only one who's really into sports, and FF has become nice bonding material between father and son. "We talk about it all the time. He leaves me notes on developments around the legue and meets me at the door with news like 'Hey, Dad, the Pats fired their lawyer!' after the Patriots released Lawyer Milloy. We're very close, but FF has made us that much closer."

In other words, Jeff sounds as if he could teach a course not only in how to raise really smart kids who will probably get into Harvard, but also in how *not* to get too obsessed with FF while, at the same time, being able to play as much as you want and even go to Vegas five times a year.

We also discuss the basic things, in his opinion, that an FF player—specifically a newbie—needs to know prior to a season: Understand the league rules. Buy one good magazine and read it from cover to cover. Get a source of training-camp and weekly updates, some sort of e-mail update. Ask questions of the other owners. Get a second opinion from a nonowner on any trade offer.

After a few more minutes of watching the "experts" draft, Jeff and I head back out into the Rio casino to meet Craig and Adam, who look exhausted from handing over their life savings to various blackjack dealers up and down the Strip. The four of us have a drink, we grab a late Mexican dinner, during which we talk about—what else?—sports, everything from Yankees–Red Sox and Cubs–White Sox (Jeff is a lifelong Cubbies fan) to, of course, fantasy football. He likes my Priest pick at #5 overall. "Big touchdown year for Priest," he predicts.

I'm in bed at 2:15 A.M.—relatively early by Vegas standards but long after most geriatrics have turned in.

I have this awful dream where Priest's hip literally comes unhinged from his body and, growing a set of bizarre, blood-covered piranha teeth, devours Priest whole, right along with my 2003 season.

Serves me right for eating two giant seafood enchiladas right before bed. Real crabmeat my ass.

After finding myself wide-awake at 4:30 A.M. thanks to jet lag and my piranha nightmare, I go for a run on the Strip. The drunks and hookers staggering home gawk at me as if I were an alien. *Who the hell does anything healthy in Vegas?* But I pay them no heed. *I'm* a fantasy football draft facilitator, dammit! Outta my way . . .

I make my way over to the Rio for the predraft breakfast.

In 2002, while commonly known in FF circles, WCOFF was a barely noticeable blip on the national sports radar. Now, after just one short year, I see four film crews setting up cameras, boom stands, lights, etc.—one crew from HBO, one from ESPN, and two independent film groups making documentaries on FF. I can't help but think that over the next few years, this will evolve from a still-semi-underground-yet-enormous convention event, into a *World Series of Poker*–type broadcast, into, finally, a yearly spectacle on mainstream network television. It's not so far-fetched, trust me.

I get my official facilitator badge, scarf down some scrambled eggs and bacon, and wait for the doors to the airplane hangar to open and this year's competitors to come flooding in.

And flood they do.

Like a general-admission Who concert (minus the trampled teens) approximately twelve hundred people come rushing into the room and find their preassigned draft tables, numbered one through fifty, twenty-four team owners per table, no more than two representatives per team. It's the largest "Christmas Day" in the largest living room in the country.

I head off to find the draft table I'll be working. But before I even have to search, Jeff, sipping a Red Bull, tracks me down and tells me that we'll be working the same draft: League #47, right up in the front of the room. And there'll be a third facilitator joining us, Rob—a thin, friendly guy who looks a bit like the singer/piano player Ben Folds and is a programmer for FantasyAsylum.com, a Washington, D.C.–based website.

We split up the duties: Rob will work the clock and announce the picks, and Jeff will write in the picks on the small draft sheet, while I take the Vanna role and stick the names up on the big board. The player names are color-coded by position—green for RB, yellow for WR, red for QB, and so on. 100 percent idiotproof. My duties aren't what you call challenging.

"Last year the facilitators were terrible," mutters one of our League #47 owners, a curmudgeonly, sixtysomething man with military-cropped gray hair. He sizes me up the way a Parris Island drill sergeant sizes up a fat, lazy new recruit—skepticism at best; contempt and borderline disgust at worst. "We had to tell them what positions guys played, what teams they played for, they didn't know how to spell the players' names. It was a real clusterfuck." He stares at me, eyebrows raised, as if to ask, Is this year going to be any better?

Not expecting to be heckled so soon, I assure Full Metal Jacket here that things will be much better this year, having no idea whether they will be. Honestly, even though I somehow retain NFL player information the way Rain Man remembered Abbott & Costello's "Who's on first?" routine, this guy's making me a little nervous.

"OK then, well . . ." Not even finishing my sentence, I walk off to join Jeff, and we introduce ourselves to the other League #47 drafters. It's a mix of young and old—ages ranging from midtwenties (two guys from Hoboken, New Jersey) to sixty-four (the Drill Sergeant). Nearly all of them are wearing football jerseys of some sort (Eagles, Vikings, Tampa Bay Bucs). There are two one-man teams, two husband-wife teams, and eight two-man teams. Everyone seems more or less friendly and excited, if a bit pensive, as they secretly discuss last-minute strategy and size up the competition. As an entry fee, $1,500-ish isn't exactly chump change, and this room is filled with some of the most obsessed, dedicated FF players in the country, all vying for more than $650,000 in prize money and, more than that, the respect that comes from being crowned champion of the largest FF league in the universe. Plus, for reasons I can't begin to explain, a grown man wearing a wizard's outfit is sitting not twenty yards away. Rob tells me the guy wore the same Mickey-Mouse-in-*Fantasia* getup last year and calls himself, not surprisingly, The Wizard.

Ohhhhh-kay.

Emil and Lenny, the event's cofounders, welcome the 2003 participants and thank them for traveling far and wide to be here, exemplified by the variety of NFL teams—and wizards—represented today through various apparel. Then they introduce Andy Mousalimas, one of the original GOPPPL members, who is standing next to an oversize, cardboard blowup that—from my view, three miles away across the convention hall—looks about the size of an FF draft sheet. Turns out, it *is* the original GOPPPL draft sheet. Lenny informs the crowd (most of whom might not have read Emil and Bob Harris's article on FF's founding) that Andy, who's got to be pushing eighty years old, had the *very first* pick in the *very first* FF draft held back in 1963 at his bar, the King's X, which would later become the country's first unofficial FF headquarters.

Lenny reads some of those first picks from the sheet: George Blanda, Johnny Unitas, Jim Brown, Mike Ditka, Jim Taylor, Frank Gifford. All of the studs of the day. Like cave paintings or crumbling biblical tablets, this draft sheet serves as a window into the past of this wonderful game, and

Mousalimas is clearly touched by how far "his" game has come. It's a borderline emotional moment—something I wouldn't have expected in this testosterone-filled room in a zillion years—and Mousalimas is applauded the way a Hollywood legend would be while receiving a lifetime achievement award at the Oscars.

After a few more announcements and introductions, including last year's champ, Chris Schussman (who stands up and gives a wave to the polite applause that says, "Yes, we respect what you did last year, and now we're going to kick your ass"), Lenny says, "And now I'll turn it over to the facilitators, and welcome once again to the World Championship of Fantasy Football!"

The drafters, chomping at the bit to unwrap their new toys, ramp up their applause from polite to thunderous and start hooting and hollering, pumping their fists.

With that, at almost 11 A.M., we're off and running.

Drill Sergeant and his draft partner, having drawn the first pick in an earlier random draft lottery, start things off by taking Clinton Portis. Nervous for no good reason other than that twenty-four people are staring at me to see if I'll screw up, I manage to stick Portis's name up there more or less at a straight angle.

Good start, Mark. Only about 239 more picks to go.

During the first big break for lunch after the eighth round, I talk to Drill Sergeant, who is actually named Patrick and turns out to be a pleasant, almost grandfatherly figure, despite looking as if he might know how to snap my neck with his pinkie finger. A computer instructor from the Detroit area, he and his draft partner—a soft-spoken, round-faced, good-natured engineer simply named Oz—have been playing fantasy football for more than seventeen years.

I ask him how the FF world has changed over the years he's been playing.

"I don't know if you remember the paper *The National*, started by that sports columnist, what's his name . . . ?"

"Frank Deford?" I offer like an excited schoolboy trying to impress the wise old professor.

"Yeah, I think it was," Oz interjects, the first words he's spoken yet.

"Yeah, Deford," Patrick agrees. "I mean, we would literally—and this was back in the old days—we would wait for that magazine to come out, and it was always like four days old, but that was all we used. Little did we know, a buddy in our league who lived in Chicago had access to *The National* and other information two days before us. He won the league three out of the first four years. But once the hobby grew, it was a whole different story. The informational playing field leveled."

So then, as it is now, timely access to the right information gave FF players a leg up. As for drafting a successful team then versus now, Patrick says that even if you *do* have access to the right information before your league-mates, "it's still a crapshoot whether or not you'll get the best/right players on your team."

Prior to the draft, one of the film crews handed out a survey asking basic questions about FF, and Oz has some simple answers:

Survey: What do you plan on doing in Vegas other than fantasy football?
Oz: Gambling, drinking, and partying.
Survey: What does FF mean to you?
Oz: Five months of heaven.
Survey: What do your friends and family think of you coming to Vegas for WCOFF?
Oz: Friends think it's awesome; family thinks I'm nuts.

That about sums up most of the participants here today: fun-loving partyers who love fantasy football and don't care what other people think. Or so I thought. Because when perusing the WCOFF message board in the days and weeks after the draft, I discover that not only do some of the participants care what other people think, they're downright embarrassed by the oddball antics of the Wizard and some of the other "characters" that the film crews seemed to focus on. Why? Because they portrayed the average fantasy football player as a dunce-cap-wearing goofball. "It's a sad day for the regular fantasy football participant," one person writes in the message board. "He made us all look like friggin' idiots." Another fears that, thanks to the slanted TV coverage, FF players will now be lumped in with another widely ridiculed, much maligned group of costume-wearing convention-goers—the dreaded Trekkies. "When they use him [the Wizard] on camera it makes ALL of us look like those Star Trek freaks, walking around with our fingers in a V shape, talking about tribbles and flipping our cellphones open dramatically and saying, 'Beam me up, LaDainian!'" But a third board member has an altogether different—and perhaps more realistic—take on the opinions of the outside world. "Who the hell cares what they think? I sure don't. This is big business. This is the future of professional sports. Why do you think that HBO was there in the first place?"

Having been there, I can tell you that guys like the Wizard were the minority. The Rio ballroom was filled with football fans, plain and true, who just love that there are others with whom they can share their love of football. Sure, people might ask, "Why on earth would a person actually want to do *that* with their time?" But we FF junkies might ask that same question of people who climb big rocks or run twenty-six miles without stopping or chase a dimpled little white ball around finely manicured patches of grass and try to whack it into a hole with a club. The answer? Because that's what they enjoy.

It's with this sense of kinship that, after five hours of drafting, I conclude my League #47 draft facilitator responsibilities. Five hours. Two hundred forty picks. None of them real head-scratchers (like Ike Hilliard in the fourth round of Draft Masters last night). All placed on the board with deft skill and accuracy, I may add.

Jeff, Rob, and I make the rounds, shaking hands with all of our drafters, and they thank us for performing our duties with something bordering on actual competence. And you know what? It feels good to have made their draft as smooth and fun as possible. It's clearly a good bunch of people, and I wish them all luck in their quest for the two hundred grand.

As Jeff drops me off at Bally's, we watch a beautiful young Asian girl wearing a tiny veil vomit out the passenger side window of a Hummer limousine while fifteen of her fellow bachelorette partygoers cheer her on.

Yeah, um . . . Vegas, baby . . . (sigh) . . . Vegas.

9

Kickoff and, Alas, Liftoff

After six interminable months of winter, spring, summer, snow, rain, heat, *Joe Millionaire*, the *Bachelorette*, Clay Aiken, Ruben Studdard, Oscars, Tonys, Grammys, Emmys, Barry Bonds, Bud Selig, the Osbournes, *Punk'd!*, and other people, places, and things that don't matter to me and never will, there is reason to celebrate today.

There is great rejoicing across the land.

The eighty-fourth NFL season is here.

(Note: Yes, technically, there was a game on Thursday, but I didn't have any players on the Jets or Redskins, so honestly, it didn't really count. Plus, I think opening the season on a Thursday is akin to playing baseball on AstroTurf or Michael Jackson fathering a child: it's just plain unnatural, and it would behoove us all if we just pretended it never happened and never spoke of it again.)

Even that my beloved Red Sox have mercilessly pummeled those infernal Yankees by a total score of 22–4 over the last two days to pull within a game of the AL East lead—not that baseball means anything right now compared to football—doesn't come close to measuring up to that today, for the first time since the seconds ticked down in San Diego early this year and "Chuckie" Gruden lofted the Lombardi Trophy, NFL games are here.

Most importantly, this also means that after countless mock drafts, real drafts, arguments, projections, predictions, and eager speculation, the 2003 fantasy football season has begun.

Hallelujah! And there was much rejoicing across the land!

Unfortunately, while these wonderful games are being played from Buffalo to Seattle, I'm currently being held captive by the evil, unfeeling bastards at Continental Airlines as I make my way back from Vegas and WCOFF. I'm operating on four hours of sleep over the past day and a half, traversing three time zones, eating microwaved airplane sandwiches of some frightening meat-based substance that's been pounded into more or less patty shape, and of course, more than anything, I'm absolutely dying to know how my 2003 Acme squad is playing.

It's actually not Continental's fault. Like a complete moron, I scheduled my return flight so that I'd miss all the games today. The helpless "not knowing" feeling is killing me. Absolutely *killing* me. I mean, come on, people, I know not everyone on the plane is a football fan, but is it really too much to ask for them to show the Bills-Patriots duking it out at Rich Stadium in Buffalo instead of Harrison Ford glaring at people in *K-19: The Widowmaker*?

The NFL is back for godsake! Is anybody listening to me here?! Hello?! God, I hope I'm just thinking this and not actually yelling it aloud.

Thanks to the good people at Sprint PCS, I *am* able to check some scores and stats during an all-too-brief layover in Houston, and I discover that my Acme Fantasy Football, Inc., is starting out pretty well.

Priest is blowing up yet again (knock on wood), with 2 TDs, 60 yards rushing, and 40 receiving in the first half alone. God, I love that Priest! If he stays healthy, I see him leading all of FF in scoring for the second consecutive year. Trent Green's already thrown a TD, which is a good start to what I think will be a surprisingly studlike season for him. Stephen Davis has about 55 yards rushing on only 9 or 10 carries, a nice little average, though I'd like to see him pop one into the end zone against the Jags. Heap and Plaxico, playing against each other in Pittsburgh, haven't done much yet, but it's still early.

And my opponent? The Dream Team, owned by two former coworkers, Steve and Joe, has Portis who already has a TD and 50-plus yards on 3 measly carries, so he's looking worthy of the first overall pick in many leagues so far, including almost half of the WCOFF leagues that drafted just yesterday. But other than Portis's already big game, from what I can tell, I'm ahead as of 2 P.M.

So, to take my mind off the sheer agony of *not* knowing what's happening on football fields across America, not to mention trying to digest my processed-squirrel-meat sandwich or whatever the hell I just ate, I give

K-19 a shot, but after approximately fifty-three instances of Harrison Ford glaring intensely at someone, I fall asleep.

Exiting Logan Airport a few hours later, the anticipation is devouring me from the inside out, like some sort of flesh-eating virus. I have absolutely no idea what's happened to my beloved Acme squad. None. This is not good.

As my cabbie and I sit in Callahan Tunnel traffic (*Where the hell are all you people going and why do you have to go there now?!*), I squirm in the backseat like a caged rat, grinding my teeth, taking deep breaths, generally trying to remain calm while secretly wanting to smash my head through the Plexiglas partition and find some NFL coverage on the radio, even though we can't get any reception in this godforsaken tunnel, anyway.

I mercifully get home about forty-five minutes later (note: it's approximately four miles from Logan to my place . . . thanks, Big Dig!). While I am, of course, dying to see my beloved wife and tell her all about my trip, she's out, so I'm immediately in front of my computer.

At first glance, things look good.

Priest exploded for 85 rushing yards, 90-something receiving, and 2 TDs, good for 37 points (did I mention that I'm in love with Priest?). Plaxico got 116 yards, no TDs, for 21 points. Davis got 111 yards rushing, 30-something receiving, no TDs, for 24 points. Green, Heap, Jackson, Wilkins, and Tampa chipped in for a weak total of 42 points, but in the end I'm looking at a nice, high Felon League score of 124 points. As I peruse the other games in my league, it turns out this is the second-highest score in the league in Week 1. Yes, folks, I have assembled a veritable FF powerhouse! Project Kick My League's Ass is on its way to a perfect, 16-0 '72 Dolphins-esque Super Bowl campaign! I will not be stopped!

Except for one tiny problem: the Dream Team, my opponents, thanks to the dangerous and unstoppable Clinton Portis of the Broncos, just happened to rack up the *first* highest FFL score in Week 1, a whopping 174. To make matters worse, I also got hosed by several this-shit-only-happens-to-me performances by Dream Team players. Kurt Warner suffered a concussion and fumbled like 13 times but still managed to rack up over 300 yards. Tiki Barber played, and played well, with a dislocated finger. And finally, Mike Shanahan—or Satan, as he's known to FF players—defied all

NFL head-coach logic and, despite the Broncos already having blown out the Browns, left his superstar (and smallish, injury-prone) RB Portis in for the entire fourth quarter to rack up *even more* points against me than he had already. Meanwhile, my own team saw Priest finish a piddly 15 yards short of our 100-yard rushing bonus, and 2 measly yards short of our 100-yard receiving bonus. I soon learn that, unlike the robotic Shanahan, weepy, touchy-feely Dick Vermeil rested Priest for most of the second half after he scored those 2 TDs. Not that I would have been happy had Vermeil left Priest in the game (a Chiefs blowout) and gotten him hurt, and it was the right move in *real* football. But screw real football . . . this is fantasy, and I needed those goddamn bonus points!

I fall to my knees and shake my fists at the ceiling.

Curses, foul FF gods! Why dost thou forsake me?! Why, oh why, must I fall victim to stupid, blind luck every single season?!

Seriously, I ask you, is this how the season is going to go? Are the FF gods going to crush the very soul out of me one week at a time by leading me *ever so close* to victory, so close I can almost taste it, and then yanking it away? Will I be like poor, tortured Tantalus, condemned to spend eternity in Hades cursed with a dying thirst while, ironically, standing up to his chin in a pool of water, and yet, whenever he tries to drink, the water teasingly lowers itself, over and over and over, never once quenching his thirst throughout his cursed afterlife? *Will I?*

I swear to you, FF gods, if you continue to curse me like this, I will never play your foul, wretched game ever again!

Ah, who am I kidding? I'll always play this stupid game. And, hey, all's not lost, especially since just this year we added two extra playoff spots for the highest-scoring teams who *don't* make the playoffs based on win-loss record (a rule enacted to combat the "pure schedule luck" factor that's killed some great teams in the past).

So, despite this crushing, frustrating loss, I'm taking a page out of the real NFL teams' notebooks, putting Week 1 behind me, and looking ahead to next week.

Because in fantasy football, there's always next week.

10

FF: Friend or Foe?

The Week 2 games are here.

Unlike last Sunday, when I was being held captive in the sky after making the dumbest travel arrangements in airline history, I have my first full day of football ahead of me.

Celia, keenly sensing that staying home will be like being stuck in a padded cell with a manic, teeth-gnashing lunatic, has agreed to go shopping at the Wrentham outlets with her friend Holly for most of the day. Thus, I have the living room, television, refrigerator, and eight straight hours of quality "me" time to do with as I please.

As always, I start with some last-minute information-gathering on the Huddle, Rotoworld, and other sites. Then I tune into *Sunday NFL Countdown* on ESPN. I flip back and forth between the Fox pregame show with Terry Bradshaw, Howie Long, James Brown, and some token smoking-hot bimbette weather girl wearing what looks like a slightly larger doily as a shirt, and CBS's pregame show with Jimmy Johnson, Boomer Esiason, Dan Marino, and Deion Sanders. Don't know why, but I get a kick out of Deion. Maybe it's because he's a gazillionaire and still attempted to sue his mechanic to get out of paying a $500 car repair bill.

Both pregame shows are sorta painful, honestly, but, hey, information is information, and I'm just excited to be sitting here once again after a full year, awaiting the start of my NFL television season. And speaking of information, there's more FF info in the mainstream media now than I've ever seen before in my FF lifetime. Fox, CBS, ESPN, all of them are now adding more frequent news and notes for FF players.

"Experts" share their start/bench advice, sleeper picks, all that. You know that FF awareness has skyrocketed in the mainstream media when Fox's ninety-seven-year-old correspondent Dick Stockton is telling fantasy football players to take note of Kansas City tight end Tony Gonzalez. About 99 percent of the field is one step ahead of you there, Dick, but thanks for the tip, buddy.

Over the next one-third of a day, I'm prepared to watch three full games. (While I'd love to have the NFL Ticket and watch all the games, three is all I can get on network TV. But, making do with what I have, I'm determined to stay up all the way through the ESPN Sunday-night game, whether it ends sometime around Tuesday morning or not.) And, of course, I'll log endless computer time checking on my team, praying that I don't run into some hard luck like last week.

Worse than my luck, however, was my inability to check the game updates for my teams. And, yes, you read right, that's *teams*, plural. For the first time ever, I've taken on a new lover, so to speak, and joined a public Yahoo! league. I feel that I'm cheating on the Felon League, but my buddy Craig needed another owner for a public league and I figured, what the hell. It might be fun to follow a different group of players. I've never been in a Yahoo! league before. I'm curious to find out whether they're as bad as people say, so I signed up. So far, it's been just about what I expected. Aside from one or two guys who seem to know what they're doing, this league is a fucking train wreck.

When we held our draft a few weeks ago, three absentee owners trusted the "auto draft" function to pick their teams based on preranked players, which led to such strategic selections as bottom-tier kicker Matt Bryant in the fourth round and the Packers defense in the fifth. It was hilarious. Meanwhile, using my silly little human brain, I loaded up on running backs and wide receivers and ended up with a starting squad of Daunte, Ricky Williams, Deuce McAllister, Eric Moulds, Chad Johnson, Hines Ward, Marcus Pollard, Carolina's defense, and Jason Elam, with a bench—*a bench!*—of Steve McNair (who I think has a huge season ahead of him), William Green, Moe Williams, Peerless Price, and the injured Donald Driver, all guys who may or may not be the studs they're projected to be, but were taken by the sixth round in my Felon League draft. Granted, it's a seven-team league, so *everyone* has all-star teams and some solid players are still available on the waiver wire (Garrison Hearst and Curtis Martin, for two). In this league, I won my Week 1 game, beating another all-star team made up of McNabb, Plaxico, Henry, Jamal Lewis, Toomer, and other studs. And while it helped in its oh-so-tiny way to ease the sting of my bitter Felon League defeat, it really didn't mean a hell of a lot to me. This is a league of juggernaut teams owned by strangers with questionable, at best, FF acumen. How much fun can winning under such circumstances be? Beating strangers in cyberspace pales in comparison to making your close friends miserable and, subsequently, rubbing their faces in it. "I don't need the respect of a bunch of clown strangers," Cenk tells me. "I need the respect of my peers. I'm unconcerned with the pain of strangers, but when it's my friends in pain, that's the spice of life."

While I hope Cenk's exaggerating (otherwise he might be a sociopath), I couldn't agree more. I want Felon League glory, dammit! I want to see my friends in tears! I want to prance around like Elaine's crazy actor boyfriend on *Seinfeld*, wearing a big crown, holding a golden staff, and yelling, "I'm the Whiz! IIIIIIII'm the Whiz! And nobody beats me!"

But today, in Felon League play, I have an *extremely* tough game against my pal Josh and his team, the Rat Bastards, a formidable squad of Air McNair, LaDainian Tomlinson, Jamal Lewis, Torry Holt, Rod Smith, Randy McMichael, Kris Brown, and the Ravens defense. I thought he had the best draft of all of us, and my Acme squad has its work cut out, even though McNair has a knee injury and has been questionable all week. Of course, with my luck, this means he'll go for 350 yards and 4 TDs. Bank on it.

Still, I'm hoping Priest will pick up where he left off last week. I pray Plaxico has another 100-plus yard game and throws in a TD for good measure. I need Heap to add a TD to his solid 55-yard game last week. Maybe Darrell Jackson busts out against Arizona and throws up 80+ and a TD or two? And I hope that Stephen Davis—Tampa defense or no Tampa defense—manages to push one across the goal line and gets maybe 75 yards rushing. This was my biggest decision of the week: whether to bench Davis in favor of Detroit's Olandis Gary, who, while not an RB of Davis's caliber, might put up as good if not better numbers against Green Bay than Davis will versus the hellacious Bucs. But as of now, 12:01 P.M., I'm putting my faith in Davis and hoping he pulls off a minor miracle. I have to trust my original draft, at least until I start to panic. Always start your studs, as they say.

Is all that too much to ask, you bastard FF gods? Can you please grant me one week of good luck to even my record at 1-1? Can I *please* have some of the pure, dumb fortune that you granted my opponent last week? Or will you smite me down once again in your evil, vengeful, petty little way?

Wait, I'm sorry, I'm sorry! I take that back. I love you, FF gods. Really, I love you like my own mother. Can I get you anything? An Italian-sausage sandwich? How 'bout a Fresca?

Well, the clock strikes one. Here we go; my *real* NFL opening day has begun. Up here in Boston, with the Pats playing at Philly in the late game, we have Jets-Fins and Rams-Niners. You bet your ass I'm going to watch the Rams game and stick pins into my Torry Holt voodoo doll. No offense Torry, but FF is all business, and considering you play for my enemy today, I need you to snap your leg in half on your first pattern.

Wish me luck, folks.

Ten minutes later I'm screaming, Oh God oh God oh God NO NO NO NO NO NOOOOOOOOOOOOOOOOOOOOOO!

I said wish me luck, not "wish me pain and misery"! And certainly not "wish that Jamal Lewis rushes for an 82-yard TD on the second fucking play of the game and Trent Green throws an INT in *his* first series"! Oh. Mah. Gawd.

I kid you not, this is how my day has begun. Can someone please dig out my eyeballs with a melon scooper?

The CBS ticker scrolls by with an update. Am I hallucinating or did I just see it read the following:

Baltimore 10, Cleveland 0 . . . 9:24, 1st quarter . . . Hey, Mark St. Amant . . . yeah, you, up there in Boston . . . don't look now, but you're totally fucked, man! . . . Jamal Lewis now has 111 yards rushing . . . plus that long TD . . . and it's *only the first quarter* . . . seriously, I wish I were kidding . . . wait, no, I don't, this is hilarious! . . . oh, oh, and get this, Holt just caught a TD, too! . . . and I hope you're drinking already, because there's more . . . ready? . . . Pittsburgh 7, Kansas City 0 . . . Chad Scott, INT of Trent Green for a TD . . . oh, man, are you going to get your ass kicked today! . . . why do you even play fantasy football? . . . seriously . . . why do you do it to yourself? . . . you're down 57 to minus 2 and the day is like ten minutes old! . . . oh, this is too funny . . . hold on, I'm sorry, I need to wipe my eyes . . . man, do you suck at fantasy football! . . . my stomach's killing me . . . and I hear you quit your job to write a book on this shit?! . . . oh, that's priceless! . . . yeah, good decision there, Lombardi! BWAAAAAAA ha ha ha ha ha ha! . . . Minnesota 7, Jacksonville 0 . . . 8:34, 1st quarter . . .

What did I do to deserve this? I beg of you . . . what!? I pay my taxes! I call my parents about once a week! I've been a good husband, brother, son, friend! Sure, on long, boring drives I've sometimes daydreamed about picking up a hitchhiker, robbing him, duct-taping his mouth shut, and leaving him for dead tied to a scarecrow in the middle of a remote cornfield, but I've never *actually done it*!

So I ask you again, *why dost thou forsake me, oh, bitter, cruel FF gods!* Your latest evil minion, Jamal Lewis, is ripping my heart from my chest and, worse, seems to be enjoying it! Oh, sweet Jesus, I'm in for another long goddamn afternoon. And maybe, if this keeps up, an even longer season!

Kill me! Please kill me!

OK. All right. Deep breaths. A couple of hours have passed, and with the help of some rhinoceros tranquilizers and a shot of 700-proof grain alcohol, calm is being restored, at least partly anyway.

Just as I thought all hope was lost for the day, Priest has torched the Steelers for 122 yards rushing, 3 TDs, one of them a 31-yarder (yahtzee!), racking up a whopping 62 points! Meanwhile, in the same game, Plaxico, whose Steelers were playing from behind for most of the second half, hauled down 115 yards and a touchdown, a bonus baby no less (33-yarder), giving me 41 more points!

Still, despite these monster performances, I trail the Rat Bastards. Jamal Lewis has an NFL record-setting 295 rushing yards and 2 TDs, *both* of them long ones. Do you frigging be*lieve* that? A guy breaks the NFL's all-time single-game rushing record . . . and he's playing against *me*! Seriously, this kind of stuff *only* happens to me! While defeat isn't guaranteed, right now, as the old Magic 8 Ball would read, *Outlook not so good.*

I'm down 22 points with Stephen Davis, Darrell Jackson, and the Bucs D going against the Rat Bastards' Tomlinson and Rod Smith. Stay tuned, it might be close. Then again, lemme guess: Davis will finish with 99.5 yards rushing, .5 short of our 10-point bonus. Jackson will get pushed out of bounds on the 1-yard line after a 55-yard reception. The Buccaneers team bus driver will fall asleep at the wheel on the way to the stadium and smash through the front of a Hooters (which, as far as places to die go, wouldn't be *all* bad).

I know this will happen. I *know* it. Losing is my destiny. I am destined to be an FF also-ran until I die, at which time I will lie rotting in the ground being devoured by worms and maggots who feast on my loser flesh despite the rancid, gamy taste of loserish loserdom, while six feet above, my tombstone reads, "Here lies Mark St. Amant. He was average in every way. C-plus/B-minus was all he could ever muster up. And boy did he suck at fantasy football."

God. I. Hate. This. Game.

11

FF: Sex or Marriage?

God. I. Love. This. Game! Did I mention that I love this game? Love it! Sometimes it just makes me feel like singing until little cartoon animals surround me in woodland bliss. So I will. *Zip-a-dee-doo-dah, zip-a-dee-ay . . . My, oh my what a wonderful day!*

How can I possibly be happy this morning? Well, last I reported I was getting my ass handed to me. I was down 22 points heading into the late games, and the Rat Bastards had a total stud (Tomlinson) and a good player (Rod Smith) going for them. All seemed lost. The FF gods had napalmed me back to the Stone Age yet again, and as a result, Project Kick My League's Ass was off to an inauspicious 0-2 start.

But then, get this . . .

Koren Robinson, Seattle's #1 WR, got suspended for being late to a meeting on Saturday—what's worse, Coach Mike Holmgren didn't tell anyone about it, thus screwing millions of Robinson owners out of production from that position and earning Holmgren Public Enemy #1 status in the FF world, previously occupied by Mike "Try to Guess Which RB I'm Starting Today" Shanahan. But with Robinson out, this meant that my man, Darrell Jackson, was put in a great position to step up as Matt Hasselbeck's primary target. And step up he did: 133 yards receiving and not 1, but 2 long TDs (55 and 66 yards, for hellacious Felon League bonus points!). And what of Stephen Davis? Well, while Priest and Plax might get all the ink on my squad, Davis is my workhorse, plowing away, piling up the yardage without all the fanfare. After posting a solid 111 yards on opening day, as the late-day sun set over Charlotte's Ericsson Stadium, he put the nail in the Rat Bastards' coffin with 142 rushing yards (against the vaunted Tampa D no less!), good for 24 much needed points.

OK, some more thoughts on Davis. I know it's only Week 2, and I know this relationship is new, and I don't want to rush things and scare him off. But I simply can't help how I feel. Redskins coach Steve Spurrier—who isn't long for NFL coaching, if you ask me—was a complete idiot to let him go. But Davis is still relatively young and, as his first two games prove, quite capable of being a feature back, thank you very much. I had this feeling that Davis would be a big sleeper RB this year, rushing behind a monster offensive line and playing in Panthers coach John Fox's pound-the-ball-thirty-times offense. Yes, folks, despite feeling sort of icky, I think I'm falling in love with Stephen Davis. In fact, right now, I'm scribbling some possibilities for our future together on my Trapper Keeper notebook . . .

Mark Davis . . . ?

Mr. Mark Davis–St. Amant . . . ?

Mr. Mark St. Amant–Davis . . . ?

Mark S. A. Davis . . . ?

I digress.

Anyway, after the devastating beginning, my final score for Week 2 is:

Acme: (a staggering, sending-a-message-to-my-league-that-I-mean-business-this-year) 211.

Rat Bastards: (a very-impressive-but-unfortunately-the-wrong-week-to-be-playing-Acme) 161.

Yes, good readers, Acme is in the win column! Project Kick My League's Ass is back to .500! (I also won my Yahoo! league game, but, honestly, who cares? This is a league where the Bears defense was autodrafted in the fifth round—and yet I *just* picked up Marc Bulger off the waiver wire.)

But it's a long season, and it's time to start preparing for Week 3, when I'll face my first real challenge: my man-crush, Stephen Davis, has his bye week, meaning it's time to find a decent replacement #2 RB or face the horrifying possibility of starting either Olandis Gary or Michael Pittman. Not good.

•   •   •

Out of sheer boredom I check my baseball team to see how it's doing. Lo and behold, while not even paying attention for the past month, I discover that I'm still in first place by a whopping 27 HRs. Yippee. Hoo-rah.

Zzzzzzzzzzzzzzzzzzz . . .

Sure, the money will be nice ($650), but baseball has virtually no relevance in my life right now. None. Not even with the Sox trying to hold on to the AL wild-card lead over the Mariners. Baseball, with its interminable 162-game season, just doesn't get my blood pumping the way the week-to-week NFL does. Frank Deford said it best: "[Fantasy] baseball is more like marriage; [Fantasy] football more like sex."

So, considering my total lack of interest in baseball, let's just keep this between ourselves, shall we? No need to let Celia in on that little nugget. The last thing I need right now is to end up on *Dr. Phil.*

12

Trader Mark

Cenk is off to an 0-2 start in the Hershey Highway League and he's agitated by the early-season failures of Donovan McNabb, his starting QB and second-round pick. When a team starts off slowly, the urge to shake things up and make a trade can be overwhelming. But Cenk knows that a good FF owner must resist the urge to make panic moves and lose a stud player while his value is lower than usual.

Early-season heart murmurs are a common ailment for FF players, and a number of players are making their owners wash down handfuls of Pepcid AC with gallons of Mylanta. Tomlinson, the number one overall pick in a lot of leagues, isn't performing up to snuff in the early going, sitting twenty-first in the latest Huddle RB rankings. McNabb is looking lost, tentative, and just very, very bad. Kurt Warner, a comeback-player-of-the-year candidate in most FF circles (and a risky third-round pick by the Dream Team in my Felon League draft!) has already been benched in favor of Bulger. My own inconsistent QB, Trent Green, is making me want to drive all the way to Kansas City just to key his car and egg his house. Curtis Martin is looking as if he were seventy-three years old. Supplement-crazed, 270-pound middle linebacker—er, wide receiver—David Boston, another guy who got lots of preseason hype, has already missed a game, leading me to once again wonder how his knees can support *that much* muscle. It's amazing he hasn't turned green, shredded his uniform, and started swatting army helicopters out of the sky yet.

On the other hand, some early-season surprises have crept up out of nowhere and made their owners happy. Cards rookie Anquan Boldin snagged 200-plus yards in his first game (and looks as if he ain't gonna be stopping anytime soon). Dolphins wide receiver Chris Chambers, and my own Darrell Jackson, join Boldin in the top five WR rankings, while Marvin, Moss, and Owens are nowhere to be found. Moe Williams has plowed his way into the starting RB role in Minnesota. Jay Fiedler, Tommy Maddox, Jeff Garcia (despite the back injury), Doug Johnson, and Quincy Carter are right up there with Daunte Culpepper as the top QBs so far. Jamal Lewis leads in yardage over the likes of LDT, Portis, and Ricky. The top TEs? If you guessed Gonzo, Shockey, or Heap, please beat yourself about the head with a frying pan, as I feel like doing as a Heap owner. Try Alge Crumpler, Josh Norman, and Freddie Jones. Toughest defenses? Bucs? Eagles? Panthers? Nope, more like the Giants, Niners, and—get this—the Chiefs.

And what does this all mean? Bubkes.

If you're a newbie, please write this down and, for lack of a more creative term, call it **Newbie Strategy Tip #1: Don't panic if your stud looks sluggish out of the gates. If healthy, nine studs out of ten will always rise to the top, so hold on to them.** On the other end of the spectrum, it means that the fortunate owners of fast starters and pleasant surprises can't exactly start gloating yet. I mean, do you really think the Chiefs defense will stay on top all year? Will Jay Fiedler finish the year ranked ahead of Peyton? Please.

Still, one can always look to improve one's team. So, I make my first trade offer of the season. With the injury risks of Priest and Davis, I need a more solid backup/emergency RB, especially this upcoming week, than Michael "I Might Be Thrown in Jail for Beating My Wife Any Day Now" Pittman or Olandis "I Can't Even Land the Starting Job on the *Freaking Lions*" Gary.

Scanning the Felon League rosters, I notice that All-American Angus has what looks like the best overall group of startable-right-now RBs (Deuce, William Green, and Charlie Garner), but nothing great at WR (Peerless Price, who isn't settling into the #1 WR slot down in Atlanta with Vick out; Tai Streets, the inconsistent #2 in SF; and Charles Rogers, the Lions' promising but unproven rookie). But, I'm wary of trading with Angus owners John and Grady: they're the ones who gladly took Harrison and Henry off my hands for the useless Faulk and Hines Ward last season, which cost me a playoff berth and a Super Bowl title. Yes, even a year later, I hate them more than poison. (Well, maybe not *that* much, but I at least hate them more than running back by committee.)

Nevertheless, I make my friendly, soft-peddle pitch. "Despite getting completely hosed on our Faulk deal last year, I'm willing to get back on the horse and do some more business with you guys if it means making a win-win trade." Of course, I start off portraying myself as the still-wounded little gazelle limping across the Serengeti and them as the hungry cheetah who, last year, chased me down and devoured me. Sometimes this guilt strategy works, but hardly ever. I offer Darrell Jackson (coming off an astronomical 63-point week) for William Green (semistud running back who had a fantastic second half of 2002).

Now, did I think they'd go for it? Not really. It was a good opening shot, but it wasn't my best offer, which leads us to **Newbie Strategy Tip #2: Always make your first offer a good one, but never make it your *best*.** I *do* think Darrell Jackson will have a huge year while defenses pay more attention to his heavily hyped teammate Koren Robinson. For All-American Angus, losing William Green would be bad, but starting Peerless Price and Tai Streets every week might be worse. I always try to provide some rationale as to why the trade might work for both teams. You can't just say, "Duh, wanna trade Green for Jackson?"

Despite my fine tactics, Grady and John aren't interested. They believe Jackson might be a one-game wonder and his value coming off a huge week might be inflated.

I can't say I blame them for giving me the Heisman. I wouldn't have accepted that trade, either. But I notice that they didn't say, "No thanks, and kindly fuck off." They did what good owners should do and responded with their own rationale, keeping the door open for further talks down the road. But was it an *awful* offer I made? No. And if their WRs continue to shit the bed, and Jackson keeps blowing up, this window to acquire him will soon close for them entirely. That's the risk they take. And as I've discovered many times, sometimes the trades you *don't* make hurt you as much as those you do.

Trading is half the fun of FF for me. Even when trades are rejected—which they usually are because most owners are so chickenshit to make a deal unless it's clear they're getting the better deal—I still enjoy the back-and-forth of trade talks. The negotiating. The posturing. The reasoning. The bartering. And the smack talk that can often result from even the most rational, win-win offers.

Heading into Week 3, it seems I'm not the only one with the trade bug. I receive my first offer of the season, from Ron, owner of the Pound Dawgs (a nod to his beloved Cleveland Browns). And, boy, lemme tell ya, it's a doozy. "You get Amos Zereoue, Peter Warrick, Terry Glenn, Jay Riemersma, and I get Stephen Davis, Darrell Jackson, and Todd Heap," he suggests, presumably biting down on his hand to keep me from hearing his stifled satanic giggles. "What do you think?"

What do I think? Did he just ask what do I *think*? Hmm, well, Ron, let me tell you what I think: I think that *you* must think I'm sitting here at my computer wearing a crooked bow, smeared lipstick, blue eye shadow, torn panty hose, a tube top, spiked heels, and a tight Naugahyde skirt because, apparently, you're trying to screw me like a two-dollar Tijuana whore! *That's* what I think! This is how I *want* to respond, but I restrain myself. And here's **Newbie Strategy Tip #3: Always be as polite, sane, and respectful as possible when turning down a trade so as not to damage any future trade relationship.** After all, there might come a time when you'll need a player on his team, but if he remembers you as the guy who was foaming at the mouth and calling him an irrational, greedy, brain-dead asshole when he made *his* offer, however justified that reaction might be, then he's likely to ignore you in the future. And if possible, don't just give him a curt, one-word no either. Remember, no matter how bad the offer is, he took the time to write it up and e-mail it to you, so you should always give some concrete reasons why you're rejecting the (shitty, one-sided, makes-no-sense-whatsoever) deal. So, even though I want to verbally kick Ron in the nuts, I instead give him a syrupy, candy-coated, rational response: "Sorry. Amos scares me with Bettis' fat ass still hanging around; I fear Glenn's a one-week wonder; Warrick might have his best year yet 'cause Kitna looks good, but he's still inconsistent; and I can get some TE's like Riemersma off the free agent scrap heap. Sorry, I can't do that one."

I think I handled that well, especially considering my urge to scream, "*Do you think I'm a fucking moron?!*" I gave my reasons for turning him down, and while I did subtly trash some of the human toxic-waste containers that he was offering me (Glenn and Riemersma specifically), I did it nicely, calmly, leaving the door open for future trade talks. Basically, sometimes FF players are like two dogs meeting up in a park and sniffing each other's ass to see if they're friend or foe. (Thankfully, the ass-sniffing in the Felon League never makes it beyond the metaphorical level, and now that I think of it, this is the last time I'll use that particular metaphor.) But, I'll still probably never hear from him again. As I said, while there are some wild-eyed traders like Shergul, most owners are fearful of change.

Trade fallout is yet another reason why it's virtually impossible to judge fantasy football acumen. And that's why a league as large and respected as WCOFF is so intriguing.

Is it the single standard by which all FF players should be measured? No, not yet at least. However, it is the largest single league in the country, with the largest single payout, and, therefore, a damn good measuring stick for FF skill. For all intents and purposes, the person who wins WCOFF can be considered the FF national champion.

And last year, that person was a machine operator from Wisconsin.

13

200 Grand

Chris Schussman doesn't have to be in to work until 2 P.M. Sleeping in is one of the perks of his otherwise demanding job as a machine operator in Hortonville, Wisconsin, about a half hour southwest of Green Bay.

This is hard-core Packer country. Someone foolish enough to sport a Vikings or Bears hat in the center of town is at risk of being hog-tied, thrown into the back of a pickup, driven to a remote spot, beaten, and tossed into a quarry. Chris, not surprisingly, is a die-hard, lifelong cheesehead. From Bart Starr and John Brockington to Brett Favre and Ahman Green, he's been wearing the green and yellow, and next to his wife, Melissa, and their two boys, nothing means more to him.

Well, nothing except perhaps his other true love: fantasy football.

Chris has proven himself to be awfully good at fantasy football over the years. How good? He's the 2002 WCOFF champion. Last year (the WCOFF's inaugural season), he won more money playing fantasy football for five months than most people make over several years.

Like any defending champ—the 2003 Tampa Bay Buccaneers can certainly relate—Chris is realizing that the feel-good story of his unlikely run to glory has quickly faded into fending off jealousy, animosity, and everyone's desire to see him fail. He's the one everyone's gearing up to beat now. After all, if there's one thing America loves more than the rags-to-riches story, it's a rags-to-riches-*to-rags* story. Why else would *E! True Hollywood Story* and VH1's *Behind the Music* be so popular these days? Because we want to see a poor, young, innocent Stanley Kirk Burrell work hard to become zillionaire megastar "M.C. Hammer," buy a $20 million mansion with a gold statue of himself in the front yard, but then lose it all thanks to a bloodsucking posse and shady financial advice.

And for the time being, Chris is the M.C. Hammer of WCOFF.

"It seemed so easy last year, and this year, jeez, I'm pulling teeth," he tells me in a soft-spoken Midwestern accent straight out of *Fargo*. "I actually put *more* time into it this year because I wanted to be able to at least look like I'd be competitive again. I actually prepared more this year than last year—and I prepared a ton last year—but it's been tough so far."

Chris first got into FF eight years ago with a local ten-team league composed of a bunch of work buddies. They borrowed a points system out of an FF magazine, added a few twists of their own, and they were off and running. For a "high-profile" FF player, Chris typically plays in a small number of leagues (compared to my air-travel buddy Joe and his nine leagues). But this year Chris is playing in four thanks to the proliferation of high-stakes games that are being formed on the heels of WCOFF's success.

"I *lovvve* playing fantasy football for high stakes," he says with guilty reverence, much in the same way a man would say "I *lovvve* porterhouse steaks" or "I *lovvve* Jennifer Garner." Last year he "only" shelled out the cash for WCOFF, which runs about $1,700, including the entry fee, hotel room, and postdraft party at the ESPN Zone. As a result of the WCOFF championship, he was asked to join a high-stakes league called Fantasy Jungle, which has a $700 entry fee. And he's in two other leagues with larger-than-average entry fees, in the $500 range. So, all in all, this not-exactly-rolling-in-it Wisconsinite is shelling out somewhere in the neighborhood of $4,000 this season.

WCOFF is his baby, though, as it's clearly the most prestigious. Having won his hometown league's Super Bowl four out of the first seven years, Chris immediately jumped when he received an e-mail from a website called footballguys.com announcing that there was going to be a world championship of fantasy football—for high stakes.

Thus begins our *E! True Hollywood Story* rags-to-riches segment. While certainly not destitute, he and Melissa, as is the case with many young couples with two children to raise, didn't have a spare $1,350 waiting to be used on something frivolous like, say, a fantasy football tournament in Las Vegas. So they went to a finance company and borrowed the entrance fee and an extra thousand for expenses. Being casual gamblers—they occasionally put some cash on their beloved Packers just for kicks and visit the ubiquitous Native American casinos every now and then—they try to make it to Las Vegas about once a year, anyway. So they figured, what the hell, let's just make the WCOFF weekend our yearly Vegas trip.

Needless to say, the gamble eventually paid off. In true Vegas fashion, they showed up on the Strip with little more than pocket change and parlayed it into two hundred grand.

But it wasn't as simple as it sounds. After all, he had to draft a good team first against some of the stiffest competition on the planet. Then, he had to cozy up to Lady Luck and hope his players stayed injury free, which they did. And third, he had to make a couple of those key free agent moves throughout the year that help an owner pull away from the rest of the pack. "If you can combine those three things," he says, "that's pretty much what it takes, in my view, to win a championship."

Chris's key sleeper in the original draft was Bills running back Travis Henry, whom he snagged in the fourth round, fantastic value considering how well Henry did all year. But the nail in the coffins of the 599 other WCOFF owners was a key free agent pickup. At the time, Chris wasn't exactly in great shape at QB—the Redskins' Shane Matthews was his starter . . . blecccch—so, considering even the most mediocre starting QBs were already taken, he, like any savvy owner, started scouting the backups around the NFL to see who might have the best chance of stepping in and putting up good numbers. And just like that, a ray of light shone from the Jersey swamps halfway across the country to Hortonville, prompting Chris to make a bid on the Jets' backup QB, Chad Pennington. "Vinny [Testaverde] was playing really bad and I figured it was only a matter of time before they made a change," he tells me. "So I bid a good chunk of my free agent cash on Pennington the week before [Jets head coach Herm] Edwards benched Vinny for good." While Shane Matthews flatlined, Pennington went on to finish as one of the top-rated fantasy QBs in the entire league and, along with Henry, led Chris to the promised land.

This season, however, Chris was forced to alter his WCOFF draft strategy a bit, primarily due to his draft position. In his 2002 championship season, he had the eleventh overall pick, so he was virtually guaranteed two good-to-great running backs—the cornerstones of any successful FF team. But this year, he drew the third overall pick, so he had to scrap his backfield-focused MO because, by the time a draft snakes back to the 1-4 owners for their second-round picks, there are typically no ultrareliable running backs left. So, Chris had to substitute the reliable "stud running back theory" with a "best player available" theory in the second round. After all, if an owner has a choice between, say, a fair-to-middling running back like Garrison Hearst and a stud wide receiver like Randy Moss, that decision is pretty easy. "You gotta take what the draft gives you," he advises. "Normally, I take two running backs—I've done that the last eight years—but you can't waste a second-round pick on someone who will barely start. You gotta get a stud you can count on every week. That's why I went with Culpepper." And we might as well make that **Newbie Strategy Tip #4: Always take what the draft gives you. Never get so locked into a draft strategy that you're flustered or thrown off when the draft doesn't go as expected.** In other words, have some backup strategies in place, because drafts never, ever go as planned.

While Chris makes all final fantasy-team decisions, running the Point Mongerers—the team name, which he and Melissa had printed on their matching dark orange jerseys at this year's WCOFF draft—is definitely a team effort. Melissa helps Chris track players during the draft, mostly to keep him abreast of which competing owners have already filled what positions, and which positions they're therefore likely to fill next, information that helps Chris chart his own draft needs. But where Melissa helps Chris most of all is *after* the season begins. "When we're at home, she takes the brunt of the load with the kids, which gives me the time I need to do research on the Internet or free agent bidding. I just couldn't do it without her. She's an amazing comanager."

OK, right now some of you might think, "Big deal—so he's a caveman who wants Melissa barefoot and pregnant and doing all the child-rearing/house work while he watches football and plays on the Internet." Sure, maybe this semi-old-fashioned arrangement wouldn't fly with most couples in this day and age. But if you could hear the honest appreciation and respect for Melissa in Chris's voice, you might have a change of heart. The Point Mongerers are a team first and foremost—he is always quick to point out that his wife is a "comanager"—and Melissa knows that her husband has a talent and passion for FF and, as their run to the championship proves, has an ability to take this passion and talent and turn it into financial gain, one that, while it certainly isn't enough to retire on, can clearly help make a better life for themselves and their children.

And just what did the Schussmans do with the $200,000? Sorry to disappoint anyone hoping for the big *True Hollywood Story* crash where Chris and Melissa piss away every penny in one bacchanalian lost weekend of coke, champagne, Humvee limos, strip clubs, and Hilton sisters, but their tale just isn't that sordid. After Uncle Sam took his bite, they paid off some bills and invested the rest. In other words, no solid-gold statue of Chris in the front yard. "Our big treat was a sixty-five-inch wide-screen TV to watch football on this year," he says laughing. "That's about it."

I know I'm obsessed with fantasy football. My friends and leaguemates know it. Celia—bless her heart—knows it better than anyone. So, I can't help but wonder how much time the reigning national champion puts into team management, information gathering—all the aspects of FF that drive wives and bosses insane the world over—in an average season. This is a question Chris gets a lot, and his answer might surprise you. It certainly shocked the hell out of me. After all, I figured that, to win WCOFF, one has to be a veritable Internet vampire, staying up to all hours of the night scouring waiver wires, daily reports from NFL team practices, anything at all, and sleeping only when completely necessary (in some sort of creaky wooden box, most likely).

Not so.

"Right now I spend about an hour a day," Chris admits. An *hour*? That's *it*? Christ almighty, I spend an hour on ESPN's injury report alone! Then again, I don't have kids. I don't have a machine-operating job. Maybe an hour is all Chris can afford to spare right now? After all, his voice echoes with pride when he talks about his boys—four- and two-years-old—and Melissa, so he clearly has other priorities. In fact, FF has become quite the family affair: Chris's dad comes over every Sunday to watch all the games—the Schussmans typically have two TVs set up side by side, both with the NFL Sunday Ticket—and spent every waking moment with his son during those final few weeks of last year's WCOFF season, when every point mattered, and when it started to look as if Chris could possibly win the whole thing. The elder Schussman got so excited for Chris last season, in fact, that he entered his very first fantasy football league this year. "He's sixtysomething years old and playing for the first time," Chris tells me with pride. "Amazing."

It *is* amazing, considering that, more often than not, hobbies and passions for certain teams and sports are passed down from father to son, not the other way around. That said, as for his own two boys, Chris doesn't plan to push them into FF, but he does hope that they'll see how much he enjoys it and possibly get into it themselves someday. The whole family loves NFL football, and for Chris and Melissa, FF just adds excitement to watching not just the Packers but all the games. But he's going to let the boys decide for themselves. "Maybe someday they'll want to be comanagers of our 'family team' along with Melissa, but I just want them to do what makes them happy," he says, before adding, with a conspiratorial laugh, "but, hey, I'd be lying if I said that I'm not secretly hoping they'll get into it." He laughs again, perhaps imagining a time somewhere off in the future—the 2023 WCOFF draft?—when all four Schussmans, wearing their matching rust-orange Point Mongerers jerseys, huddle up at the draft table over their cheat sheets, conducting a hushed family conference to decide whether to take Barry Sanders Jr. or John Elway III with their first overall pick.

Don't let the family-friendly demeanor fool you, however; Chris is still on the warpath to repeat as champion, and his current hour-a-day fantasy football research schedule is the exception, not the rule. "So far, I've probably put more time into this year that I did last year . . . and I put a *ton* of time into it last year. I don't want people to read this and think that I didn't put the time in." Not surprising. The stakes have been raised for Chris this season. Last year he was just another one of the six hundred anonymous entrants. This year, he's the defending champ—the first WCOFF champ ever, in fact—and like his beloved Packers coming off their Super Bowl I victory, he has a reputation to uphold. He wants to prove that his two-hundred-grand win wasn't a total fluke.

The Pack, of course, won Super Bowl II. Can Chris repeat?

"Here's the thing," he says. "You can have all the knowledge in the world, you can be more prepared than anyone at your draft, but if you draft players that get hurt, you're not going to win. It's that simple. This year, I've already lost early games thanks to Daunte and Portis being out, and if I lose one more game, I'll probably be out of it for good. WCOFF is such a short season—eleven weeks—so you can't lose more than four games or you're not going to make it."

While Chris isn't bitching about his bad injury luck and is taking it all in stride, his fellow WCOFF owners—at least the more verbal ones on the message boards—are clearly enjoying the champ's early-season struggles. He recently posted a topic in the boards entitled "Enjoy It at the Top," in which he wishes the current top teams good luck, good health, and tells them to enjoy it while it lasts because FF is a funny game and you never know what kinds of fluke injuries or plays can haunt you.

Well, this genuinely good-natured post led to an unexpected backlash of verbal abuse from the masses, accusing him of making excuses for a bad draft by blaming his poor start on the banged-up Daunte and Portis.

Basically, they want to hear the defending champ say, "Okay, you got me, I had a shitty draft." But he is standing firmly behind his draft decisions and, while not making excuses, can't *not* point to injuries as the cause of his early-season struggles. "I don't know why that's so hard for those guys to understand," he says, more bewildered than bitter or resentful toward the cyber-beating he's enduring. "They're saying that my third-through-eighth-round picks should still carry me, but that's just not the way it works. You take out your first- and second-rounders, you're not going to compete."

It doesn't seem fair to me. Chris seems like one of those salt-of-the-earth guys, the kind who'd come over and help you haul bags of mulch, or install a new bathroom sink, or clean up after an all-day barbecue long after everyone else has eaten their free food and split. Bottom line, he's been a gracious champion. But this is the part of the *True Hollywood Story* that makes people salivate most: the fall from grace. So it's not surprising that the forum hyenas are starting to pick at his carcass.

Still, though his current struggles, and the popular reaction to them, might be discouraging and baffling to him, they don't dampen his memories of last year's championship. And what does it feel like to learn that you just won two hundred grand? True to his soft-spoken form, there was no obnoxious hooting and hollering or fist-pumping in the Schussman household. He didn't chug a keg of Blatz and streak down Main Street. He didn't take out billboard space on local highways to gloat over his victory and stomp on the throats of his competition.

While there was certainly joy and excitement, more than anything at all Chris felt one thing: relief.

The Point Mongerers were in first place when the playoffs started in

Week 13 and stayed in first place all the way through Week 16, which meant they spent the playoffs trying to hold the other teams off. Just like this season, they were the hunted, and along with being hunted comes stress. "The emotional ups and downs for that whole month were insane. There were about ten or fifteen teams who had a chance to win. It was close. At one point, I actually got passed by the guy who eventually finished in second place."

But when, on the last ESPN Sunday-night game of the season, Point Mongerers quarterback—er, Jets quarterback—Chad Pennington put up monster numbers in beating the Patriots at Gillette Stadium, Chris took a commanding lead into *Monday Night Football*. And when his opponent couldn't erase the nearly sixty-point lead, he had the two hundred grand wrapped up.

Speaking of winning, let's get to the crux of the matter here: What, in his proven opinion, can an average FF player like myself do to win his league? First and foremost on my mind is the Priest dilemma. Should I ride my stud until he drops or trade him while his value is still sky-high? "Oh, jeez, sure," Chris responds, "I'd ride Priest until he drops—but I'd make sure I had both Derrick Blaylock and Larry Johnson, too, just to cover myself."

Check. I already have both Priest's backups just in case.

Next, what to do with Stephen Davis?

"Do you have Foster?" he asks immediately, his urgent tone letting me know that if I don't have Davis's backup, DeShaun Foster, I'd better get him, and fast. "You definitely want to handcuff Foster to Davis."

"I'm about to trade for him," I answer proudly. I'm oddly proud to have Chris's approval on some of my moves. He's my fantasy football J.D. Power.

For all your newbies out there, the "handcuff" theory—making sure you have the backups to your injury-prone stud running backs—is a common strategy, one that the WCOFF champ adheres to. But he takes it a step further: instead of carrying a slew of productive extra receivers he'll rarely start, he'll carry *other owners'* backup running backs that have the *potential* to be studs if something happens to their starter. **Newbie Strategy Tip #5: Backups to other owners' injury-prone studs make (a) great trade bait to those very same owners and (b) might turn into studs themselves if the starter gets hurt.** "Why have players who are going to just sit there?" Chris asks. " Sure, those backup running backs might not play much either, but their upsides are far higher should something happen to the starter." Case in point, he currently has *nine* running backs on his roster (WCOFF is twenty-three spots deep, mind you). If a key RB injury happens, guess who'll be there to reap the benefits? "And injuries do happen," he says. "This is the NFL, not golf."

So, will Chris Schussman repeat as champion? The odds of him doing so are just as astronomical as they were the first time—perhaps even greater now that he's won once. And the fact that he's already started out with injuries to his top two players (Portis and Daunte) doesn't help matters. So I'd have to say no, he won't repeat. Not a chance. But he's already reached the pinnacle of the fantasy football world. Do I mean the two hundred grand? Sure, that's a nice perk. Hell, I just want to win my league once, and it's only six hundred bucks. (OK, maybe I'd like to win twice. And then I promise I'll be happy. Maybe.)

No, I'm talking about the *real* pinnacle of the fantasy football world: standing mere inches from my football dream girl, Suzy Kolber, at the WCOFF awards presentation, shaking her hand, perhaps even slipping an arm around her waist while posing for the publicity shot with the crystal WCOFF trophy and oversize novelty check. I have so many questions for Chris I can't even begin. *Does Suzy look as good in person as she does on camera? What type of perfume does she wear? Does she even wear perfume? Did he also imagine giving her a piggyback while she giggles and whacks him with a riding crop?*

Sorry . . . oversharing.

14

Hanging by a Nail

We're attending the wedding of a friend of Celia's family's in her hometown of Niskayuna, New York. For five straight hours, I pretend to be concentrating on the lovely bride, the proud groom, the ceremony, the flowers, the food, the dancing, and the various words emanating from the mouths of those around me.

The man sitting next to me—Bob or Rob or Russ?—tells me that he's a computer consultant and has a three-hour commute to Rochester every morning. Do you believe that? *Three hours!* He must be crazy! But get this: he fools those thieving bastards at E-ZPass because he gets on and off the highway at certain strategically chosen exits that somehow mess with the E-ZPass system and, in doing so, saves himself about $800 per year in tolls. Do you believe that? *Eight hundred bucks!* He explains how this diabolical plan of highway deception works. It has to do with either advanced chaos theory, county zoning laws, or global warming, but honestly, it goes way over my head, mostly because I'm not listening to him. BobRobRuss could be telling me that he used to be a go-go dancer named Claire, or that he has twelve young boys buried in a crawl space beneath his house and often dresses in a clown suit, and I'd *still* just be sitting here nodding, smiling like a dope, and adding requisite conversation filler like "wow" or "you don't say" for good measure.

Running through my head is this: "My God, I have to start Michael Pittman tomorrow. . . . Do you believe that? *Michael Pittman!* . . . Don't I have any better options than Michael freaking Pittman! . . . Shit, I don't. . . . Olandis Gary sucks. . . . Mike Anderson and Derrick Blaylock don't get any carries. . . . My God, I have to start Michael Pittman. . . . Do you believe that? . . . *Michael Pittman!"*

I desperately try to counter with some positive thoughts: "Michael Pittman might have a good game. Not likely, but you never know. He's starting to distance himself from Thomas Jones, and even though Alstott is the TD vulture, Pittman's still The Man between the twenties. Priest will play, even with bruised ribs. No force of nature can stop a fantasy juggernaut like Priest from playing. Heap will finally get in the end zone, you can count on it. Plaxico is a stud. Darrell Jackson is emerging as the sleeper WR you thought he'd be when you giddily drafted him in the seventh round. Green, heretofore a total gimp, will finally get a piece of the KC points pie. And the Tampa defense will make Atlanta quarterback Doug Johnson wish he'd never been born. So, relax. Have a piece of this delicious chocolate-vanilla cake. Have another Stoli-and-tonic. Dance with your beautiful wife. Join the other hillbillies out on the dance floor for a rousing, clapping, shimmying Electric Slide. Enjoy yourself for godsake, you're at a wedding! Fantasy football can wait until tomorrow."

But the thing is, it *can't* wait until tomorrow. Fantasy football never waits until tomorrow. Not when you're starting Michael Pittman. Do you believe that? *Michael freaking Pittman!*

Stoli. Tonic. OJ. Heavy on the Stoli. I have this strange feeling I should just keep on drinking straight through till Monday.

Exclamation points are funny things.

Just yesterday I was using an exclamation point to say, "I'm starting Michael Pittman!" And today, as I track the early games, I find myself using the same sentence, but a very different exclamation mark: "I'm starting Michael Pittman!" On the surface these sentences look exactly the same, sure, but the meanings couldn't be more different.

Why the lesson in punctuation nuance? Well, the recently maligned—mostly by me—Pittman just finished racking up 82 yards rushing, 82 yards receiving, including a 68-yard touchdown, for . . . drumroll please . . . a whopping 36 Felon League points. Wait, I mean, "Eighty-two yards rushing! Eighty-two yards receiving! A 68-yard touchdown! Thirty-six whopping Felon League points!" He was a difference-maker today, pure and simple, a true stud.

As for the rest of Acme's early games, Priest not only played, but he racked up 2 more touchdowns—giving him an NFL-leading 7—and 156 total yards for another great afternoon of 34 points, which, believe it or not, is somewhat of a down day for a stud like him. But he played, he stayed healthy, and I'm not going to sneeze at that kind of performance. Plaxico had a less ignorable day with a pedestrian 55 yards receiving and no TDs (how a guy six foot five inches doesn't get used in the red zone is beyond me), but the Tampa D manhandled the Falcons and racked up a respectable 14 points.

Bottom line: it's only 5 P.M. and I already lead 89–7.

However, my opponent, Ivan, with his SoCo team, has most of his squad yet to play in the late games—Marshall Faulk, Koren Robinson, Favre, Moulds, and Bubba Franks—so by no means is this thing over. After all, if there's one thing we learned last week when Jamal Lewis beat the shit out of me in the first five minutes of the day, it's that no lead is safe, anything can happen in the topsy-turvy world of FF. The final whistles must blow in every single game.

As I sit alone in my mother-in-law Sally's living room, watching the Pats run out the clock in a grinding, tense 23–16 win over the Jets, I realize I've been biting my right thumbnail until it's just about hanging off. Since the Pats are about to win, however, I leave it that way. I have to; I have no other choice. To bite it all the way off and spit it across the room like some kind of savage—being engrossed in the game, I might usually do that without even noticing—would jinx the luck that the hanging nail has obviously brought to my Pats, not to mention my Acme squad, who, as I've detailed, have had a monster set of early games led by my new best friend, Michael Pittman. (I mean "Michael Pittman!")

The nail must stay.

Later, somewhere on the Mass Pike heading through the Berkshires, Celia notices the grotesque, nibbled thing and stares at it as if it were something I'd lifted from the urinal at the last rest stop. "Um . . . what's with the nail?" she asks in an almost fearful tone.

"It was hanging like this when the Pats won and my team kicked ass in the early games," I explain, as rationally as a grown man purposely clinging to a gnarled, hanging thumbnail possibly can. "So I have to leave it this way until after all the games, because the team I'm playing has four or five good players going for him, and I only have two, maybe three good ones left, so I don't want to jinx it."

As the changing, early-fall leaves whiz by in a blurry greenish-brownish-reddish montage out the window behind her, she looks at me for a few pregnant moments, in which I imagine her doing some quick math to calculate how much she'd net after divorcing me and selling our condo. After determining that her best course of action might just be to have me committed to an asylum, pay off another patient to stab me with a Popsicle stick during arts and crafts, and then collect the insurance, she finally shrugs. "That's warped," she says, laughing despite herself. "I don't know what to . . . that's just . . . warped."

I have no rebuttal. It *is* warped. Hugely warped. But there's nothing I can do about it. Nothing. That nail simply has to hang there by its few remaining sinewy white strands until the ESPN game is long over, the stats are compiled, and I see the final tally of Faulk, Moulds, KRob, Favre, and Franks did *not* top Green, Jackson, Heap, and Wilkins, at which point I'll probably burn the nail with some incense and chicken blood in a solemn sacrifice to the benevolent, protective FF gods.

But, if that nail comes off *before* the late games are over—maybe gets accidentally dislodged while switching the radio stations or pumping gas—oh, boy, look out. Those FF gods could turn on me and strike me down with great fury and vengeance for depriving them of their rightful thumbnail sacrifice.

I'm sorry, Celia, I want to tell her, I really am. I know it's hard to be married to a freak. But I'm in a no-win situation here: if I keep the nail like this, I might lose my wife; but, if I lose the nail, I'll *definitely* lose my game. *That* I know.

So, of course, my decision is a no-brainer: keep the nail. I'll take my chances with Celia later. She can be tough, but she's not nearly as wrathful and merciless as the FF gods.

"Sorry, I have to keep it this way," I conclude weakly, knowing that she's probably searching for an ejector-seat button.

I also want to tell her that I am not the only freak out there who does stuff like this. This is the kind of dilemma that often faces FF players throughout an average season. Fact is, sports fans in general—but FF players especially—can be some of the oddest, most superstitious birds on the planet. Athletes don't change socks during winning streaks. Wade Boggs used to eat chicken and only chicken before every single game. Michael Jordan wore his powder blue Tar Heels shorts under his Bulls uniform during every game. Just look at the hyperkinetic spectacle that Nomar Garciaparra is every single time he steps into the batter's box, adjusting and readjusting and adjusting and readjusting his batting gloves over and over and over.

And for an FF player changing *anything* while his team is winning—his spot on the couch, the beer mug he's drinking from, his shirt, the room temperature, his remote-control hand—well, that would be suicide, a tempting of the fates that could be downright disastrous. "I have four seats in my living room," one Huddler says, "left, middle, center of the couch, and a recliner. If my team is doing well with me sitting on the left side of the couch, I'll stay there. If they start off sucking, then I'll move to the center, then the right side, then to the recliner. Then, if they still suck, I'll start the cycle all over again." Another no-no for many FF players is bragging or gloating. There's a general feeling that once you start saying how great your team is/players are, you're setting yourself up for a big, fat jinx. "I always say my team can be beaten every week," another Huddler adds. "I go in expecting a loss, so I'm pleasantly surprised by a win. I'm optimistic in every other facet of life, but when it comes to fantasy football, it pays to be a pessimist." Whether it's giant foam fingers that they throw at the TV or golf club-head covers with team logos on them, FF players often rely on little game-day trinkets to get them through. "I kept a Patriots 3-wood cover on my desk all through the 2001 season," another Huddler chimes in. "It stayed in the same spot—wedged behind my keyboard—right through the Super Bowl. Obviously, it worked."

See? You just can't fuck with a good-luck charm.

And why? Because good-luck charms work!

It's official. Another week is in the books. And in the end, the fearsome fivesome of Faulk, Favre, Robinson, Moulds, and Franks that I was *sooooo* worried about while driving home yesterday only combined for 39 points. Final Week 3 score: Acme 137, SoCo 53. Hence, my beloved Acme squad—actually, come to think of it you've been patiently bearing with me all these pages, so you know what, we're going to start calling it "our"

Acme squad—*our* beloved Acme squad is 2-1 with a commanding lead in total points.

Here's where Project Kick My League's Ass now stands:

Team	W	L	PF	PA
Bonesky Crushers	3	0	340	159
Account Guys	3	0	316	223
Acme FF, Inc.	2	1	472	393
Rat Bastards	2	1	374	354
Funk Soul Bros.	2	1	285	281
The Dream Team	1	2	368	365
The Pound Dawgs	1	2	277	301
All-Ameican Angus	1	2	222	290
Big Dogs	1	2	221	287
SoCo	1	2	218	311
Charlemagnes	1	2	215	253
NH Hillbillies	0	3	204	295

Ha! *See*, I want to gloat to Celia, *the keeping-the-nail-on-the-thumb ploy worked, didn't it?* Sure, I may have looked like a derelict— okay, downright unhygienic—at the time, but hanging on to that raggedy-ass thing until all the games were finished paid off, and the FF gods rewarded me for my selfless sacrifice of a body part (albeit one that would quickly grow back; I wonder what they'd give me for one of my legs?).

So, if not for a little bad-schedule luck in Week 1, I'd be 3-0. But, I'm also leading in points *against*, which is a tad troublesome. The two teams ahead of me, while not scoring badly, are 1-2 in *fewest* points against, the lucky bastards. But this can't keep up all year long, can it? I mean, will I catch every single team on its most productive day for the rest of the season? That would make me want to gnaw all my nails off. Toes included.

15

Off to See the Wizard

Several historic events took place in 1981.

Ronald Reagan took the oath as the fortieth president in American history and, three months later, took a bullet from some wackjob trying to impress the future star of *The Silence of the Lambs*. A hungry little bugger named Pac-Man devoured his way onto the video game scene. Casting aside his family's centuries-old policy of inbreeding, Prince Charles married a common lass named Diana Spencer. A band called The Buggles informed us that video, indeed, killed the radio star and launched an upstart channel called Music Television. *Chariots of Fire*—oddly, a movie about neither chariots nor fire—won Best Picture. The first DeLorean rolled off the assembly line, with standard features like cruise control, power windows, and bags of cocaine in the glove compartment. Women everywhere were seen in public wearing headbands, leg warmers, and anything else that would let them get physical, physical. And in the sports world, the East and West Coasts divvied up the major sports crowns, with my beloved Celtics and the NY Islanders winning the NBA and Stanley Cup, respectively, and the 49ers and Dodgers taking the Super Bowl and World Series.

As for yours truly, I was a scrawny, high-strung eighth-grader trying to woo a cute little blonde away from a dance in a cramped gymnasium and into the squash courts for a ham-fisted make-out session. (Despite what Rick Springfield claimed, it was Lisa Higgins—and not Jessie's Girl—that I wished I'd had.)

Meanwhile, twenty-two hundred miles across the country in Albuquerque, a young man named Emil Kadlec began going to a friend's house to watch *Monday Night Football*. More often than not, his buddy would say, "Hey, Emil, check out this game I've been playing," and would take Emil through the rules and scoring for something he'd never heard of before—a "fantasy football" league.

Emil was intrigued.

So much so that, the following year, he had not only joined his friend's league, but had started up one of his own. But, he was soon disappointed to learn that whenever he'd go to the local newsstand to grab a few football magazines to help prepare for his drafts, none of them had any coverage whatsoever from a fantasy perspective. Nothing. So, being a smart guy, like any good entrepreneur with a budding idea, he kept an eye on the marketplace over the next few years. By 1990, still noticing a huge void in the marketplace, he finally decided it was high time someone filled it. Fantasy Sports Publications, Inc., was born.

Using a little start-up cash he'd saved, he began with his flagship, *Fantasy Football Pro Forecast* and, over time, added three more: *Fantasy Football Draftbook* (1996), *Fantasy Football Cheatsheets* (1998), and *Fantasy Football Experts Poll* (2001). Today, FSP is the largest publisher of fantasy football annuals in the country, distributing over nine hundred thousand total fantasy football magazines in 2003.

In the pre-Internet days, FF magazines had a corner on the predraft preparation market, and as you might expect, Emil's business flourished. But, surprisingly, despite fantasy football's wholesale move to cyberspace in the mid/late 1990s, his magazine empire is still a viable business. "Internet or no Internet," Emil says, "people still enjoy having a magazine in their hands." But this doesn't make him a Ted Kaczynski–esque, antitechnology zealot, ranting against the World Wide Web and building pipe bombs in a remote cabin in the New Mexico desert while pining for the "good old days" of paper and glue. Fantasy Sports Publications has a large Web presence—www.fspnet.com—providing subscribers with e-updates on players and NFL/FF developments, and the Internet's actually been great for his brick-and-mortar magazine business. With all the commissioner and league-hosting sites that have come out over the past five years, people can join leagues and run their teams more easily, meaning, with the heavy lifting eliminated, more people than ever before feel encouraged to play. "And the more people that play, the more people there are to buy magazines," Emil sums up. "The Internet's helped more than it's hurt."

But Fantasy Sports Publications and fspnet.com aren't Emil's only FF-related ventures. He's one of the brains behind the largest—and richest—fantasy football league in the world: the Las Vegas–based World Championship of Fantasy Football, or WCOFF (or "whack-off," as David Dorey and Whitney Walters endearingly call it).

That second brain is Lenny Pappano. In 1999, Lenny cofounded a fantasy football website called Draft Sharks and, soon afterward, started advertising in Emil's *Fantasy Football Pro Forecast*. Eventually, their conversations turned from small-space-ad insertion rates to more specific discussions about their industry, particularly, what was missing?

After all, here was a hobby—fantasy football—that, even in 1999, already boasted millions and millions of participants, but, surprisingly, lacked a single, genre-defining event where all these people could join together and celebrate their common love of/obsession with their hobby. Sure, there had been a few conventions, but while they attracted the businesspeople like Emil, Lenny, and the Huddle's Dave Dorey and Whitney Walters, they failed to lure the masses who made it tick. Why? Because even though these conventions were billed as "world championship" events and featured high-stakes leagues and drafts, the teams were all owned and drafted by industry "experts."

Realizing that, everything finally clicked for Emil and Lenny in the fall of 2001. "It was like a shining light," Emil says, laughing perhaps because, having a good sense of humor and being a realist, he knows that devising a better fantasy football championship wasn't exactly on par with curing cancer. Still, this was his livelihood, and a growing industry, and a hobby that brought joy to millions of people every year, so while Emil can downplay his contributions all he wants, this was an important development in the ongoing genesis of FF.

Anyway, the problem with the few previous attempts, he and Lenny realized, was that those events involved "common people" paying to come watch the "experts" draft or watch the "experts" talk about FF strategy, industry developments, et cetera. What's the common denominator here? *Watch.* Let's face it, Emil and Lenny concluded, people don't want to come *watch* somebody else play fantasy football; they want to come and be part of the event *themselves.* "It's the same principle behind the World Series of Poker," Emil tells me. "People don't come from around the world to watch *somebody else* play poker, they come to have a chance to be the champion themselves. And they'll throw down big money to be part of that show."

So that—having people *be* the show, not *watching* the show—was, and still is, the concept behind the WCOFF. And, beginning in the 2002 season, after a year of planning and preparation, the "people's event" was ready for play.

Prize money was the first major hurdle. Many of the previous contests that had billed themselves as "world championships" didn't get the required number of teams to participate, thus lowering the prize money for the teams that *did* join. So, naturally, FF players became inherently skeptical of big-money leagues and the lofty prizes they advertised. Knowing this, Emil and Lenny guaranteed the WCOFF prize money, even if it meant losing $100,000 out of their own pockets if not enough teams signed up. "The guarantee made all the difference."

For Emil, the WCOFF is about celebrating the entire hobby. All of a sudden, we FF junkies have a single place where we can go every year and join a thousand or so other enthusiasts from around the country.

Unfortunately, not everyone shares the enthusiasm for fantasy football that Emil, I, and millions of others do. Case in point, the aforementioned HBO *Real Sports* segment that, in the view of many WCOFF participants, was an absolute hatchet job on the hobby, portraying FF players as antisocial, dangerously obsessed (okay, that might be true) freaks and geeks. And Emil agrees HBO missed the boat by depicting FF as a bunch of "Wizard"-esque social misfits. "You have to realize that it wasn't journalism; it was a TV show," he says. "They're trying to get people to watch, so they took the angle of making it a freak show." In fact, prior to the broadcast, HBO producers asked him if he could recommend people to be interviewed or featured in the segment. He showed them Web photos of some of the participants, and naturally they gravitated toward the most bizarre, oddball characters that fit their predetermined stereotype of the fantasy sports enthusiast. In other words—the Wizard.

But where HBO failed, and the reason there's such an uproar within the FF underbelly, was their decision *not* to focus on understanding the love for a hobby, the passion for football, and the camaraderie within the community. Rather, they focused on the small percentage of extreme cases of obsession-gone-pathetic. (Having been there in person, I can tell you—that percentage *was* small.)

"Even after the piece, when [*Real Sports* host Bryant] Gumbel was kind of smirking, as only Gumbel can do, Deford hit the nail on the head," Emil tells me. "He [Deford] said, 'Hey, these people woud play for nothing, they love it.' So *he* kind of understood, at least. But HBO has to do whatever it can to get people to watch, and that's by showing the Wizards of the world."

The problem, as Emil and I see it, is that most people on the message boards—WCOFF's, the Huddle's, wherever—want to be recognized as legitimate, whether they'll admit it or not. And when a well-known personality like Bryant Gumbel rolls his eyes, smirks, and says "fantasy football" as if he can't believe something so lowbrow and pathetic is actually passing his lips, *that's* when the masses start getting a burr under their shoulder pads. Because it means they're not being taken seriously. And this is odd in the scheme of things, considering how so many segments of NFL fandom are considered more "legitimate," and taken more seriously, than the fantasy players. I mean, for crying out loud, what about the shirtless, fat guys in the stands at Lambeau Field in the middle of December, painted green and yellow from head to toe and spitting Blatz all over each other? What about the grown man wearing a giant, rubber dog-mask in Cleveland's end-zone Dawg Pound, or the guys wearing flowered muumuus, wigs, makeup, and pig noses to pay homage to their beloved "Hogs" in D.C.? Are you telling me that *these* wing nuts are somehow kosher in the media's eyes, but the guy who plays fantasy football somehow *isn't*? Are you telling me, Bryant Gumbel, that the first group are almost revered and respected as passionate superfans, and yet fantasy football players—who are just demonstrating the same level of passion for the sport, albeit in another arena—are mocked by the likes of you and your Chia-headed older brother, Greg?

The answer, Emil says, is yes. "Bottom line, the fantasy guys just aren't accepted yet. Period."

He also takes issue with the way HBO edited the segment, something that, while not surprising—after all, as he said, their goal was to entertain—nevertheless still irks him. While he really enjoyed being interviewed by a sports journalism legend like Deford, respects him a great deal, and truly believes that Deford was trying to understand FF ("It was a highlight of my career in the business so far," he admits), nearly all of their interview was left on the cutting-room floor. Why? Emil thinks it's because he explained to Deford that the WCOFF participants are just people who love NFL football, have found this hobby that makes them feel much closer to the game, use their mind in a strategic way, and in some cases escape from everyday life for a few hours on Sunday—none of which was controversial or edgy enough to make the final broadcast.

"That's not quirky and doesn't make good TV," Emil says. "No one's getting shot or solicited by a prostitute."

What's worse, Emil felt that Deford also asked him leading questions, trying to get Emil to admit that the WCOFF participants are freaky, weird, get-a-lifers. He wasn't biting. He didn't want to give Deford anything HBO could edit into a quickie sound bite because he was afraid that whatever he said would be technologically twisted to suit what he saw as their entertainment-over-fact, style-over-substance agenda.

For instance, Deford finally came out and asked Emil if, when you get right down to it, all the WCOFFers are just geeky, off-the-wall, bizarre human specimens. "I wanted to say, 'OK, Frank, I guess you *want me to say* that they all masturbate in closets and wear pocket protectors, right?'" Emil pauses and laughs incredulously. "But I didn't, because *that* would have made the show, because I knew HBO would have then edited my words to make it *sound like* I said, 'They all masturbate in closets and wear pocket protectors.'"

Instead, however, Emil told Deford, as plainly as possible, that the WCOFFers are just people who love football. Blue-collar, white-collar, male, female, black, white, green, blue, old, young—doesn't matter. They're just people who've found this thing they really enjoy and want to share it with others, just like any hobby. "But that's just not an exciting quote, so they put on that roto baseball guy saying disparaging things about fantasy football," Emil concedes, referring to a roto baseball expert that HBO interviewed for the piece and indirectly—not to mention erroneously—gave credit for starting fantasy football. This account of the origins of FF, more than anything else, absolutely floored Emil.

HBO implies in its piece that fantasy football was more or less started in the late seventies by the father of rotisserie baseball, Dan Okrent, even though they not only had a copy of the article Emil and Bob Harris wrote for *Football Pro Forecast* on Bill Winkenbach et al. and the founding of GOPPPL (again, the definitive article on the hobby's founding), but had also *physically met* an original league member right there at the WCOFF—former King's X bar owner Andy Mousalimas, whom Emil and Lenny had flown in for the draft as guest of honor.

But it didn't matter. They ignored the information right before their eyes and, assuming these facts are all correct, gave more credit than they should have to Okrent—admittedly a fantasy sports pioneer and the genius behind rotisserie baseball—and presented him as the brains behind the growth of fantasy football.

"While I was being interviewed by Deford, he specifically mentioned this rotisserie baseball guy," Emil tells me. "I went, 'Ohhhhhhh, I get it now.'" Off camera, Emil told Deford that they might have mixed up the facts, and that HBO might be interested to know that the man who is credited with creating fantasy football (Winkenbach) also started playing a version of fantasy baseball in the *late fifties*, about twenty years before Okrent created rotisserie baseball. But, again, he says, they outright ignored it.

"And why?" Emil asks. "Sure, he said funny things about a fantasy football player following him into the bathroom, standing up on the toilet in the next stall, and leaning over the divider to ask him questions about his fantasy baseball team while the guy was trying to pee, but I bet it was a little embellished for TV. Okrent belittled fantasy players, patronized them, more or less said, 'Can you believe these fantasy weirdos?' while I didn't say anything like that." Emil pauses and chuckles almost sadly. "And guess who got on TV?"

And Emil says HBO's behavior at the WCOFF got even more incredible.

Bob Harris, noted fantasy football writer, appeared in the *Real Sports* segment as an example of not only the FF media, but also of the obsession people have with FF (and, in my opinion, was also portrayed as a socially inept, borderline insane person who lives life attached to his computer at all times with an "umbilical cord" that allows him to write in bed, while sitting on the toilet, wherever . . . it was honestly kind of creepy). Anyway, Harris, who's been writing for years and has probably forgotten more about FF than I'll ever know, told Emil that the HBO people flat out didn't believe the account of FF's founding in their original article, a revelation that once again floored Emil.

"Didn't *believe* us?" Emil exclaims. "How much more evidence do you need? We have an eighty-one-year-old man [Mousalimas] who was at the original draft standing not ten feet from your cameras! We've got a copy of the original draft sheet! Even if we'd *wanted* to fake it, do you know how impossible it would have been to create that thing from scratch and find all those names? We have dated newspaper clips about the league. We have letters from the commisisoner in the midsixties talking about the draft and who's going to be in it. How much more proof did HBO need?"

What frustrates Emil the most is not that they painted FF players as weirdos, freaks, and losers. And it's not that a television program—gasp!—chose entertainment and shock value over facts and substance (I know, hard to believe in this day and age of Paris Hilton and Omarosa). Rather, Emil feels worst of all for Andy Mousalimas, his special guest at WCOFF. Here's an elderly man who actually started getting emotional onstage during the predraft introductions, clearly touched and honored at the reception he'd received from the appreciative, respectful FF attendees. Andy was proud to be one of the people behind a hobby that brings so much joy, amusement, and fun to people's lives nowadays. *That's* what gets under Emil's skin the most—that HBO was, in essence, calling Andy Mousalimas a liar, too. "Fantasy football is a big village, a community," Emil says. "With Andy, I wanted to see the guy who picked the first draft pick *ever* fortysomething years ago stand with the modern people at the biggest fantasy football event ever. That was the most special moment of the entire weekend . . . and HBO completely ignored it."

One thing HBO didn't ignore was the whole "productivity at work" issue. The piece had "experts" claiming that employees doing fantasy football research on the Internet at work are costing companies around the world millions and millions of dollars in man-hours. If you believed them, you'd think that FF is going to be responsible for another October '29 crash. So, while HBO and Deford more or less implied that there are legions of insane football nerds bringing the nation's economy to its knees, they ignored one fact: people will abuse their work time anyway, whether it's fantasy football, Quake, naughtyjapaneseschoolgirl.com, whatever. It's up to the individual companies to regulate that. "They want to make it all out to be fantasy football's fault," Emil says. "It's a problem, sure, but it's not a new one; it's the *age-old* problem of getting your employees to do their freaking jobs."

Naturally, the HBO *Real Sports* piece has been a hot discussion topic on the WCOFF message boards. Most aren't happy (that's an understatement) about how it focused almost exclusively on the infamous Wizard and some of the "weirdos," without featuring much of Lenny and Emil or anything else of substance. "The message they sent," one guy posts, "was this: Dress up in costumes, act like you're a professional wrestler, tell people you have no life, and show that you have an IQ of 16, and you can be on television next year." The Wizard is a lightning rod, no doubt. Deford even closes the piece by asking him what would he rather do (and I paraphrase): sleep with a supermodel or win a fantasy football championship? Of course, our Mickey Mouse in *Fantasia*-looking character answers, "Win a championship." That's the impression viewers are left with. But had he answered, "I'd rather treat Tyra Banks like a mechanical bull," that wouldn't have fit with HBO's predetermined message: FF players are complete fucking nerds.

But, as with any large group of people, there are bound to be differing opinions, and some of the WCOFF participants weren't surprised one bit by the HBO piece. After all, HBO's goal is *not* to promote the WCOFF; it's to get people to think, "Okay, I'm entertained, and I'm going to renew my twenty-three-dollar HBO subscription."

Even cofounder Lenny Pappano says that he wasn't expecting a straight journalistic piece from HBO and isn't shocked by the approach they took. But, like Emil, what bothered Lenny most was HBO's version of the founding of fantasy football. "Andy [Mousalimas] played in a fantasy football league which predates the founding of rotisserie baseball by about eighteen years," Lenny writes in the forums. "But while they messed that up, in the end, Deford basically got the conclusion right: FF players are hard-core fans who play FF for love of the sport and for competition. As he said, it's not about the money . . . most people who love FF would play for free."

Maybe Deford isn't the enemy here. Maybe it's the editors/producers/creative directors at HBO who should be taken out to the woodshed and bitch-slapped. At one point in the piece, Deford quotes an unnamed "critic" who says that in the minds of many, fantasy football players are dweebs, nerds, shower-loathing, Star-Trek-convention-going recluses who sit about two notches above the Unabomber on the great chain of social being." Okay, so there *was* a guy in a wizard costume, I'll give you that, and chances are he hasn't ever washed said wizard costume, which most likely smells like a wet dog about now. But come on now, folks—the freaking *Unabomber*? Gimme a goddamn break. The Wizard, for all his antics, is just a guy who loves fantasy football and is just having fun with it in his own bizarre way.

Ridiculous, sensationalistic comparisons aside, even a slanted HBO piece won't affect the growth of FF. Millions will continue to play no matter what people outside the hobby say about it. It's kind of like Star Trek. Everyone cracks on Trekkies, calls them geeks, losers, and worse. Yet year after year, convention after convention, Trekkies keep coming back, undaunted. I admire the Trekkies' resolve, truth be told. They're loyal. They're passionate. They buy a lot of merchandise. They watch a ton of TV. They're an economic force unto themselves. So, shouldn't the media in general be more kind to them? No. Why should they? Trekkies, just like FF players, will keep shelling out the dollars no matter how they're perceived, so, naturally, the media opts for entertainment.

Despite what's clearly an unstoppable socioeconomic force, many in the mainstream media still take an old-school stance on the growth of FF.

Take the aforementioned Chia-head, Greg Gumbel.

I was out jogging recently—working from home, I feel a lot less "Unabomber-ish" if I get out into the real world and see other humans at least once a day—and Gumbel was a guest on WEEI sports radio's Dale and Neumy show. They asked him whether the increase of entertainment and humor in sports coverage (e.g., the sports anchor/comedian that has mutated out of the Keith Olbermann/Dan Patrick/Craig Kilborn–era *SportsCenter*) is tainting how the networks cover the NFL. Not to be outdone by his younger brother, Gumbel let fly with an answer that nearly made me run straight into an oncoming rollerblader.

"The big problem is this fantasy football," Gumbel said with the same smirky disdain as Bryant. "You have the NFL catering to these computer geeks who would rather watch a game at their computer than in front of the TV. So now, the networks have to cater to people with an attention span of five or ten minutes."

No offense Greg, but that might quite possibly be the second-craziest thing I've ever heard in my lifetime (the first being Celia saying, "Yes,

Mark, I *will* marry you"). CBS Sports—which just happens to be the logo on Greg's paychecks—also runs CBS SportsLine, which generates, oh, about a gazillion dollars a year* from fantasy football.

And yet, Greg Gumbel has the balls to insult the very people who fork over those dollars? Talk about biting the hand that feeds you.

Let's face it: the popularity of the NFL has risen right alongside the popularity of fantasy football, and the popularity of the NFL—a league that can pretty much print its own money at this point—is one reason why reason Gumbel even has a job in the first place.

"What a gross overgeneralization and misconception," a Huddle poster concludes. "Ask DirecTV if the explosion of their NFL Ticket package has been affected by 'geeks' with the attention spans of humming-birds watching games in front of a computer."

Uh-oh. The natives are getting restless.

---

*Give or take a zillion. Truth be told, in October '03, SportsLine reported that its fantasy football products generated revenues of $12 million, a 36 percent increase from the previous year's $8.8 million. Not a gazillion, no, but still some seeeeerious coin.

16

Luck vs. Skill

Before my Week 4 game, I make my first big trade of the season.

Capitalizing on the huge week from Michael Pittman, I deal him and the steady but unspectacular Jay Fiedler to Karl's NH Hillbillies team in exchange for—you're not going to believe this—Peyton *freaking* Manning!

Move over Trent Green; there's a new starter in Acme town.

Is it a panic move on Karl's part? Yes. Peyton has shit the bed the first three weeks, sure, but he's still Peyton *freaking* Manning. Does Karl need a starting running back? Yes, very badly. The injured Travis Henry, the even more injured Duce Staley, and the ancient Emmitt Smith make up his backfield. Nuff said. Noticing that, I pull the old "sell-high" move (dealing from my strength, running back, to fill a weakness, quarterback) and make my pitch: Gruden has named Pittman the Bucs' starter for the rest of the season, he'll consistently put up 80–100-yard games with a TD or two, and as last week showed, he can bust the long ones. And I also add that Fiedler, at the time of the deal, is the Felon League's third-rated quarterback (a statistic that has about as much chance of lasting all season as Fred Taylor's groin or Charlie Sheen's *Two and a Half Men*, but I leave that part out).

But, to my utter shock, Karl goes for it! No negotiating. No haggling. Nothing. But I guess that's why he's our league's That Guy.

Peyton is mine! I'm heading into Week 4 with a starting crew of Peyton, Priest, Davis, Plaxico, D. Jackson, Heap, Bucs defense, Wilkins. Can you say juggernaut-in-the-making? I'd say I now have the best starting eight this side of the Rat Bastards' steamroller of McNair, Tomlinson, Jamal Lewis, Moulds, Holt, McMichael, Ravens defense.

On Sunday of Week 4, Peyton introduces himself to his new Acme teammates in fine fashion: 314 yards and 6, count 'em, 6 touchdowns against the Saints (two of them long ones) for an astronomical 82 FFL points. But it's all for naught as, once again, *I lose to the week's high scorer!* Can you believe that? This has got to be a joke.

After Jamal Lewis tried to crush the life out of me in Week 2, I once again have the pleasure of facing players who decide to have career days. Randy Moss goes for 171 yards and 3 TDs, two of them long ones (for 77 FFL points!). Marvin Harrison goes for 158 yards and 3 TDs, two of them long ones (for 75 FFL points!). And for good measure, the FF gods allow Hall of Fame–bound Troy Hambrick, who hasn't scored a TD all year, to (a) play against the woeful Jets run defense and (b) rack up a long TD and 124 yards rushing, all for a solid day (41 FFL points).

Yes, despite the heroic performance from Peyton, and yet another monster effort from Stephen Davis—I haven't yet decided whether I will hyphenate my last name to St. Amant-Davis or just take Davis—I still manage to lose. And worst of all, my victorious opponent is—the Big Dogs.

Dumb luck strikes again.

Thus, our beloved Acme squad and Project Kick My League's Ass is back at .500, with a 2-2 record. I'm having some blasphemous thoughts about trading Priest while his value is sky-high. This would be the equivalent of the 1927 Yankees trading Babe Ruth, but there are already whispers about the dreaded hip that knocked him out last season. He might be a running time-bomb. We'll see, we'll see. I'm sorry to even be thinking this, Priest, but I have to put personal feelings aside. If there's one thing I've learned over the past few months, it's **Newbie Strategy Tip #6: FF is all business. Never let emotions dictate how you value a player.** It's hard, I know, especially if that player is on your home team. Hell, I love Tom Brady, Troy Brown, and the rest of my Pats guys, but would I ever want them on my fantasy team? No. Bottom line, those of you who play with your heart and not your head are at an immediate disadvantage.

That said, I hold off on trading Priest. I just can't bring myself to go there. Yet.

Speaking of trades, I get an e-mail from Karl, owner of the now 0-4 NH Hillbillies. Perhaps having some seller's remorse on Peyton, he has resigned himself to another year in the cellar. "There should be some sort of booby prize for the last place team," he writes. "My team could be the worst in league history."

"Well," I desperately want to respond, "now that you've traded me Peyton, it is." But I hold off. No sense rubbing it in.

While Karl seems to have a good sense of humor about possibly giving up on a stud too soon, he begins to receive angry e-mails taunting him for what is seen as an idiotic, knee-jerk move to acquire Pittman. Shergul, sounding like Bud Selig, suggests that we contract the Hillbillies due to gross mismanagement, especially if Karl doesn't start paying more attention to injury reports (a reference to Karl's starting Travis Henry in Week 4 despite reports that Henry would not play).

This attack does not sit well with the normally mild-mannered Karl. "FUCK OFF, all of you! Henry was a game-time scratch. And about Peyton, none of you were offering anything worth a damn (or you were trying to rape me). I needed a running back upgrade, so I took the best offer. Until last week Manning hadn't done squat. Have you bastards noticed that everyone tries to get something for nothing in a trade? You fuckers want to run my team, go ahead. This is two years in a row I've had to listen to this crap. My team sucks. Deal with it. If I get one more email about the league taking over my team, I'm done, and fuck all of you."

I can see the *Boston Globe* headlines tomorrow: "Tragedy Strikes Boston Ad Agency. Employee Kills 37 People, Self, After Smack-Talk-Fueled Rampage." In Karl's defense, Henry *was* questionable on Sunday, and the Bills were being typically guarded about his condition, but it wasn't the game-time decision he claimed it was; Henry was ruled out in plenty of time for Karl to substitute one of his other ass running backs.

Still, I guess there's something in the FF air this time of year that causes leagues to begin their seasonal infighting. Maybe it's because we're at the one-quarter point of the season, and this is when owners usually start to step back, evaluate their teams, and discover whether they're contenders or pretenders. And when they see that they're pretenders, and furthermore, when their league-mates rub that horrible fact in their faces, tempers flare. Hopefully, though, intra-office killing sprees will be kept to a minimum.

17

Wunderkind

Nineteen-year-old Jeremy has been playing fantasy football for ten years. If you do a little quick math, that means he loved fantasy football enough to start playing when he was—your abacus does not lie—nine. That's fourth grade to you and me. When I was in the fourth grade I barely knew my name, and this kid's tackling fantasy football? Holy Doogie Howser.

This blows my mind. So far, I've just assumed that FF "experts" are either (a) older men, grizzled veterans of the FF trenches who've done and seen it all, guys like Dave Dorey, Whitney Walters, Emil Kadlec, and all the other (relatively) old codgers who shot it out in the Wild West days of the industry, or (b) the guys who have proven their FF mastery in "experts leagues" and other respected FF battlefields, such as WCOFF champ Chris Schussman.

But now? Is it possible that I could glean some useful information from someone considerably *younger* than me? This is a kid who was literally coming out of the womb when I was taking (and in sadly comical fashion, failing) my first driver's license test. I'm beginning to think that, yes, it's possible that all the secrets to my FF success just might reside inside the mind of this FF *wunderkind*. After all, young kids have always done amazing things. Mozart was cranking out concertos for European royalty at age four, for godsake. Tiger Woods was shooting under par in grade school. And don't even get me started on the Olsen twins.

Anyway, originally from Chappaqua—"Where Bill and Hillary live," Jeremy jokes. "That's how we get our notoriety now"—he's a Georgetown University sophomore who's just baaaarely squeaking by on a 3.8 GPA, this after bungling his way through the SATs with a perfect 800 on math and 670 verbal. Math has always been his thing. He's one of those John Nash–type freaks who just "gets it" when it comes to numbers. A natural corollary to this is that he loves gambling, loves Vegas, and often uses his savantlike mastery of numbers to his advantage. "I'll see players sitting on a sixteen with the dealer showing a seven and they'll hit," he tells me with a mix of amusement and shock. "That's not going to work because the odds are two in three that they're going to bust, and second, the dealer could have a ten under his seven, but if he has anything *other than* a ten— nine, eight, seven—based on the pure odds, he'll eventually bust himself. You following me?"

"Sure," I answer, by which I mean, *No, not at all.* I typically curl into the fetal position and soil myself when faced with any sort of math. If this were a *Simpsons* episode, this would be the point where they zoom into my brain and see nothing but a scraggly mule passed out beneath a tree after drinking a bottle of moonshine.

But it doesn't take a genius to sense that Jeremy might quite possibly be the future of not only fantasy football, but of real football: a new breed of youth raised on the love of the NFL *and* the competition and challenges of fantasy football. He wants to become the youngest general manager in NFL history. And he's not kidding.

He first started playing FF at age nine, when he joined a league he found in the back of a *Sporting News*, and was hooked immediately by the football-based competition, the challenge of beating older guys, and the gambling element (a small element, he says, but it's there) rooted in his love, and mastery, of numbers. Since then, he's been amazed by how huge FF has become. "When I started playing at camp that year, fantasy football was nothing. I had to calculate my salary cap on my own and send in my team and roster moves by mail." He laughs. "And then to see the spectacle at the WCOFF this year? My God, it's gotten ridiculous."

Playing FF *at camp*? A salary-cap league, no less? No wonder he's some sort of FF wunderkind: while all the other boys were having canoe races or raiding the girls' camp, he was holed up in his cabin, assessing sleeper kickers and calculating how much he had left for his backup tight end. So it's not surprising that he wormed his way into the WCOFF this year through a loophole in the rules, which state that team owners have to be twenty-one or older. "Technically, my dad co-owns my team," he chuckles, "but I went out to Vegas and drafted alone. He doesn't even know who's on our team."

Like many college students, Jeremy plans to study abroad—right now, it's looking like Denmark—but he says he will *not* go first semester because he'd have to miss all his beloved Atlanta Falcons games. "I just liked those gross red uniforms," he says, explaining how a kid who grew up in Jets/Giants country became a die-hard Falcons fan. How die-hard? His license plate reads FALCONS. His cell phone number (which he'll be glad to know I didn't share with the world) is distinctly Falcons-related, his e-mail address includes "FalconFan." "My parents think I'm crazy," he says. "But I've just had an obsession with football since I was literally four, five years old."

Sundays have become sacred to Jeremy, so much so that he recently woke up extra early to squeeze in Yom Kippur services so he could get back home and take care of the necessary pregame fantasy research. In other words, on the most important day of the Jewish religion, he did a little "turbo atoning" so he'd have time to take care of his fantasy football business. Good for him, I say. Let's not let little things like religious faith or sacred holidays get in the way of our fantasy football Sundays, shall we, folks?

Along with clearly being a bright kid and an FF veteran at nineteen, there's one more little gem that tells me Jeremy is a good brain for me to pick: the *one* sport he really knows nothing about is hockey. He hates to watch it—"They score like once in three hours," he complains—and doesn't even understand some of the penalties. Yet, when he entered ESPN's fantasy hockey league for the first time, just for kicks, he came in ninth. Not ninth in his league, mind you—ninth in the *entire country.* Does he even realize how many people he defeated? How the hell did he pull this off? Being a pretty self-deprecating kid, he says he just got lucky. But I'm dumbfounded, impressed, and more intrigued than ever, mostly for selfish reasons, as in, "Mini–Rain Man here can be a definite asset to Project Kick My League's Ass."

So, what's Jeremy's secret to fantasy success? One is knowing the difference between fantasy sports and *real* sports. And believe me, he says, there's a big difference.

"When you first start playing fantasy football," he explains, "you're inclined to say, 'OK, Troy Aikman's the best quarterback in the NFL, so

I'll make him my number one pick.' But fantasy-wise he was below average, a one-hundred-eighty-yard, two-touchdown kind of guy." In other words—and this makes a good **Newbie Strategy Tip#7: The biggest names in football aren't always the best fantasy players.** Tom Brady would be a more current example of Jeremy's Avoid the Troy Aikmans of the World Theory—great real quarterback, no doubt, but just an average *fantasy* quarterback.

Also, he warns, never underestimate your league-mates. In some of the national, online leagues he's played in, he's often received the "Doogie Howser" treatment from older players, i.e., being treated like a stupid little kid despite having proven himself numerous times. Even at twelve, thirteen years old, he'd already won his share of T-shirts (ESPN often gives T-shirts to league winners) and had a good number of miniature trophies scattered around his bedroom. Still, he'd constantly have to fend off the "seasoned vets" who figured a kid like him wouldn't know the difference between good fantasy players and good football players and, therefore, be susceptible to stupid trade offers. "I can't tell you how many times I was offered Aikman," he sighs.

Meanwhile, more often than not, he'd end up beating them.

As for this year's WCOFF, Jeremy had a dilemma from the start, having drawn the twelfth pick in his league. This, he says, was a big problem. "A lot of people said, 'Oh, you have two in a row at twelve and thirteen.' Getting two out of the top thirteen wasn't the problem—getting two out of the top thirty-five, *that* was the problem." (There are those numbers again.) Those first two picks ended up being Marvin Harrison and Corey Dillon. Hindsight is twenty-twenty and all, but Jamal Lewis (who was also available when he selected Dillon) would have been the better pick there, and as a result of other slow starters such as Chad Johnson, Marty Booker, and Matt Hasselbeck, Jeremy's Vick Our Savior squad sits at 2-4, a pretty substantial 100 points out of first place in his league, and only 483rd out of the 600 WCOFF teams in total points (the team with the best record *and* the highest-total-points scorer from each league make the playoffs, so Jeremy's hurting on both fronts). Not exactly future NFL GM material, some might say. But not me. There's just something calm and driven at the same time, if that makes sense, about Jeremy. He knows he's going to do it, and if you could buy stock in the future of human beings the way you can the future of companies, I'd be emptying my retirement account right now and buying a zillion shares of "Jeremy Wien, Future NFL General Manager."

Not only is he sporting a near 4.0 GPA (which I would have, too, had I been able to multiply my GPA by approximately two), majoring in finance, and planning to pursue a law degree after Georgetown—he's also obsessed with, and intrigued by, the nitty-gritty GM aspects of fantasy football, which most FF players enjoy, but few hope to use in an actual career. He knows that for a *real* football GM, decisions are far more complicated than they are in fantasy, more than just "OK, I'll give you this guy for so-and-so." When putting a team together, a real GM has to consider additional elements such as team chemistry, a player's off-field life, his mechanics and work habits (or lack thereof), how strongly a player may have finished a particular season, and what kind of situation a potential trade or free agent acquisition is coming from. "Is Jake Plummer going to be good now that he's on the Broncos?" Jeremy asks, providing a hypothetical GM conundrum. "Or, was he really just a bad quarterback all those years and we just made excuses for him because he played on a bad team?"

Jeremy was light-years ahead of the kids at camp, so it's no surprise that he's light-years ahead of most college sophomores in terms of planning his career. (I should know—when I was a sophomore, all I cared about was whether the Phi Tau party fund had enough left for a keg of Schmidt's Classic, which tasted more or less like moose urine.) He's ceaselessly picked the brain of a Georgetown professor, Susan O'Malley, who is also the first female president of an NBA franchise in history (the Washington Wizards, who changed their name from Bullets after realizing it probably wasn't a wise choice for the murder capital of the country). He had a sports marketing internship this past summer and hopes to get one with Gene Upshaw's NFLPA this summer. He's already sent résumés to every NFL team—proactive, yes, but a process that has shown him that even an impressive educational background and incredible drive doesn't guarantee success: most inquiries came back negative, except one. "The Arizona Cardinals said that if I transferred to Arizona, I could have a job with them during the school year," he tells me, laughing. "Yeah, *that's* what I want to do—leave Georgetown to work for Bill Bidwell, the second-worst owner in professional sports behind Donald Sterling [the notorious cheapskate LA Clippers owner]." And he's spoken to Bruce Allen, who runs the Raiders under Al Davis and might help Jeremy land an internship with the Raiders.

In other words, he's already working it, and something tells me he's going to succeed. Maybe because he's not all about just numbers and grades—he's a funny, good-natured, typical nineteen-year-old who likes going to concerts, has a girlfriend, plays poker with his buds, and most important, has proven himself resourceful in the past when it comes to getting what he's after.

Take 1998, Miami. During the Falcons-Broncos Super Bowl week, there was a party in a trendy South Beach hot spot that the then fourteen-year-old Jeremy wanted to crash. He could have paid his ten bucks for general admission and been herded off with the other little kids to throw footballs through hoops and get an autographed hat, but Jeremy was having none of that: he wanted into the VIP tent where all the NFL players and execs were hanging out. So what did he do? He paid someone five bucks to drop a glass to distract the security guards just long enough for him to sneak past them and under a back flap of the VIP tent. Within minutes, he was playing video games with (then Packers rookie DT) Vonnie Holliday and other NFL stars.

He also started chatting up a former Falcons offensive-lineman-turned businessman. As they shook hands, he gave the guy one of his dad's business cards (which only an überprepared kid would have on him). Two weeks later, the O-lineman calls Jeremy's dad for something business-related, and it turns out he knows Gene Upshaw, whose office is in D.C., where, coincidentally, Jeremy will just happen to attend college a few years later. Hence, his connection to the possible NFLPA internship this summer.

Point is, nothing is coincidental for Jeremy: he makes things happen. Without that smashed martini glass, he has no connection to Gene Upshaw (and never gets to kick Holliday's ass in Tecmo Bowl). And if he gets some experience with the NFLPA, combined with his already impressive résumé, he'll have a damn good head start on that GM career.

"I'm going for youngest GM in professional sports, ever. Maybe I'll pass [twenty-nine-year-old Boston Red Sox GM] Theo Epstein and make a new low bar," he says with a laugh, but again I can tell he's only half-joking . . . mostly because he really wants a Super Bowl ring and has ever since he attended his beloved Falcons' first 1998 playoff game (against the 49ers). While waiting for the players to come out of the locker room after the game, he ended up chatting with the father of then Atlanta safety Eugene Robinson (of course he did), who was wearing his son's Super Bowl ring from his days with the Packers. "I got to hold that Super Bowl ring, and I've been kind of enamored with it ever since," Jeremy admits. "A Super Bowl ring isn't about being flashy or the whole bling-bling thing, it's about accomplishment."

I want a ring, too. A Felon League ring. So, what kind of immediate advice would "Doogie Howser meets Vince Lombardi meets Frank *Catch Me If You Can* Abagnale" have for me and our beloved Acme squad?

First off, he says that I might want to take what the "experts" say with a grain of salt. The difference between an expert and a regular fantasy football fanatic is the sheer amount of time they put into it . . . because it's their *job*. "How do they know, say, whether Josh Reed is beating out Bobby Shaw at Bills training camp?" he asks. "Because they have contacts within the teams who tell them, not because they have an innate skill or talent. Not to take anything away from these guys, but luck always comes into it, and the 'experts' probably aren't *that* much better at fantasy football than you or me. During the regular season, every single day, you gotta be following who's in, who's benched, who's hurt, who you should pick up and why. You can't be that guy who just grazes box scores."

So, if what he's saying is true, the fact that I now have copious amounts of free time *alone* should give me an immediate advantage over my league-mates. This makes me feel good.

He also tells me that under no circumstances should I *even consider* trading Priest. The hip will be fine, he says, Vermeil is being extracautious, and Priest will end up leading the league in touchdowns when all's said and done. "With that offensive line they have in KC now," he continues, "I think Priest will even break Faulk's TD record this year. Don't trade him. You'll regret it."

He has to get to a statistics quiz now, one that he'll probably ace. Then he'll probably go play poker with his buddies, count cards, and rake in a couple hundred bucks. Then he'll go get a job with the Raiders and continue on his path to being the Theo Epstein of the NFL. And then he'll celebrate the day's accomplishments by slamming down a couple of beer bongs and having sex with Britney Spears, followed by the aforementioned and now legal Olsen twins.

Oh, to be nineteen again.

18

Remote (out of) Control

OK, here's the Week 5 deal: I had a pretty good day on Sunday, but my chances of winning the matchup against my cyber-sports friend Kevin's team, the Bonesky Crushers, took a huge hit in the ESPN prime time game.

The Steelers offense forgot how to play football for a living and was spanked by the weak-ass Browns defense, meaning Plaxico, whom I was counting on for a monster game, hosed me. He had 1, count 'em, 1 catch for 19 yards. That's 1 measly Felon League point, folks. I could go out there and score more. Combine this with the inexplicable 137-yard explosion by Kevin's WR Jimmy Smith in his *very first game of the season* (he just got off a drug suspension), and a big game from his kicker, David Akers, who nailed a 50-plus-yard FG for some FFL bonus points, and our beloved Acme squad is now *down* by 24 points to the Bonesky Crushers heading into tonight's *Monday Night Football* Bucs-Colts game.

Can you believe that? After last week's explosion, I have faith in Peyton, but do the FF gods *have to* make him play *at* Tampa? Plus, he hasn't exactly thrived in pressure-packed national games over the years. Not good. Not good at all.

As if sensing my anxiety, Phil Kwan of the Hershey Highway League shoots me an e-mail. With a rotiss victory safely in hand, he has no need to worry about tonight's game. "I go away on business for a week," he writes, "and there are 20 players traded or picked up in my league; Governor Schwarzenegger is accused of groping by nearly two dozen women; a white tiger takes a bite out of Roy out in Vegas; and Rush Limbaugh is hired and fired from ESPN. But most importantly, I get to enjoy 5-0 in Rotiss with no need to watch *Monday Night Football*."

Son of a bitch. I wish I could be as relaxed and nonchalant as Kwan about tonight's game. It's huge. Combine this with the staggering enormity of the Sox-A's Game Five in the Division Series in Oakland, and by early afternoon I'm already shaking more than Katharine Hepburn after an espresso.

Peyton in Tampa. Pedro in Oakland. May the FF gods team up with the MLB gods and deliver *both* Red Sox Nation and Acme Fantasy Football, Inc., to the promised land.

I'm in the midst of one of the single greatest nights of sports veiwing in my entire life.

First off, the Sox are battling it out with the A's in the deciding game of the ALDS, and in typical Sox fashion they're making me sweat it out until the last possible out. Yes, that's right, I admit it: here, now, in the middle of as intense an FF season as I've ever had, I'm putting our beloved Acme squad on hold and throwing myself totally and completely into the Sox-A's series. I'm *so* into baseball right now I can't even stand it! With all this "Cowboy up!" and Kevin Millar "rally karaoke" stuff, this has been the most fun I've had cheering for a Sox team in my lifetime (even if "Cowboy up!" *is* a little too Village People for my tastes). All summer and into fall, I've been secretly living and dying with every single pitch. Hell, the Sox shouldn't even be playing tonight. It took new Boston hero David "Dominican Shrek" Ortiz's two-out, two-run double to complete a major comeback yesterday and knock off the A's 5–4 to force this dramatic Game Five. *That's* the kind of season it's been. If we win tonight, we go on to face the Evil Empire—those goddamn Yankees—in the ALCS.

Meanwhile, as if that weren't enough, over on ABC, the Colts are playing the Bucs on *Monday Night Football*, a game in which I need some serious points from my boy Peyton in order to knock off the Bonesky Crushers this week. I've been flipping back and forth all night, but, because the Bucs have pretty much manhandled Indy thus far, I've resigned myself to another loss.

But, it's funny: even though our beloved Acme squad is about to fall to a lame 2-3, I'm oddly jazzed up, in a nervous, freaked-out kind of way.

Somehow, the Red Sox having a chance to move on to the ALCS makes the inevitable Felon League loss a little easier to swallow. Not easy, mind you, but just . . . easier. Two crucial great games in one night. This is the sports equivalent of being double-teamed by Tyra Banks and Ali Landry. (Or, if you're a Cowboys fan, Tyra Banks and Tom Landry.)

Celia, knowing from experience that I'll be an absolute wreck throughout both games, and not wanting to be present when the paramedics have to bust down the door and restart my heart, has kindly left me alone for the early part of the evening and gone out to grab dinner with her pal Holly. A wise move.

Anyway, through the first few innings, Sox-A's has been a pitcher's duel, with both aces, Barry Zito and Pedro Martinez, looking abso-fucking-lutely dominant, only a few scattered hits and walks to speak of. But then they get to Pedro in the fourth. A walk to Scott Hatteberg followed by a double to right center by Jose Guillen, scoring the former Sox catcher (how fitting).

Fuck. A's, 1–0

Instinctively, I groan—a low, feral growl that, if Celia were here, might make her lock the bedroom door and dial Animal Control. As a lifelong Sox fan who is used to having his heart ripped out of his chest with rusty pliers, I know that this single run—and subsequent growl—means the game, and the season, is officially over. It's a rule. Oh, well. Thanks for the memories, 2003 Sox. I might as well pack it in now. I wonder what's on Lifetime. Maybe there's a Meredith Baxter Birney movie about a man who does something bad to her because, well, men are evil.

But then, a tiny voice in the back of my head angrily flicks my skull with its index finger and dresses me down. "Hey, fair-weather, don't be such a pussy," the voice says, sounding oddly like Denis Leary. "These Sox aren't the Sox of your miserable past. Do you see Bill Buckner out there? No. Bob Stanley? No. Calvin Schiraldi? No. They've been cowboying up and coming from behind all year long, and they'll do it again tonight. So take off your skirt and start cheering for them!" Denis Leary's voice pauses, and I imagine he lights a cigarette, takes a long drag, and exhales. "That said, I agree with you about that whole 'Cowboy up!' thing. It *is* a little too 'Y.M.C.A.'"

He's right. They *have* been a kick-ass comeback team. And now is not the time to jump ship. I'm in this till the bitter end!

As if rewarding my newfound faith, in the top of the sixth, the Sox finally get to Zito. Varitek rips a homer to right, and after a walk and a hit batter, Manny Ramirez not only launches a Zito fastball into the left-field seats, but also stands still in the batter's box, admiring his work.

- I leap up and high-five the air, the wall, anything I can reach. Ho-lee-shiiiit! Just like that, it's Sox, 4–1. But, of course, just to test the limits of my aortas and ventricles, the Sox try to give the game right back to the A's . . . but not before things take a bizarre, scary, violent turn in the seventh inning. Chasing a pop-up to short center, Damian Jackson barrels directly into Johnny Damon, nearly decapitating Damon. Damon's not moving. His head rolls into right field, where a fan jumps out of the stands to scoop it up. Might get a couple grand for it on eBay, especially if it's autographed. And just as paramedics are taking Damon's headless corpse off the field on a stretcher, some sort of brouhaha breaks out near the Sox dugout. Sox players (led by Dominican Shrek) look as if they're about to charge into the stands (reminding me of a similar incident in New York involving the Bruins, who jumped the glass and battled drunken Rangers fans, one of whom defenseman Mike Milbury apparently hit with some lady's purse). Fans are screaming at them, giving them the finger, spewing pure venom. A's players are screaming at Sox players. Sox players are screaming at fans, A's players, cops, everyone. Security gathers. It's pure chaos, the culmination of two weeks of bad blood. And in a sick way, I love it. I love seeing baseball teeter on the edge of the violence that makes the NFL so much fun to watch!

Wait, speaking of football . . . I flip to the Colts-Bucs. Same old story. Bucs 21, Colts zippo. Peyton is being eaten alive. I'm screwed. But strangely, that's okay. My Sox are going to pull it out, goddammit! It's not a World Series—hell, it's not even the ALCS—but it's a step in the right direction.

I flip back to the Sox and watch them immediately take two steps backward. Pedro, clearly out of gas, gives up two runs in the eighth to bring Oakland within one.

Oh, fuck. Uh-uh. No way. Can't watch.

Flip back to *MNF.* Holy shit! Peyton to Marvin for a bee-you-tee-ful 37-yard TD! Seventeen points for Acme, baby! Plenty of football left to play. Come on, Peyton, buddy! There's hope yet!

Flip back to Sox. Bottom of the ninth, 4–3, Sox. New closer Scott Williamson comes in, faces two batters, and channeling the ghost of Calvin Schiraldi, walks two batters. There goes that whole "hope" thing. *Double* fuck, I can't watch.

Flip back to *MNF.* Ronde Barber picks off Peyton and returns it for a TD: 35–14, Bucs. *Triple* fuck!

Flip back to Sox. Two A's on, none out. So this is it, huh? This is how I die—alone, in my boxers, on my couch, remote in hand, my last words being "*Triple* fuck." That should impress Saint Peter.

A sac bunt puts the tying run at third, series-winning run at second. Still only one down. Williamson out, Derek Lowe, a closer-turned-starter because his psyche was too fragile for the closer's spot (oh, perfect), comes in. Bang! Just like that, strikes out a pinch hitter. Two out! But then he intentionally walks the bases loaded (just to cause any remaining blood to seep out of my heart).

Mommy, mommy, can't take the pressure . . . flip back to *MNF.*

What's this? Just four minutes to go and –bada bing! Bada boom!—a James Mungro TD makes it 35–21, and before I can even blink, Peyton drills a 28-yard TD to Marvin again! It's 35–28, Bucs. Oh, my . . . oh . . . my . . .

Flip back to Sox.

"I can't believe it, but I'm actually into this," a nervous voice next to me says. "Is this what you go through every year?" Shocked, I turn to see Celia sitting beside me on the couch.

"Whoa," I say. "When did you get home?"

She stares at me, then at the top of my head, perhaps looking for signs of blunt trauma to the head. "About fifteen minutes ago. You even said hi when we came in."

"I did?" I have no recollection of that. "And who's 'we'?"

Just then I hear a toilet flush, and seconds later, Holly emerges from our bedroom and joins us on the couch. "Did they win yet?" she asks us both, excited.

Good Lord. What the hell's going on here?

Before I can figure it all out, Lowe throws an 0-1 pitch that stays up in pinch hitter Terrence Long's wheelhouse and he sends it—and my abdomen—down the right-field line, deep, deep (*fuck, fuck, please no, please no, fuck*) . . . and . . . *foul ball!*

I swallow my vomit back down and sigh. Lowe recovers, sighs himself, sets. It all happens in slow motion now: windup, release, perhaps the most beautiful pitch I've ever seen floats, floats. It's a sinker, Lowe's bread and butter, and totally freezes Long, whose knees buckle as the ball tightrope-walks the inside corner.

Silence for a nanosecond . . . then chaos.

Strike three! Series over! The Sox mob Lowe and pile on the mound! I leap up once again and start high-fiving Celia, Holly, myself, screaming, pumping my fists. Downstairs in the 21st Amendment we can hear legions of drunken Sox fans losing their shit right along with me. It's on to face those pin-striped bastards in the ALCS!

But then I remember . . . my other supermodel is still waiting for me! Frantically, I flip back to ABC. (At this point, Celia and Holly lose interest and disappear into the bedroom to watch something else. Amazing how women can just turn their nervous sports energy on and off like that. I typically need at least forty-eight hours to recover from even the most mildly pressure-packed game.)

For the love of all that's holy, you've *got* to be kidding me—the Colts have tied it up! They show the replay of the "other" Ricky Williams plunging into the end zone from a yard out. While Lowe was busy dealing with the A's, Indy scored 21 points . . . in four minutes . . . *at* Tampa Bay! If you'd asked me whether a comeback was possible down 21–0 at Tampa, I'd have told you that Ali Hilfiger has a better chance of winning the Nobel Prize for quantum physics. Al Michaels and John Madden are simply beside themselves, raving about the onside kicks, turnovers, and clutch plays that made it all possible. Why on earth don't I have TiVo! Can someone answer me this? Why?

Sitting in stunned rapture, still drooling and shaking from the Sox victory, I watch as Indy sends it to overtime, where Mike Vanderjagt first misses a game-winning field goal, but the play gets called back for—of all things—a defensive player (Simeon Rice) leaping to block the kick. The refs think he used another player's back to propel himself into the air. He didn't, but that doesn't matter. The refs give Vanderjagt another shot and he nails it.

Game over! Colts 38–35 in OT. Un-bee-leeve-a-bull. My head hurts. My eyes sting. My stomach feels as if it's been stopping cannonballs for the past few hours. My remote-control thumb is practically pulsating, black-and-blue, throbbing with dull pain, as if I'd been whacking it with a hammer for the past two hours. I feel like yelling, *"Cut me, Celia, cut me!"* like Rocky to Mickey.

That, my friends, was one of the single-greatest blocks of sports viewing I've had in twenty years. It's not often one gets to watch not one but two ESPN Instant Classics right as they unfolds.

And the cherry on the sundae? Despite Plaxico's weak-ass Kevin-Bacon-in-*Hollow-Man* act on ESPN Sunday night, Peyton's ballsy, improbable 386-yard, 3-TD Monday performance propelled our beloved Acme squad to victory over the Bonesky Crushers. After five NFL weeks, Project Kick My League's Ass stands at 3-2.

Now . . . where the hell did I put that Advil?

19

Norman Chad Attacks!

Uh-oh. Looks like we have another member of the mainstream media who's trashing fantasy football, à la Frank Deford and the HBO *Real Sports* piece.

Norman Chad recently wrote a column for the *Houston Chronicle* accusing fantasy football of, among other things, "destroying the very fabric of this nation . . . if this fad continues unchecked, I wouldn't be surprised if America were not under communist or fascist control by 2010, or certainly no later than Super Bowl XLVIII."

Clearly, his tongue is planted in his rather large cheek—after all, I'm no history scholar, but I don't recall fantasy football ushering in the rise of Hitler, Stalin, and/or Mussolini—but I see the point he's making: fantasy football, and fantasy football players, are ruining the NFL fan base.

After he goes on to explain how FF works (to the three or four people out there who are still unfamiliar with it)—the rules, the leagues, et cetera—he then describes an insufferable (to him) afternoon of watching the games at his local sports bar alongside FF fanatics who wield "clipboards and legal pads, feverishly working their cell phones up until opening kickoff." He cringes as they take over his favorite watering hole, screaming at the TV screens, cheering on their fantasy players, caring not about who wins the game, but "only about touchdowns and interceptions and various statistical debris." Norman clearly views himself as "Norm" from *Cheers*, the loyal, old-school regular sitting in "his" seat in "his" corner of the bar, and these FF players as obnoxious, *nouveau*-fans who've suddenly invaded his personal space. And he doesn't like it one bit.

Chad does admit fantasy football has replaced the point spread as the single thing that keeps viewers glued to TV sets until the final gun goes off, whether it's a blowout or an overtime thriller, and notes this as a positive for the NFL. "Because, even if the betting line is decided," he writes, "fantasy participants stay to the final snap to see if their players are accumulating points." But that's where his severely limited approval of the hobby ends.

He clearly hates FF, and if you do even the most cursory Google search for "Norman Chad" and "fantasy football," you'll see this is a bizarre vendetta he's been pursuing for years. He was spewing his anti-fantasy-football vitriol in columns as far back as 1997, when there were only an estimated 470,000 people playing. "Fantasy football freaks," Chad wrote in the Las Vegas *Review-Journal*, "please take your stats and your charts and your sad-sack lives and go sit in a sandbox in your own backyard, out of sight, out of your minds and out of my harm's way. Some people call them 'fantasy geeks.' I prefer to think of them as 'reality losers.' Fantasy football is part of the numerical rubbish of the '90s, stats and figures signifying nothing. People don't reason and deduce anymore, they just add and subtract."

Come on now, Norman. Why are stats discussions— "numerical rubbish," as you call it—suddenly taboo when, for decades, sportswriters, fans, broadcasters, anyone with any opinion on sports whatsoever, have used stats like OBP, WHIP, field goal percentage, batting average, yards per carry, free throw percentage, goals against, TD-to-INT ratio, unforced errors, forty-yard-dash times, plus-minus ratios, and *countless* others to determine a player's very value? Without stats, how do writers like you back up your opinions in your columns on which players are good, bad, undervalued, overvalued, peaking, declining? And if these "reality losers" are out in a social setting *en masse* enjoying a hobby together while they watch every snap of every game—you describe them as basically taking over your local sports bar while you're trying to enjoy your Sunday games—how have they "lost touch with life as we know it" any more than you, yourself, apparently have, slumped in the corner by yourself, casing the joint like a freaking serial killer, sipping your manhattan or whatever other bitter-old-guy drink you're drinking, and sneering. Perhaps you're just angry that (a) these fantasy football "losers" are sharing an enjoyable, active, high-spirited group activity while you sit alone, and (b) the stuck-up waitress won't give you her phone number, despite your *very* attractive Caesar haircut. Bottom line, Norman, you sound like a man who likes to criticize from afar, but doesn't truly understand what goes on inside the hobby. After all, if you knew even one thing about it, you'd know that reason and deduction are a huge part of fantasy football. Hell, just setting a lineup every Sunday requires far more insight than just "adding and subtracting."

Worst of all, according to Chad, fantasy football has spawned a generation of nonfans—conflicted individuals who no longer root for the Packers or Raiders or Rams, but, rather, root only for the individual player and his point production, regardless of his uniform color or logo on his helmet. Why are the fans conflicted? Because one's fantasy players will eventually face one's *real* hometown team. "So," Chad complains, "you sit there, rooting for your favorite team, but also rooting guiltily for your [fantasy] quarterback to put up big numbers against your favorite team. By game's end, you're an emotional mess."

On this, he's not that far off. I'll admit, there have been times when I have, say, the Dolphins defense, and they pick off a Tom Brady pass and take it back to the house, and I'm glad my defense got some points. But it's not at the expense of my Patriots allegiance. If anything, I feel *more* connected to reality, in that, hey, if Brady's going to get picked off—and he will, because this is the NFL and there are great athletes on both sides of the ball in every single game—it might as well be my defense doing the picking. Am I actively rooting for Brady to get picked off, as Chad suggests? Not a chance in hell. I'd rather he torch the 'Fins for 350 yards and three touchdowns every time, even if costs my fantasy team. But it just takes the sting off the interception if it's Sam Madison doing the intercepting, and Acme benefiting. However, Chad sees fantasy football as a form of pigskin treason, causing former fans to turn on their home teams. Yet he doesn't seem to mind the fan who often bets that his or her favorite team will lose. Take a diehard Detroit Lions fan. If he's smart, he will *not* bet his kid's college tuition that his 1-10 train wreck of a team will upset the 10-1 Vikings. Rather, he will bet that his beloved Lions will *only lose by a certain number of points*. In other words, every Sunday, using a few seemingly arbitrary plus or minus numbers set in some back room in Las Vegas, "real" fans are essentially abandoning their home teams as egregiously as Chad believes fantasy football players do. So, to angrily claim that one group is ruining football while completely absolving the other is preposterous. If Norman talked to even one FF player, which he clearly didn't before making these blanket statements about their collective psyche, he'd have heard affirmations of home-team loyalty such as this one from a Huddler from Minnesota: "If I lose my FF matchup one week, I just shrug it off and plan for my next opponent. But if the Vikings lose their game in a particular week, I'm depressed for days. A true fan has to root for his real team first."

Any FF player will tell you that no matter how obsessed one might be with fantasy football, a true fan will never, *ever* cheer against his or her home team. "I always root Steelers first," says another Huddler. "If a win for the Gold and Black means sacrificing my fantasy team's win, I'd do it in a second." That said, like me he sees fantasy football as a way to hedge his bets and take some solace in a loss by the home team. "But if they're playing the Titans and I have Derrick Mason and he scores," he continues, "after cursing furiously and scaring my wife and dog, only then will I think, 'Well, at least he was on my fantasy team.'"

Now, I can't disagree with Chad that FF has diluted the *more casual* fan base a bit—the people who weren't loyal to begin with and root for whichever team is hot and/or has the coolest uniforms. (How many bandwagon hoppers were suddenly Niners fans in the eighties or Cowboy fans in the nineties?) But, overall, fantasy football has been nothing but a positive for the league, and for the game of football, and has only solidified the serious, less wishy-washy fan base. "FF is an extension of peoples' love for the NFL," says David Dorey. "But when I watch, I am always pulling for the Cowboys to win. I think people who believe that FF 'waters down' the NFL are smoking crack."

I know of few people who would consider themselves FF fans *first* and fans of their home team *second*. Yes, in Chad's defense, there certainly are NFL fans who've gotten so engrossed in FF that they've abandoned their home team. But, as a Huddler explains, "that just shows what kind of fans they were to begin with." In other words, the aforementioned bandwagon hoppers are going to be wishy-washy anyway, while true NFL fans are going to stick with their teams till the end.

Basically, in his rants against fantasy football over the years, Chad sounds like the bitter old parent complaining about his kid playing his gosh-darn rock 'n' roll music too loud. I can almost see him in an upstairs window, wearing a button-down Mr. Rogers cardigan and screaming at the neighbor kids, *Hey, you fantasy football players with your cell phones and clipboards, get out of my yard!* Face it, Normie, FF has almost single-handedly caused the NFL to explode to supernova-like proportions in this country, and all over the world. FF lines the NFLPA's pockets with merchandising revenue; fattens the league's coffers thanks to DirecTV Sunday Ticket and other licensing/marketing agreements; increases player salaries—in short, extends the overall life span of one of your main subjects: the NFL. So who cares if someone in your sports bar is rooting for Keenan McCardell to get a touchdown? (Would you rather have that mouthy, overrated, underachieving slug Keyshawn Johnson hitting pay dirt?) Does a guy cheering about one of his players getting a sack ruin your ability to gulp down—and I'm only judging by your picture in the *Houston Chronicle*—your fourth bacon-double-cheeseburger-and-onion-ring platter of the afternoon?

As Bill Murray said in *Stripes*, "Lighten up, Francis." Like the HBO *Real Sports* piece, Chad has only succeeded in generalizing and over-simplifying the image of FF players to make this game/hobby/obsession easy to understand for the ever-shrinking millions who *don't* play. He relies upon the convenient caricature of the obsessed, socially retarded loner toting his clipboard to make his point and create an entertaining read while abandoning the truth. So, who's out of touch with reality here—the FF player, or Norman Chad, with his hands clapped over his ears, shaking his head and refusing to acknowledge the true nature of the FF fan? Ninety-five percent of the FF players out there are normal men and women with jobs, wives and husbands, kids, all the things that keep them in touch with life as we know it. How do I know? I saw them at WCOFF. I saw them in New Jersey. I've been talking to them pretty much nonstop for going on three months. And I'm one myself.

If anything, columnists like Chad should be thanking these "reality losers" because fantasy football enhances the overall marketability of *real* football. Which ramps up the excitement of sports in general. Which makes these "freaks" want *more* information about sports and, now, fantasy sports. Which gives columnists a whole new world to write about and makes people buy *more* of the newspapers that pay their salaries.

Essentially, Norman, you work for the very people you bash. So, if I were you, I'd shut my burger-hole, give up this windmill-battling quest of yours, and accept that fantasy football is growing at alarming rates and isn't going anywhere anytime soon.

20

Holy Shit, I'm Actually Starting Jerome Pathon!

I gottta be honest with you, nothing very interesting has happened lately in the Felon League. I've been sidetracked by, of all things, the American League Championship Series between the Sox and the dreaded Yankees.

Baseball has actually continued to interrupt fantasy football. What nerve! I just hate when other things dare to rip my attention away from my FF business at hand. The only thing I ever thought would get in the way of tending to my Acme team would either be Celia going into labor or . . . well, Celia going into labor.

But *baseball*?

Ever since the A's series, I've been surgically attached to every single Red Sox pitch, every throw, every run. And, let's face it—with all due respect to Michigan–Ohio State, Harvard–Yale, and Dr. Dre–Suge Knight, there is no better rivalry on earth than Sox-Yankees. I don't care what I said about baseball earlier—about how it's fat and old and getting its ass kicked by football—it's redeemed itself 100 percent over the course of August and September.

Of course, the Red Sox will soon rip the collective heart out of New England and stomp it to a bloody pulp, like something out of a novel by number-one Sox fan, Stephen King. But I don't care. That's what we Sox fans have come to expect every year since 1918, so why should 2003 be any different? I'm just enjoying the ride . . . and trying not to kick in my TV set whenever the Yankees get a lucky break.

However, something interestingly FF-related *does* occur as we head into Week 6.

Celia and I are at a family wedding—her cousin Wick—at a golf club in her hometown of Niskayuna, New York. Typical scene: cheese and fruit hors d'oeuvres, DJ playing "Celebration" and "Old Time Rock 'n' Roll," Uncle Lenny accusing Uncle Terry of bilking his share of grandma's estate—the staples of any good family wedding.

Wick is not just a nervous new groom, he's also an FF rookie whom I've been helping out a bit this season. He's playing in a free Yahoo! league with a bunch of buddies and, during preseason, asked me to help rank his players for his draft, help with lineup and trade decisions, stuff like that. And because he's about to head off to Aruba for the next two weeks, he's asked me to look after his team (as if it were his child).

So, naturally, about halfway through *his own* wedding reception, he wants to talk FF.

"I think we start Booker one more week, and if he sucks again, we cut his ass," Wick says, standing at the adjacent urinal as I release a few gallons of the Stoli-and-tonic that my bladder's been holding hostage. He flushes, walks to the sink, and looks back at me in the mirror. "What do you think?" he asks, pumping some pink liqui-soap into his palm.

What do I think? Bro, I think it's your wedding reception and you should probably be dancing with your new bride. I think you should be thinking about the wonderful future you'll have together, and the amazing honeymoon you're about to go on. I think you should be thinking about *anything* but Marty freaking Booker. But, honestly, I'd probably be worrying about my team, too, if I were going to be out of commission and, presumably, nowhere near a computer for two straight weeks. (Then again, I found no fewer than two Internet cafes on my own honeymoon in Costa Rica, this in a remote surfing town that makes Aruba look like Silicon Valley.) Such is the curse/obsession of FF: it's never fully out of one's mind—at a wedding reception, lying in bed half-asleep at 2 A.M., running a shareholders' meeting, operating heavy machinery, performing open-heart surgery, whenever. Hell, Wick and I could be stranded in the Andes Mountains after a plane crash deciding whom we're going to eat to survive and *still* find the strength to debate the pros and cons of starting Marty Booker.

"I don't know, man," I say, zipping up, walking over to the sink, and washing my hands next to him. "Moulds might be out this week, which'd mean Bobby Shaw might get a few more looks from Bledsoe. Buffalo plays the Jets, too. I might start Shaw if I were you, but, hey, it's your call."

He's 4-1 (thanks, in part, to some of my coaching, truth be told). I don't want to be the reason he falls to 4-2.

"It's all in your hands for the next few weeks," he says. "I trust you. Start Shaw if you want."

Gee, thanks. As if I'm not worried enough about my own team, now I have the added pressure of not screwing up the team of a happy new groom on his wedding day—a groom who's family no less.

But I signed up to help him out and, well, I can't leave him in the lurch now.

Little did we know, a third guy has been in the bathroom with us, using one of the back stalls. He flushes, emerges, walks over to the sink, pumps out his own pink liqui-soap, and gives his hands a quick scrub. "Sorry to eavesdrop," he says, yanking out a few brown paper towels and drying his hands, "but I'd go with Shaw, too. The Jets can't stop anyone, and it sounds like Moulds's hammy is pretty bad. I own Moulds in one league and I picked up Shaw this week."

The oddly helpful stranger then crumples up the paper towels into a ball, tosses it free-throw-style toward the trash can (it rims out), and fixes his slicked-black hair (I almost expect him to give himself the imaginary double-guns-and-wink combo). Satisfied, he finally congratulates Wick with a slap on the back and leaves.

"Who was that?" I ask.

Wick shrugs and adjusts his bow tie. "No idea."

But alas, I *do* know who it is—a celestial messenger of the FF gods, sent via the handicap stall with a message from on high: Start Bobby Shaw, and go ye and prosper.

And so it was decreed: Wick and I will start Bobby Shaw. Amen.

We head back into the ballroom. The sweet dulcet tones of Buster Poindexter singing "Hot Hot Hot" wash over us *(Conga line alert! Conga line alert!)*. I tell Wick not to worry, that I've got it all under control. Just enjoy your honeymoon, man! You'll be 6-1 when you get back and getting ready for your playoff run.

Honestly, at that moment, I'm more worried about the upcoming Sox-Yankees Game Three at Fenway and, a few hours later, am watching with a mix of amusement and pity as, in the aftermath of several bean-ings and subsequent retaliation, Pedro Martinez tosses Don Zimmer to the ground like some sort of a drunken, disoriented weeble-wobble. But that's the only victory for the Sox as the Yankees, behind Roger Clemens (aka evil traitor), beat the Sox to go up two games to one. Worse than the loss is that I'm forced to watch the game at Celia's aunt Susan's house in a crowd of obnoxious, pompous, smirkingYankee fans.

Oh, come on, I'm kidding—they're perfectly nice people . . . for band-wagon-riding starfuckers. How can anyone root for the Yankees and claim to have a human soul? Boggles the mind, really.

But another Sox-Yankees bloodbath is about all the sports excitement in Week 6. Football-wise, sadly, it can't be more dull. In absentia Wick wins his game in a landslide. However, despite the FF gods' bathroom messenger assuring us that Bobby Shaw is a safe start, the Bills WR doesn't do a hell of a lot against the Jets: 50-something yards, no TDs. But at least he plays better than Booker, who hurts his ankle in the first quarter and doesn't do squat. So we made the right call.

And in Felon League play, I win my own game—bringing Project Kick My League's Ass to 4-2. But the game itself is about as exciting as Ben Stein reading James Joyce. Final score (if you can call it that) is 85–50, my lowest point total of the season.

Peyton, coming off the monster Tampa game, only manages 17 points against the tough Carolina defense. Davis and Priest have OK games. Plaxico and Darrell Jackson have 60 and 55 yards respectively, which is annoyingly becoming par for the course. And Todd Heap once again does zilch, mainly because Ravens rookie QB Kyle Boller doesn't realize he has a right arm attached to his body and, if he does, certainly doesn't plan on using it anytime soon. The Baltimore game plan is clearly Jamal Lewis left, Jamal Lewis up the middle, Jamal Lewis right. However, the Bucs defense is my saving grace, racking up a great 19 points. But the real kicker is that I win despite leaving Trent Green on my bench, who blows up a whopping 59 points against the Packers in a thrilling overtime game at Lambeau Field.

So, I don't have much more to report here in Week 6, other than the scary reality that I'm now facing Week 7 with two starters—Peyton and Plaxico—on their bye weeks. But that's okay; Plaxico isn't doing dick any-way. And I can replace Peyton with the red-hot Green, who, as I said, is coming off a huge game and, this weekend, faces a Raiders squad that's giving up approximately 627 points a game.

All things considered, I'm feeling good.

And by feeling good, I of course mean I'm totally screwed.

If you'd told me before the season started that, in Week 7, I'd be starting Jerome freaking Pathon at wide receiver, I'd have told you I was clearly in the midst of an 0-16 season. But that's just what I have to do, thanks to Plaxico's bye week. I have no other options at WR. Bad planning on my part. In my desire to stockpile RBs, I've left my WR corps decimated.

And, to put it mildly, Pathon sucks in Week 7. Doesn't catch a damn thing.

Meanwhile my opponent, All-American Angus, watches their own backup WR, whom they've started on a hunch, Terry Glenn, strut through the Swiss-cheese Lions secondary for 3 touchdowns—bang, bang, bang!—like daggers to my heart. Meanwhile, their Vikings defense is going Ike Turner on Broncos backup QB Steve Beuerlein, bitch-slapping him for 5 sacks and returning an interception for a touchdown, all to the tune of a whopping 23 points. Combine this with a great game by their stud RB, Deuce McAllister, and you have the makings of a painful afternoon for yours truly.

Meanwhile, my unholy man-crush, Stephen Davis, is shut down for the first time this year, held to only 20 yards rushing. Darrell Jackson does squat. The normally reliable Bucs defense craps out with only 4 points. And while Todd Heap *finally* shows up with 129 yards receiving, I'm still down a whopping 145 to 51 as the Sunday games wrap up.

I still have Priest and Green going in Oakland on *Monday Night Football*, but even though the Raiders defense couldn't stop a Pop Warner team right now, unless my guys rack up 95 points, I'm looking at a loss, and a 4-3 record.

Not good.

And it isn't. In the 17–10 Chiefs win, Priest has a pretty studly game (123 yards rushing, 50 yards receiving, 1 TD, for 37 points), but Green comes back to earth after his huge Green Bay game with a typical "Green-like" day (low 200 yards passing, 1 TD, blah blah blah, for a piddly 13 FFL points). It's not nearly enough to make up the 94-point difference.

Final score: All-American Angus 145, Acme 101.

Our beloved Acme squad is now an extremely pedestrian 4-3. Man, that's just embarrassing. But at least the FF gods have stopped bending me over and treating me like their own personal carnival ride. That was sarcasm. Prior to our game, All-American Angus had been averaging a paltry 96 points per game. But this week? One hundred forty-five. And in my previous loss? The Big Dogs *had* been averaging 89 points a game, yet went totally and inexplicably Chernobyl on me with 236. Hey, FF gods, at least take me to dinner and get me drunk before Adebisi'ing me! Is that too much to ask? Can you believe this keeps happening?

Here's how we stand:

Team	W	L	PF	PA
Account Guys	7	0	777	570
Rat Bastards	6	1	1,019	582
Funk Soul Bros.	5	2	711	637
Acme FF, Inc.	4	3	948	906
The Dream Team	4	3	894	751
Bonesky Crushers	4	3	685	616
Big Dogs	3	4	737	788
SoCo	3	4	636	761
All-American Angus	3	4	631	733
The Pound Dawgs	2	5	561	618
Charlemagnes	1	6	490	762
NH Hillbillies	0	7	473	838

Okay, so I lost to a 2-4 team. And I'd rather chew tinfoil than have Shergul ahead of me in the standings. But to quote the Red Sox—and perhaps the Village People—I gotta "Cowboy up!" and hope for better things in Week 8.

Speaking of, we're almost halfway through the NFL season. Most FF league playoffs, like mine, take place Weeks 14 through 16, but some end at Week 15 because NFL teams who've already clinched playoff spots often rest their stud starters. This is an FF owner's personal hell. I bring this up because even though there's a lot of football left, I'm already worried about the 7-0 Chiefs and how they handle Priest. If they clinch home field early—and it's looking good considering the shoddy competition in the AFC West—they might be inclined to rest their stud (and, more important, my stud), Priest. Come fantasy playoff time, he could potentially play one half, *maybe* three quarters a game. This would be devastating.

But I should try to look on the bright side: it's been four months since I officially quit a perfectly good job to devote 24-7 to playing fantasy football, and there's not any gainful employment in sight. Which is good. I'd have a hard time being thrust back into an office environment after pretty much being my own boss all day, every day, for the last 120 days. Sure, a steady paycheck would be nice, but we're doing okay . . . for a while, anyway. We've cut some corners, obviously: clipping coupons, no eating out, whoring Celia out to visiting Japanese businessmen. (Just seeing if you're paying attention.) One Saturday afternoon, looking like two fairly well-dressed and showered homeless people, we wandered up and down the Quincy Market food court and gorged ourselves on the free samples at the food kiosks. Hey, why should tourists get all the free eats? After two or three reps, we'd managed to incrementally inhale a three-course meal, although the lady pimping baklava in front of the Athens Café was starting to get a little suspicious.

Celia, bless her heart, has been the primary trouper. She's put on a brave face and volunteered for some market-research focus groups, the poor kid. God, does she loathe focus groups. Then again, anyone who's sane and/or not lonely and looking for attention would hate them—sitting in a stuffy conference room, being gawked at by a bunch of ad guys hidden behind a two-way mirror, getting mentally probed (thankfully not anally, unless, perhaps, it's a medical-product focus group), answering asinine questions about razors or online shopping or flavored coffees or ATM banking. This is an educated, talented professional woman we're talking about here, folks, not some slobbering derelict who's dragged herself in off the street looking for a few bucks to support her crystal meth habit. No, it's not selling her blood or internal organs, but it still represents an extra sacrifice on her part for the good of my holy quest for an FFL Super Bowl title. I can't tell you how much I appreciate her understanding, patience, and most of all, the insightful opinions she's given the marketing community to aid in its holy quest to create a more aerodynamic ladies' razor.

But she's reaching her breaking point with focus groups.

"The Staples one I could take, because it was only an hour, it was right near work, and I got a hundred bucks," she said recently. "And the electric toothbrush one was all right, pretty painless. But that bagel one nearly killed me. I had to eat those disgusting friggin' bagels for two straight hours, and then go back the *next* day for two *more* hours and eat *more* of those gross things. *And* it was only for sixty-five bucks. That was awful."

I could tell by the beaten look in her normally lively brown eyes that, sure, she's willing to sacrifice for the team . . . but not for much longer. I'd better get my fantasy shit together, and fast.

I just hope that she hasn't divorced me come playoff time.

21

Resignation of a Red Sox Fan

It happened. Again. The Red Sox did it to us *again*. How many times can we play Charlie Brown trying to kick that goddamn football, only to watch that sneaky broad Lucy yank it away and send us toppling over onto our asses?

I won't go into all the horrific details; they're just too painful. Plus, I don't want to veer too far away from the fantasy football tale at hand again. But I can't *not* report what those merry prankster Red Sox did to me in the ALCS Game Seven last night, and assuming you live anywhere other than the Galápagos Islands, certain parts of the Australian outback, or Neptune, you know exactly what I'm talking about: Grady Little, Pedro, eighth inning, Tim Wakefield, tenth inning, Aaron Boone, 1918, Bucky Dent, Bill Buckner, Satan, Hell, Death, Purgatory, Eternal Damnation, Fuck.

The Curse lives on. The Red Sox are done.

They were up three runs, with only five outs left . . . *five outs!* . . . and *still* lost. How can a team possibly lose that way? *How?* you ask. *BECAUSE THEY'RE THE FUCKING RED SOX, THAT'S HOW!* Serves them right for spray-painting the 2003 World Series logo behind the home plate at Fenway before the first pitch of Game Seven was even thrown in the Bronx. Talk about adding one more unnecessary jinx to a franchise chock-full of 'em.

I feel as if I've had my internal organs ripped out, rearranged like mismatched puzzle pieces, and haphazardly jammed back into my body . . . without anesthesia. My heart is somewhere near my bowels. My stomach is firmly lodged in my trachea. My foot is still stuck in my TV screen. I have no idea where my spleen is.

This being the case, the only thing I can muster is the following letter. (I'm sorry. This is the last time I'll mention the foul plague that *is* pro baseball, I promise, and then it's right back to Project Kick My League's Ass.)

TO: Theo Epstein, John Henry, Larry Lucchino, Tom Werner
FROM: Mark St. Amant
RE: My official resignation as a Red Sox fan

Dear Sirs,

The purpose of this letter is to inform you of my resignation from my current position as "Boston Red Sox Fan," which I have held since leaving my mother's womb in the Impossible Dream season of 1967. After much thought, and serious discussions with friends and family, I have decided to pursue a different team and have accepted a position as "Detroit Tigers Fan" beginning in April of 2004. My last day of work with your fine organization will be this Friday.

However, I would like to take this opportunity to express my sincere appreciation to you and your predecessors for the thirty-five wonderful years that I have worked as a Red Sox Fan. My decision to root for a different baseball team holds no relation to my experiences here with the Red Sox. Well, other than annually coming as close as humanly possible to victory, only to watch it slip away in the most spirit-crushing possible manner due to inexplicable and heart-wrenching human error, fate, destiny, mystical curses, and, of course, the inevitable intervention from Satan himself (who, by the way, wears pinstripes). I know that I have been fortunate to have been associated with such great teams as the 1975 Sox, the 1978 Sox, the 1986 Sox, the 1995 Sox, the 1999 Sox, and, most of all, these recent 2003 Sox. So please know that I have learned a great deal during my tenure in Boston.

For instance, I've learned that a human foot can fit neatly through virtually any television screen, with or without a shoe. I've learned that dogs and/or babies get very scared when you hurl coffee tables across the living room in their general direction. I've learned that chanting "Yankees suck!" during a Red Sox–Orioles game in May at Camden Yards has no bearing whatsoever upon the psyche of the Yankee players themselves. I've learned how to curl up into the fetal position, defecate on myself, and weep quietly while muttering incoherent sentence fragments about Jorge Posada, Grady Little, Alan Embree, Aaron Boone, Chuck Knoblauch, Derek Jeter, Tim Tschida, Roger Clemens, Bill Buckner, Mookie Wilson, Ray Knight, Calvin Schiraldi, John McNamara, Bob Stanley, Jeff Reardon, Roberto Kelly, Bucky Dent, Mike Torrez, Don Zimmer, Ed Armbrister, Carlton Fisk, Larry Barnett, Bob Gibson, Lou Brock, and countless others. Most important, I have also learned how to heal self-inflicted steak-knife wounds and lighter burns, a valuable skill that might lead to a possible career in nursing once my tenure as Tigers Fan has ended.

I thoroughly enjoyed my time employed with Red Sox Nation and would recommend the experience to anyone looking for a fair and rewarding job, or hoping to have his/her very soul ripped from his/her body and shoved directly up his/her rectum in an extremely painful manner every year for his/her entire life until he/she mercifully expires from sheer misery. Please use the address on this letter to send my final paycheck and any other official communications that may be necessary as I make my transition to Detroit Tigers Fan.

I wish the Red Sox continued success—and by "continued success," I of course mean I wish for you and your entire organization to rot in hell for all eternity—and I want to thank you for allowing me to be a part of your team. Please feel free to contact me at any time if I can be of further assistance in helping with a smooth transition for the masochistic son of a bitch who takes my place.

Thank you, again, and best of luck as you continue the utterly futile, Sisyphean quest for a World Series championship.

Kind regards,
Mark St. Amant

P.S. Thank you for losing. I can now turn my full attention back to my fantasy football season.

22

Stalking Joe Horn, Part I

It's snowing in mid-October, the earliest it's snowed in Boston in like twenty years.

This is New England, a place whose residents should be used to inclement weather, but most of the people down on Beacon Street are running for cover, holding newspapers over their heads. Come on, folks, it's not a meteor shower. It's not Atlanta, where panicked residents hoard bottled water and canned goods in a wild survival frenzy at the first sign of precipitation. It's just . . . a little . . . snow. You're New Englanders for godsake! Buck up!

It's kinda pretty, actually (easy for me to say, sitting here in my flannel pajamas in my warm apartment). But that it's snowing this early in the year bodes for a wacky day. I can feel it already. Something just feels . . . wacky. But seeing the white stuff falling from the sky evokes some more familiar feelings as well. The 1967 Packers-Cowboys "Ice Bowl" at Lambeau (which I don't actually remember, being only ten days old at the time). The 2001 Pats-Raiders "Snow Bowl," featuring the infamous Tom Brady tuck (or fumble, if you're from Oakland) and the Lonnie Paxton celebratory snow angels in the end zone. And how can any New Englander forget Mark Henderson, the convict on work release who drove a plow across Schaefer Stadium's snowy turf to clear a path for Pats kicker John Smith to boot a game-winning field goal against Miami in 1982? *This*, my friends, is football weather.

And, it's Wednesday. Wednesdays are typically big trade days in the Felon Fantasy League. Free agent picks are flying. Teams are rushing to fill holes. It's always a good time to exploit another team's weakness and use it to improve your own team. The following is a brief anatomy of a typical trade negotiation in the FFL, in this case an attempt on my part to pry the undervalued (in my opinion) New Orleans Saints receiver Joe Horn from the Bonesky Crushers.

I e-mail Kevin first thing.

```
Me: I've been working on some trade scenarios and
I think this one is pretty fair considering both
of our needs: T.Green and D.Jackson for J.Horn?
You still have Jimmy and Toomer as starters,
Jackson is a solid startable backup, and you get
the QB upgrade you (sorely, in my opinion) need
while I get my WR upgrade (and take on Horn's bye
Week 10). Also, we don't play each other again
unless we both make the playoffs . .

Kevin (the Bonesky Crushers primary negotiator):
We definitely won't do Horn, too valuable to us.
We might do Toomer if he interests you.

Me: If you drop from Horn to Toomer, I'd need a
little something extra. Green for Toomer and your
free agent pick, maybe?

Kevin: We're interested but don't know if we
can sacrifice our FA pick. We would need a WR
in return. So possibly D Jax/Trent Toomer/FA?
```

So, it's going to be a tug-of-war, eh? OK, I can play that game, brother.

```
Me: You want me to throw in DJax now? OK, then
we're back to Green-DJax for Horn. The other way
makes no sense for me. DJax has been BETTER than
Toomer this year. . . . OK, fair enough, no Horn.
And no solo Toomer for Green. What about Green
solo for Toomer & your FA pick? I just need a
little sweetener if I'm going to lose all my QB
```

security for a question mark like Toomer (Giants
offense sucks). . . . I wanted Horn, as you know,
but would take Toomer if you threw in your pick.

Kevin: If I trade Toomer and FA I will have
Green/Gannon and only 2 WR left. IF I don't get a
pick this week that leaves me with a MUST-PICK WR
pick next week. SHIT! I just noticed that I don't
have a D this week too. I am hosed.

Uh-oh, Kevin's starting to come unraveled. Time to play hostage
negotiator and convince him he'd be getting great value for what he's giving up.

Me: Green is a valuable backup, a starter on most
teams in this league. I'd be screwed if Peyton
went down, so there's value on both sides.
Toomer's too big a drop from Horn. Not ruling it
out, but maybe we'll talk tomorrow after you see
how your FA QB search pans out . . . 'til then,
enjoy starting Kurt freaking Kitner. ☺

Kevin: OK.

Oh, but it's not OK. If I can't get Horn, I want to go in for the kill on
a blockbuster to improve my RB corps, under the guise of trying to
improve my WR corps.

Me: I've been thinking of a blockbuster also, to
really send a jolt through the league. I give:
S.Davis, T.Green, DJax. You give: Ricky Williams &
Toomer. Davis is FIVE points behind Ricky in total
FFL points. They've both had their byes. Green is
your new stud QB. DJax has been better than Toomer
and can replace Horn Week 10. Plus, you keep your
FA pick to pick up a defense. Win-win.

I click send, sit back in my chair, and wait for the inevitable response that says "no way we trade Ricky if Priest isn't involved." And not thirty seconds later . . .

Kevin: Sheesh. My brother told me never give away your #1 draft pick, ever! Unless we get back a #1.

Jason (Kevin's brother, and Bonesky Crushers secondary negotiator, who's been watching the trade talks like an offensive coordinator up in a booth above the field): Yeah, any deal that includes Ricky, must include Holmes.

Great, now I'm being double-teamed, and their logic couldn't be more flawed. We're eight weeks into the season and they're *still* judging players based on when they were drafted? I counter with:

Me: The whole #1 pick thing is out the window at this point in the season. Is Edge a #1 now? Faulk? They were picked third and eighth overall, Ahman was ninth overall. But would you trade Ahman for Faulk or Edge right now? No way. My point is that RBs like Davis, Jamal Lewis—second rounders—are playing better than most first-round RBs not named Priest, Ahman, and Portis. Davis and Ricky have virtually identical stats, with the 2nd half edge to Ricky, which is why I'd get him and you'd get the new stud QB (Green) you desperately need.

I nod my head emphatically while sending, like a defense attorney resting his case. But then, lo and behold, Kevin reveals that they have another suitor. *Nooooooo!!!!!*

Kevin: Actually, we just got hit with a MONSTER offer which would shake things up more than your offer. A #1 for a #1, so just what we want. But we

```
have to work on the back half. This potential deal
is much better than yours, sorry. We'll need you
to spice yours up to even consider it now.
```

Greedy motherf%#*ers!! Smart of them to shop around, yes, but I still feel like head-butting my iMac. I'm now the sucker at the bar who's been buying the hot chick drinks all night, only to have some other, better-looking dude saunter in, sit down, and start laying down a rap that I can only dream of. He's an investment banker. He has a house on Nantucket. And a yacht. And a Porsche. And a private jet. He can give her any freaking thing she wants. Me? I work at Arby's, drive a Hyundai, and live with my parents. I have to keep the suave dude with the killer rap away from the hot chick (Bonesky). He is *not* leaving with the hot chick!

```
Me: OK, we have the players to make this work,
let's think about this . . . downshifting into a
less sexy but still very good deal . . . Green &
DJax for Toomer & Warrick Dunn?

Kevin: Maybe Toomer and Amos Zereoue. Still
interested?
```

Translation: you've bought me expensive drinks all night; now I want you to buy me dinner at Nobu, a Cartier diamond watch, and a Porsche, the way the suave dude can. And, by the way, I will give you no sex in return. Deal?

Man, this is one gold-digging slut. Maybe I should just let the suave dude have her. But, I can't. It's a pride thing. Any guy will tell you that to lose a girl at a bar to another guy after spending all night, and all your money, trying to get her phone number . . . well, there's nothing worse. At least, that's what I remember anyway, the last time I tried to pick up a girl in a bar, which was probably, oh, 1990, and, if memory serves, ended with me getting shot down and my amused buddies telling me that it was probably best, what with her unusually large Adam's apple and all. But I digress.

Keeping Priest out of it, I try to be the voice of reason . . .

Me: OK, lots of deals flying back and forth so
let's see what we have . . . 1) Green-DJax for
Horn; 2) Davis, Green, Jax for Ricky, Toomer; 3)
Green-Jax for Toomer-Dunn (very fair, need-based
trade); 4) and I'll throw in a lesser one . . .
my FA pick for Dunn. You don't get Green but you
get an extra FA pick to grab a 1-week QB and then
light prayer candles for Gannon's health, who's
got a big fork sticking out of his back, but
that's just my unbiased opinion . . . :) I don't
think there's a QB available from another team
with more upside, and in a better offense, than
Green, and I can top any offer you get, within
reason . . . and keep in mind I'll play CIA agent
and verify whether those "other offers" are
bullshit, so no making stuff up :) . . . and care
to share the details of your monster deal? I'm
just drunk enough to try and top it . . .

Translation: Does the other guy look like Marcus Schenkenberg, drive
a Ferrari, and make $35 million per year as a bond trader?

Kevin: Not revealing anything yet. Waiting to get
back a response first. Then I will share.

Don't play coy with me, sister! You know you want me! I feel like yelling.
But yelling would be pointless. Kevin lives in Washington, D.C., and
wouldn't be able to hear me. I finally realize that it's time to play it cool.
She—he—they—whatever—needs me more than I need her. I'd like a
possible WR upgrade, but Toomer's no sure thing, and Green is a nice
backup to have in case something (knock on wood, hear me FF gods?)
happens to Peyton.

Me: OK, fair enough . . . but know that I've
already bent more than Rudy Galindo during Ice
Capades on all my successive offers, while you

```
guys seem to have offered less and less each time
(downgrading from Horn to Toomer to Dunn to the
now-benched Amos friggin' Zereoue), so the
whiskey's wearing off and I'm losing interest
quickly here, fellas . . . lemme know ASAP.
```

After a few minutes, they introduce me to the swaggering, smooth-talking a-hole who's moved in on my territory—All-American Angus! Those bastards! I can't help but picture them looking like William Zabka, who played Johnny, the cocky, Aryan dick boyfriend in all the *Karate Kid* flicks. And I am, of course, poor wrong-side-of-the-tracks Daniel Larusso, played by Ralph Macchio. As Angus's cackling toadies hold me down on the ground, pinning my arms so I can't let fly with a little "paint of fence" or "wax-on, wax-off," Angus punches and kicks me in the gut repeatedly, then makes off with my best gal (a younger, chunkier Elizabeth Shue, of course) after giving them the following offer:

```
Kevin: Angus wants to give us Jeff Garcia/Deuce
McAllister/Rod Gardner/Steelers D/their #4 FA
pick for Joe Horn/Ricky Williams/our #7 FA pick.
Can you top that?
```

Battered, bruised, my pride shattered, and that useless cocksucker Mr. Miyagi nowhere to be found, I try to pretend I'm not hurt by this turn of events. And, of course, I try to make them feel as if they have made the wrong decision. Spiteful, yes, but it has to be done.

```
Me: Um, no thanks . . . as Seinfeld would say,
"Good luck with alllll THAT" . . . they basically
traded Garcia, Deuce, and a load of spare parts
for Ricky and Horn. Very good deal for them, OK
deal for you. Deuce faces Carolina, has a bye
week, and Tampa in next three weeks, so he should
give you about 100 yards . . . combined. Davis, on
the other hand, has New Orleans (yahtzee!),
Houston (double yahtzee!), and Tampa. Green has
```

```
Buffalo this week; a bye, and then Cleveland on
the week that Garcia's on bye. Gardner is the #3
option behind Coles and, now, McCants in Wash. I
dunno. But you had to do what you had to do . . .
no biggie. But you could have kept Ricky AND Horn
and done Toomer and Dunn for Green and DJax.
```

But then, to my shock, perhaps after realizing that the other guy is nothing more than William Zabka with blow-dried-and-feathered eighties hair and a sweater tied around his shoulders, the slut comes crawling back for one last try:

```
Kevin: Last chance offer—Green and DJax for Amos
and Toomer. You basically unload your TRASH for
Toomer.
```

Bwa-ha-ha-ha-ha-ha! I love when they come crawling back. It gives me a chance to slam the door on my previous offers and make them think they screwed up big-time.

```
Me: And now starting at QB for Bonesky Crushers
. . . Kurt Kitner! :) Sorry guys, I am NOT
handing you Green and Djax for your garbage. If
you want to rethink Green and DJax for Horn,
lemme know ASAP.
```

Almost immediately, I get . . .

```
Jason: Green for Toomer, straight up.
```

Uh-oh, the double-team is back.

```
Kevin: Ahh, let's go crazy then . . .
Priest/Green/D.Jax for Ricky/Horn.
```

Priest? *Priest?!* When did Priest get back into this? Would I even consider trading Priest? I guess nothing's out of the question. He does have a bye week coming up, and Ricky has already had his bye, so I'd gain an extra game of production. And Priest has been injury-prone the past few years, and pessimistically, I assume that because I own him now, this is the year that he'll fall apart down the stretch. The Chiefs are 7-0 and if they clinch home-field advantage for the playoffs earlier than most teams, Weepy Vermeil might rest him a little more amid the most crucial weeks—the FFL playoffs, Weeks 14, 15, and 16. But come on—dare I *even think* of trading the player I've cherished since I tried to pry him loose from Big Dog and Erik's evil two-headed clutches last season? No. I can't. Not Priest. Never. As much as I love my boy Stephen Davis, I try to sell Davis some more, as the jump from him to Ricky would be worth it for me.

```
Me: Sorry, not crazy about dealing Priest. Davis
and Ricky have been basically the same RB all
year, but you guys still have the big "#1" tag on
Ricky, which is your prerogative. So the way I see
it, the big upgrade you get to Green (from shitty
Delhomme/injured Gannon) as essentially a FREE
throw-in is equaled by the upgrade I get from DJax
to Horn and the SLIGHT upgrade from Davis to Ricky
. . . remember, right now, only 5 pts separate
these guys. Still, lemme mull all this over . . .
```

I soon offer them S.Davis/Green/D.Jax for Ricky/Toomer/Delhomme. If they don't go for that, then I quit. With Gannon all but on injured reserve, they're looking at starting the immortal Jake Delhomme for the rest of the year, so screw 'em. I'm tired . . . so very tired . . . need sleep . . . Mommy . . . need sleepy so badly . . .

After a bit, Kevin counters:

```
Kevin: We were almost there. . . . We want Priest
or Manning. . . . You get Horn and Ricky, two studs,
plus backups Gannon, Amos, or Toomer, hell, we'll
give you anyone you want for Priest! You need depth!
```

Ah, the old "quantity over quality" trick. **Newbie Strategy Tip #8: Someone trying to trade you more guys than they're getting back,** claiming they're giving you "depth," is usually trying to screw you. So, no thanks, Kevin . . . I don't need a bunch of stiffs for my studs. But I *do* need sleep, food, water, basic human necessities for survival. These trade talks have lasted—I kid you not—more than *seven* hours, straight through lunch, without leaving the apartment, without leaving this uncomfortable seat, haggling and arguing and reasoning back and forth, crafting and recrafting. It was like an out-of-body experience, an absolutely frenetic whirlwind of FF logic and lack thereof. But, fueled by Dunkin' Donuts coffee and a burning desire to line up Ricky and Priest in the same backfield, I've kept at them like a pit bull, offering what I believe are *very* fair deals based on their desperate need for a QB upgrade. If I'd ever put this kind of dogged determination, zeal, and cutthroat negotiation savvy toward my actual career, I'd be a retired Advertising Hall of Fame zillionaire living in the Cayman Islands by now.

But these guys, the Brothers Bonesky, are killing me here. *Killing* me. They're like those sleight-of-hand three-card monte guys on a New York street corner—Whoa! Hey! Zim-fling-bang! Round and round she goes, keep your eye on the shell, where she stops, nobody knows! Where's the ace? Where's the queen? Now she's here, now she ain't!—upgrading here, downgrading here, asking for more here and pretending to offer more there, all the while thinking the "customer"—me—won't notice the flimflam scam whizzing before my eyes and my wallet disappearing from my back pocket. They ask for Priest while adding Horn. They say, "OK, we'll take Davis . . . but only if you give up Manning instead of Green and we give up Toomer instead of Horn." Astounding. Do they actually think I won't notice that kind of amateurish, Coney-Island-boardwalk chicanery?

But after seven hours, I barely even care anymore. I'm just spent. I'm a shriveled husk of a man hunched over a keyboard. Eyes burning, twitching ever so slightly. Wild Albert Einstein hair. Bulging Don Knotts eyes. I haven't showered, haven't shaved. I'm still wearing those flannel pajama bottoms and a tattered, red "Nantucket" T-shirt. Anyone walking into the living room right now would think I'm either an eccentric MIT professor or a deranged homeless person who's broken into Mark and Celia's apartment to send some e-mails.

But OK, fine, Brothers Bonesky, I'll gladly keep Davis and Green, and I send them an e-mail telling them exactly that.

```
Me: Well, it's clear that we're not going to get
aything done today, despite—and this is just a
rough estimate—the 27 hours we've put into this.
Maybe some other time.
```

Sure, I would have liked Ricky—who wouldn't want Priest and Ricky in their backfield?—but Davis is no slouch. Horn, though . . . there's just something unsettling about not getting Horn. I don't know what it is. I just have this weird, sick feeling that somewhere down the road, Joe Horn is going to play a major role in my season, for better or worse.

I feel like Gordon Gekko (Michael Douglas) in the final, frenzied crescendo-of-a-stock-trading scene in *Wall Street* when he realizes that Bud Fox (Charlie Sheen) has scammed him, and the Blue Star Airline stock *he thought* would go through the penthouse roof has, in fact, crashed through the outhouse floor. "What the hell," Gekko says, confidently, smugly, "so I'll only make *ten* million."

What the hell, I think confidently, smugly—so I'll only keep Davis and Green.

23

Fantasy, Meet Reality

In the "how important they are to fantasy football scoring" hierarchy, NFL positions probably rank as follows: (1) running back, (2) wide receiver, (3) quarterback, (4) tight end, (5) defense, (6) kicker. It all depends on a league's scoring system, of course, which can bump a first-tier stud QB like Culpepper or Manning above a second tier stud WR like Hines Ward or Eric Moulds. But for basic performance leagues—where points are awarded for touchdowns, yardage, and other statistical categories—the running back is king.

Which means the long snapper is the peasant shoveling horse manure in the royal stables.

Aside from making sure the ball lands safely into the hands of the holder on extra points and field goals, the average NFL long snapper has no bearing on a fantasy football team. But that doesn't stop complete strangers from harassing Patrick Mannelly, long snapper for the Chicago Bears, about their fantasy football teams. "I'll run into people at a restaurant," he says, "and within the first thirty seconds after finding out I play for the Bears, they'll say, 'I have [Bears WR] David Terrell on my fantasy team. When are they going to throw him the damn ball?' I'll be like, 'Sorry, man, can't help you—I'm not the offensive coordinator.'"

A six-year veteran out of Duke University, Patrick is considered one of the best long snappers in the league. Visiting his website, www.longsnapper.com—yes, even NFL long snappers have their own websites!—I learn a few other interesting facts: Patrick's wife, Tanya, is the daughter of former Major League pitcher Tommy John, perhaps known more for the surgery named after him than for his 288 wins, four All-Star appearances, or astounding twenty-six-year career. Patrick majored in history and minored in markets and management at Duke, a school where one can still utter the term *student*-athlete without snickering afterward. On his website, there's also a QuickTime video of Patrick demonstrating the perfect long-snapping form—he lines up footballs twelve to fifteen feet away from a goalpost, bends over, and with a seemingly effortless flick of the wrist, flings the balls behind him in perfect spirals, directly into the goalpost almost every time—*Bam! Bam! Bam!*—like Wild Bill Hickok picking tin cans off a fence post with his six-shooter (though I'd be more impressed if Hickok ever did it bent over and looking backward through his legs the way Patrick does). Cool as it all looks, I have no need for the long-snapping skill. But Patrick is clearly a well-rounded guy and has a nice little NFL career in the works.

Coincidentally, he's been in the league since 1998, when the Internet started providing the rocket fuel that fantasy football needed to blast off into the stratosphere, meaning his career has ascended right alongside the rise of FF. It's been virtually impossible not to notice the hobby getting bigger and bigger every season, and while he doesn't play FF himself, he hears about it now more than ever before. "This past training camp," he says, "A-Train [Anthony Thomas] and I were walking off the field and some guy yells, 'I drafted you this year, A-Train, gimme some points, baby!' A-Train's like, 'I'll try, man, I'll try.'"

Back in the old days of Broadway Joe and Dandy Don Meredith, pro football players were typically approached by beautiful women; now, unfortunately for them, it's mostly FF-obsessed men. Patrick can't count the number of times he's been out with someone like Bears backup QB Chris Chandler and watched with amusement as a Chandler owner—one of four in the country—approaches with some comment, question, or complaint. "They'll come up to us and say something like 'I started you this week and you sucked. You screwed me.'" Patrick laughs. "Chris is a proud guy. He's trying his best out there, but if he has a bad game, he feels bad for the Bears, not the fantasy guys who have him on their team." In other words, even though we FF fanatics would love to believe that Randy Moss, Clinton Portis, or Steve McNair have our best interests at heart when they take the field every Sunday, players are simply unaware of how many fantasy points they rack up. *Did I do everything I could to help my team win?* is what NFL players ask themselves after each game, not,

Gee, did I get Mark St. Amant enough bonus points to win his Felon League game? Some NFL players are even downright annoyed with the metamorphosis that the NFL fan has undergone, blossoming (or mutating, depending on your view) from the awestruck, grateful autograph-seeker into the brash, pushy fantasy football player. Jaguars running back Fred Taylor told the *Florida Times-Union*'s Bart Hubbuch that FF players aren't always a welcome sight. "'You better play good for me because I'm starting you this week.' If I've heard that once, I've heard it a million times," said a clearly frustrated Taylor. "I'm telling you, it never ends. Please don't ask me about fantasy football, because I don't care." Damn, Fred, that's cold. If you ask me, you should be glad that owners keep drafting your fragile ass after you've hosed them so many times over the years . . . then again, being a repeat Taylor owner in past seasons, that might just be my own personal bitterness talking.

Colts (and, ahem, Acme) quarterback Peyton Manning shares Taylor's sentiments. When people approach Peyton in an airport or a shopping mall, they barely even ask for his autograph right off the bat anymore: all they want to do is talk FF. "They just care that Marvin Harrison is their fantasy receiver, so I should throw it to him a lot, especially in the red zone," Manning says in the Hubbuch article. "They don't understand that it's more important to players to win the game than it is to put up great [fantasy] numbers. We won a game last week in which Marvin caught just three passes. Fantasy players probably didn't like that too much." OK, so maybe FF players are becoming sort of a nuisance to *real* players out in public. But even the frustrated Taylor recognizes what FF has done for the league and its players. After all, the fans love professional football, and fantasy football is a way for them to feel more involved. "Anything that can make them feel a part of it is good in my book," Taylor confesses.

Patrick says part of the problem guys like Peyton and Taylor have is that most NFL players assume that we play FF just for fun—it's just something that gives us a little extra action on each game—and are shocked and baffled by the obsession it's become. He's right . . . to an extent. The "extra action" idea is one of the lures of the hobby, no doubt. It makes that late-season Lions-Falcons game worth watching from start to finish if you have Mike Vick or Joey Harrington. But if I could tell the average NFL player one basic thing about this game of ours, it's that, more often than not, we don't play FF "just for fun." Our pride and manhood, bragging rights, the fun of watching our friends' spirits get crushed along with their teams—all that and more is on the line every week. *That's* why we badger you for information in airports and bars. Ask me how much "fun" I was having when Jamal Lewis was ripping my heart out of my chest and kicking me in the balls with every carry during my game against the Rat Bastards. That wasn't fun; that was pure hell. And if I ever saw Jamal Lewis munching on some jalapeño poppers at the Logan Airport TGI Friday's, I'd probably tell him that he almost single-handedly cost me a game . . . and then maybe, *maybe* ask for an autograph.

But deep down, in some twisted part of my soul that likes to be chained up by a busty leather-clad dominatrix and beaten within an inch of my life with a tire iron, I loved every minute of it. I decide not to share that image with Patrick, but do tell him about the level of obsession some people have for fantasy football, which would make even the most jaded NFL player's eyes bulge. "I sat next to a guy on a plane to Vegas who plays in nine money leagues," I reveal. "Some guys I know play in fifteen leagues."

Patrick had no idea people were *that* into it. "Wow" is all he can say. "*Wow.* That's insane."

However, calling it "insane" (and even occasionally wanting to stiff-arm roster-toting madmen who approach them in airports) doesn't mean that NFL players don't appreciate us fantasy football players. Not by a long shot. Players unanimously recognize how FF has increased the league's popularity. It's put money directly into the players' pockets by allowing the NFL to raise team salary caps thanks to added revenue streams like multi-million-dollar TV deals. And other types of endorsements that are typically harder to come by in a league where you don't see the players' faces regularly (unlike MLB and the NBA) have become easier to get. "Fantasy football is probably the best thing going for our sport," Patrick says. "It makes someone an instant Falcons fan or Chargers fan if they have, say, Tomlinson or Vick on their team and makes them want to watch more than their home team's games. It increases viewership, Internet traffic, magazine and newspaper coverage. It's only going to help the sport out in the long run. Bottom line, fans are the number one thing in the NFL, and fantasy football is probably the biggest fan interaction we have."

That said, Patrick does have his own stories of oddballs trying to mine him for FF gold. When he first made the Bears, an acquaintance from high school—"He graduated a year ahead of me, I barely knew the guy"—called him out of the blue and, after some requisite small talk, started peppering him for info about the Bears running game. "He congratulated me on making the team, and then, as if it slipped his mind, says, 'Oh, hey, I'm also in this fantasy football league . . . is James Allen starting this week?'"

I decide not to ask him whether Marty Booker or Dez White is getting more looks in practice. Patrick is a reasonable guy, but I don't want to push my luck.

24

Halftime

It's late October, and Halloween is almost here—the pagan holiday that brings us ghosts, ghouls, stale candy corn, Jamie Lee Curtis movies, and lots of other weird stuff.

For example, I *actually won* a high-scoring game! Can you believe that? The FF gods can be merciful after all. In fact the "anti-Acme," the Account Guys, my opponents this week, proved to be less anti-Acme than I thought—they scored the second-highest point total of the week and still lost. Hey, welcome to my personal hell, fellas. There's plenty of room. Pull up a torture rack and make yourselves comfortable. But the matchup was no cakewalk—it was the kind of game that makes me clutch my chest and stagger around the living room like Redd Foxx yelling, *"This is the big one, Elizabeth!"*

The first-place Account Guys did benefit from the luck that's been with them all season, with FF mutts like their seventy-six-year-old RB Curtis Martin rushing for 104 yards, while I got 3—3!—total points from my two ass wide receivers. But what else is new? My WRs have sucked all year long. Thankfully, though, Stephen Davis racked up 178 yards and 2 TDs against the Saints. (Did I mention that I'm back to loving Stephen Davis again? I know, I'm as fickle as a Southern belle, but FF is a what-have-you-done-for-me-lately? type of game.) Priest had 3 TDs and 83 yards rushing for 38 Felon League points. Lordy, do I love my running backs! My WRs are trouble, but I'll let them ride the victory-parade float for now.

Final score: Acme 159, Account Guys 147. At the halfway point of the NFL season, Project Kick My League's Ass now stands at 5-3.

Winning immediately puts me in a good mood, which is nice because I've been in quite a foul mood. I try not to let it affect me like this, but it does. This year I think I've gotten a helluva lot better at putting a loss behind me and moving on, but I'm still clearly agitated and depressed when my team goes down in flames.

"It's just not healthy," Celia has said on more than one occasion, "you know, mentally. It can't be good for you. It's like living with Sybil."

"But I'm doing much better this year, don't you think?"

She pauses, thinks about it for a split second. "Not really. You may have regressed, actually. I'm thinking of hiring a team of psychiatrists to watch you round the clock."

Okay, she's not buying my reformed-FF-guy-successfully-undergoing-anger-management act. I'm just as obsessed as I've always been, maybe more so. When we went to sleep Sunday night, I figured I'd lost my game to the Account Guys thanks to their improbably successful Martin–Correll Buckhalter RB combo, and I just couldn't stay up to watch their tight end (Tony Gonzalez) and defense (Chiefs) put the final nail in my coffin despite Priest's best efforts. So, I went to bed angry, which is never a good idea. But Priest came through for me, and outside my window, despite the gray, rainy following morning, a golden halo appeared around my computer and a choir of angels kicked in when I woke up and checked CBS SportsLine.

Suddenly, all was well with the world again. I had won and was back to being Good Sybil.

This raises a question, however: Should we FF players let one silly loss affect our entire week? Should we let it affect how we treat our significant others, our jobs, our kids, our pets, our electronics? If I had kids, last night they would have been saying, "Uh-oh, Daddy's got 'that look' again . . . run away! Run to your happy place!" I don't want that to happen when Celia and I *do* have kids. I don't want to be one of those sports-obsessed fathers who frightens the little ones when things don't go his way on the field, or the kind of lunatic who scales the glass, drunkenly scuttles across the ice, and pummels his kid's hockey coach when the guy doesn't give Marky junior enough playing time. But I can't help it—FF *does* affect my mood. As Cenk told me earlier in the season, "Winning your rotiss game makes the whole week sweeter. Losing the game puts a gray pall over the rest of the week. When my players perform poorly, I despise them and secretly plot to get them off my team as quickly as possible so that I never have to see them or root for them ever again."

It's true. When I lose, I feel that there's a heavy, wet, stinky wool blanket hanging over me all week until I can redeem myself *the following* week. I brood. I obsess over what I coulda shoulda woulda done differently. I curse my players and their families. I bemoan that the FF gods are always out to screw me while constantly helping out other, far less worthy owners. Basically, an FF loss can turn even the most happy-go-lucky person into a hissing, fire-breathing son of a bitch. So how does a bad FF day affect some of my fellow junkies out there?

"I am silent and seething when the day is going wrong," one Huddler writes in the forums. "I throw things, including ranting tirades toward anyone who will listen . . . [this week] I was pretty much a raving bitch lunatic all day. Good thing God made beer."

Not to promote alcoholism, but beer seems to be a viable antidote (albeit a temporary one) for postgame depression. "I do double time on the beers [after losses]," another Huddler responds. "If you ever want to know how I did on a Sunday, you don't need to check CBS SportsLine—just check my garage fridge on Monday. If it's empty, things didn't go so well."

But what if it's one of those freak losses to a clearly inferior team? Can even the mystical, all-healing hops and barley churned out by the Anheuser-Busch family cure those woes? "I hate losing anything—I hate losing playing Go Fish with my three-year-old—so if I lose to an opponent who has six no-names in his lineup and they have career days, I go nuts, and even a few beers can't calm me down," he says.

One of the more visible female Huddlers, Lisa, a Hospice social worker from New Hampshire, says, "When I lose, I do that slow simmer, which soon turns to seething, all while [her husband] just giggles at me. Of course, this just sets me off even more." Good to see that the fairer sex is also prone to FF-related sulking/anger/outbursts/hissy fits, especially a woman whose job is based on compassion, caring, and selflessness. Makes me feel slightly less like a testosterone-enraged sociopath.

And on that note I can look ahead to the second half with a new winning attitude. We're officially halfway through the NFL season, and here's how my Felon League stands:

TEAM	W	L	PF	PA
Rat Bastards	7	1	1,168	671
Account Guys	7	1	924	729
Acme FF, Inc.	5	3	1,107	1,053
Funk Soul Bros.	5	3	795	727
The Dream Team	4	4	993	911
Big Dogs	4	4	827	872
All-American Angus	4	4	791	832
Bonesky Crushers	4	4	774	765
SoCo	3	5	682	841
The Pound Dawgs	3	5	641	664
NH Hillbillies	1	7	579	589
Charlemagnes	1	7	573	868

OK, but not great: 5-3 is just too close to a fair-to-middling .500 record, and that's not going to cut it.

And who's cutting it in the Hershey Highway? Phil Kwan and "Teddy KGB" Samip are battling it out for first place with 7-1 and 6-2 records, respectively. Greg "White Monkey" Russo and "Sly" Shailesh lurk within striking distance at 5-3. And "Doctor" Tolga (4-4), Steve Oh (4-4), Cenk (4-4), "Dark Monkey" Sujay (3-5), T.K. (3-5), "Computer" Kaan (3-5), "Reckless Guy" Koller (2-6), and "Applehead" Wong (2-6) round out the remaining spots.

As you might expect, both leaders have been trying to make deals to push them over the top heading into Week 9, and beyond. But their trade tactics aren't exactly endearing them to their league-mates. "Neither one of those guys is subtle," says the feisty David Koller, who started out 1-1, but then lost five out of the next six and now wallows in the damp, musty, spore-filled basement alongside Wong. "Kwan made me one offer, and when I turned it down and explained why I didn't like it, he responded with an angry e-mail telling me that if I was going to criticize, why don't I make offers myself. I still have no idea what the hell he was talking about."

Steve Oh says he's had an enjoyable season so far, even though work has been getting in the way lately. One thing bugs him, though: the lack of trading in the league. "Personally, I'm annoyed by the ass managers who are so reluctant to trade, especially when it comes to studs. Don't get me wrong, I'm all in favor of riding my studs for as long as I can, but if there is an opportunity to trade my stud for a studlier stud, well . . . giddyap baby, it's time to go for a ride!" His nontrading angst is soon alleviated, however, as he makes a deal with Koller for Fred Taylor, giving him a solid backfield of Taylor, Tiki Barber, and Travis Henry heading into the second half of the season. "And with McNair at QB," he adds, "I have another stud I can saddle up and ride till the end." Steve's currently 4-4, three games behind Samip and Kwan, but feels good about his chances.

Applehead, on the other hand, does not. He's committed one of the mortal sins of any early FF season: he panicked on some of his slow-starting studs and traded them away while their value was lower than usual. In Week 7, he traded superstud Randy Moss to White Monkey Russo in exchange for Eddie George, who isn't exactly the Eddie George of old, and sixty-two-year-old Rich Gannon, who promptly got hurt. This is a surprising panic move, because Applehead is no FF idiot. "In my other league," he says, "I'm in first place with a six-and-two record and the highest point total." But unlike past years, when trades have always worked out for Wong, this year's dealings in the HH have been different. Why? "Because I made the trades out of desperation," he admits.

Cenk, just as I have been, is concerned about the luck factor running roughshod over fantasy football and dominating league standings. In nearly every past HH season, the team that's finished in first place has managed to not only score the most points, but have extremely low points *against*. And like me, he is throwing his arms up in the air and wondering when, if ever, this horrible trend will stop. "I think in nine out of ten years, heading into the halfway point, the first-place team has been the recipient of complete and utter schedule luck. I understand this is why they're in first place to begin with, but nine years in a row is just too freakish. Why isn't this phenomenon going away?"

Sadly, Cenk, I don't think it ever will. As Victor from Nyack told me a while back, "If you play in a league where you know more about football than your league-mates, then skill puts you over the top. But if you're in a league with guys who know as much as you do, then it all comes down to pure luck." So, I'm sorry, Cenk, but it seems that this is one of the prices you pay when most, if not all, of your league-mates are FF-savvy. As with the NFL itself, parity strikes.

Cenk and I both seem to be suffering from that maddening combination of hope (because we know we both drafted a solid team and have the players that could easily carry us to a championship) and frustration (because unseen and unavoidable factors, primarily the whims of the FF gods, seem to be conspiring against us). "Nothing drives me nuts more than when my players who *should* do well mysteriously don't," Cenk complains, "and players on other teams who have no business doing well suddenly become heroes. Brad Johnson being miraculously good while McNabb is suddenly the worst quarterback in NFL history is just too unacceptable for words." That said, he's willing to give credit where credit's due, mainly to Kwan, who, he feels, drafted a great team right out of the gates, anchored by three solid running backs (Deuce McAllister, my man-crush Stephen Davis, Anthony Thomas) and Peyton at QB. "[Kwan's] been good from day one, so I am not surprised or embittered at all."

But Kwan isn't renting out a hotel ballroom for a victory bash quite yet. Like all superstitious FF players, he knows that the second you believe that luck is on your side, it can kill you. "It's quite simple—you score more, your opponent scores less, you win. I hope that 'bizarro anomaly' continues for me all season long, although the law of averages has to be lurking around the corner, waiting to bite me in the ass."

Also typical of FF players at this point in the season, some of the HH guys have developed unholy man-crushes on their players, à la my feelings for Stephen Davis, which I clearly haven't been afraid to shout to the world (though if he ever reads this, I'm sure he'll feel more than a little bit uncomfortable). Samip, for example, like a thirteen-year-old girl, can't stop gushing about a certain Pittsburgh Steelers wide receiver. "I don't know if anyone can understand how much I love Hines Ward. If I had a younger sister or older daughter, I would try as hard as I could to have her marry Hines Ward. He's a great receiver, and just an excellent overall football player. Put it this way," he adds, "I love him as much as I despise Keyshawn."

Poor Keyshawn. He's gone from fantasy stud to fantasy dud in just a few short seasons. I also wouldn't have him—or his big mouth—anywhere near my team.

That said, it might be time to get out the old shopping cart and pay a little visit to the other Felon League rosters to see what players, if any, I *do* want to bring into the Acme fold.

25

Transcendental Negotiation

The pre-Halloween weirdness continues. Well, actually, the latest occurrence wasn't *that* weird: an NFL player was busted for—get this!—drug possession. Can you believe that? No *way*! What's next . . . wife beating?! Infidelity? *Steroids?!*

The NFL police blotter now includes William Green of the Cleveland Browns, who was arrested late Tuesday night for DUI and possession of a significant amount (3.2 grams) of the ol' wacky tabachy. Is 3.2 grams a significant amount? I don't know—thankfully I've never been pulled over with illegal substances in the car (I didn't say I've never *had* illegal substances in the car and/or my bloodstream, I've just never been pulled over)—but it's certainly more than you want to have sticking out of your ashtray while a neckless state trooper is shining a flashlight in your face.

Green's arrest leads to my discovery of one of the funnier, more creative league rules I've come across, this from a guy in the Huddle forums: "In our league if a guy on your roster gets arrested," he writes, "you have to throw $5 into the pot for bail. We call it the 'Michael Irvin Rule.'" The Michael Irvin Rule. I love that! You think in fantasy hockey they have the Theo Fleury Rule? In fantasy baseball, the Daryl Strawberry Rule? And in fantasy basketball—well, it's gotta be the Entire Portland Trailblazers Roster Rule, right?

Anyway, since starting running backs are scarce on the waiver wire, I strategically grab Green's backup, James Jackson, in case Green gets suspended or worse. Unfortunately, I can't use Jackson this week to replace Priest because Cleveland, like KC, is on bye. But maybe I *can* peddle him to the scared Green owners (John and Grady, of All-American

Angus), who might be worried that Green will be tossed into the pokey. All-American Angus has Hines Ward, who would be a big upgrade from El Busto Grande, Plaxico Burress. **Newbie Strategy Tip #9: If you keep your ear to the ground and listen for even the most random information (such as a drug bust), you can parlay someone else's misery into a joyous upgrade for your team.** And this is exactly what I do. Noticing that Angus could also use a decent wide receiver (their number one WR is Peerless Price . . . yuck), I strike while the iron's hot and offer them Darrell Jackson and James Jackson for Hines Ward. After all, this is business. It's no time to feel sorry for anyone. Capitalize while you can. Eat the weak. Kill or be killed. Don't take any wooden nickels. Wait—forget that last one. Not applicable.

Anyway, while I wait to hear back from the Green owner on my trade offer, I've decided that it's time to get out of the apartment for a while. That's right, I'm going back to nature. After yesterday's dismal, torrential monsoon-of-a-day, today is a clear, crisp, sunny fall day in Boston. So Celia, who has a rare day off, and I are heading out to Walden Pond.

While I'm presenting it to her as an opportunity to be together on a weekday and enjoy a nice romantic picnic, secretly I'm hoping that being outside amongst the trees, fresh air, and little talking cartoon birds will clear my head and perhaps get me mentally prepared for the Felon League stretch run, the second half of what's already been an up-and-down season.

Maybe I can soak up some divine inspiration from this renowned literary setting, the same tranquil locale that inspired the legendary poets Emerson, Thoreau, and their whole merry band of rockin' transcendentalists? Maybe, as Thoreau once said of Walden's effect on him, I can also start "living deep and sucking out all the marrow of life"? (Or, in my case, "going deep into the playoffs and start sucking the marrow out of my league-mates.") And the other similarities between me and Mr. Woodsy Owl Thoreau don't stop there.

He lived an experiment in solitary living and wrote about it in *Walden*. Hey, I, too, am more or less living a solitary existence as I write about fantasy football! After all, Celia seems less inclined to hang with me whenever I look as if I might shoot out our TV when something bad happens to my team.

Thoreau spoke out against the materialism and conformity in American culture. Hey, that's me, too! What's less materialistic than spending all of your time with a team that doesn't actually exist?

Thoreau believed that God is immanent in man and nature and that individual intuition is the highest source of knowledge, leading to an emphasis on individualism, self-reliance, and rejection of traditional authority. Whoa, talk about your coincidences—I *also* believe that the whims of the FF gods are ingrained in FF players and that individual intuition about the NFL, its players, their injuries, and weekly matchups is the highest source of knowledge, leading to an emphasis on individual lineup decisions and rejecting the traditional authority that sometimes tells you to idiotically start Jerome Pathon over Darrell Jackson.

And the civil disobedience stressed in Thoreau's writings eventually influenced the likes of Gandhi and Martin Luther King Jr. Wow, this is getting eerie—this is also just like me! After all, Gandhi and MLK Jr. would have been proud of the way I've risen up to battle those who have kept me down all these years, not through violence, but with my mind! And it's no surprise that they called it transcendentalism, as I truly feel I'm starting to "transcend" my traditional shitty position in the league standings!

This is all creepy, just creepy.

OK, so I'm stretching it. A lot. Still, it's a nice day to get out and walk around a pond. I just hope that Hines Ward is waiting for me when I get back.

Later On

I have good news and bad news. The bad news: after all that Thoreau talk, we never made it to Walden Pond. Well, "never made it" implies that we actually tried, which we didn't—we took a walk around the Charles River instead, which is almost like Walden Pond . . . only with more lethal toxins.

Walden just seemed like a big undertaking. Plus, after thinking about it some more, I didn't like the sound of building a thatch hut and living a solitary existence deep in the woods, as I don't ever recall Thoreau mentioning cable television or high-speed Internet.

And the good news? All-American Angus went for the trade! I could have sworn that they'd come back and demand that I give them D.Jackson and J.Jackson for Toomer, (whom they recently acquired from the Bonesky Crushers) a significant downgrade from Ward and not much better than D.Jackson alone. But they didn't. They probably figured out that with Deuce on bye next week and Green possibly being suspended, they might be stuck with only one running back and therefore decided not to try to hold a gun to my head. Darrell Jackson for Hines Ward? Hell, I'd have thrown in Jermaine, Tito, and La Toya Jackson if it got the deal done.

I happily announce the trade to the league.

Our beloved Acme starting squad now looks like so: Peyton, Priest, Davis, Hines Ward, Plaxico, Heap, Bucs D, Wilkins. I like that team. I like it a lot. Sure, throwing all my eggs into the Steelers offensive basket is risky. Bill Cowher's crew has been performing far worse than expected so far. But up until this point in the season I've only been averaging about 10 points a week from *both* wide receivers, so at least now, with Ward, I know I'll get a TD or two a week. And, if Plaxico's recent hissy-fit does him any good—he demanded to know why he wasn't getting the ball despite being open (although every WR always thinks he's open)—then the two Steeler receivers could be a nice combo down the stretch.

Upon learning of the deal, Jason of the Bonesky Crushers e-mails me.

Jason: I want to puke. This is why you win every year.

Me? Win? *Every* year? How about *no* years? I write him back to explain that I have never won. Ever. His response?

Jason: Oh, it just SEEMS like you win every year.

Interesting. Why does he think I've won the Felon League? Despite the internal rage I feel at the end of every season after having blown it, do I nevertheless project some kind of victorious outer shell? Have I won our league before? Am I suffering from amnesia, or perhaps some kind of post-traumatic stress syndrome? I quickly check my mental Palm Pilot under W for "Winners, FFL Super Bowl" and the following comes up:

1997–1998: ***Funk Soul Brothers.*** (The inaugural FFL champ.)

1998–1999: *Charlemagnes.* ("1999 was CJ's year," writes John, co-owner of All-American Angus. "I saw the fireplace set he bought with his winnings. Stunning.")

1999–2000: *Rat Bastards.* (He's well on his way this year, too, dammit. Steve McNair, Jamal Lewis, and LaDainian Tomlinson are a tough trio to beat.)

2000–2001: *Funk Soul Brothers.* ("I won in 1998, our first year, and again in 2000," my fantasy nemesis Shergul writes. "Happiest memory ever: winning on *MNF* with Warner/Faulk helping me overturn a 73-point deficit!")

2001–2002: *The Dream Team.* (The first of the dreaded two-headed monsters to win. I'd always hoped that these co-owned teams would fail miserably so as never to rear their ugly heads again.)

2002–2003: *Big Dogs.* (Thanks to NOT trading me Priest!)

2003–2004: *Acme Fantasy Football, Inc.* (Because he quit his job, spent every waking moment playing FF, and *had* to win, otherwise he'd look like a complete jackass.)

Oops, a little premature on that last one. But sorry, Jason, clearly I have never won this league. Maybe it just *seems like* I have because I talk the most smack, much like a Super Bowl champion can/should? I don't know, but what this tells me is that it's time I started living up to that reputation of a champion. And after my Ward trade, I'm on the warpath. I'm reborn.

I scan the FFL rosters to see whom else's injuries/fears/weaknesses I can take advantage of—**Newbie Strategy Tip #10: Always, *always* scan your fellow owners' rosters to spot weaknesses you can exploit in a trade**—and hidey-ho there, neighbor! What's this I see? At QB, the Bonesky Crushers have Gannon (injured/benched), Garcia (injured), and Rattay (starting this week for the injured Garcia, but still basically a rookie). Hmmmm . . . . are they willing to roll the dice that Garcia's ankle injury, being reported as a partially torn tendon, doesn't turn out to be worse? Probably not. Do Kevin and Jason really want to attempt a playoff run with Tim Rattay at quarterback and leave their entire season in the hands of an unproven backup? Probably not. Do they wish they'd traded for Trent Green when they had the chance? Probably.

I think it's time to pay another visit to the Bonesky camp.

```
Me: From SI.com . . . "Tests have revealed that
Garcia has a partially torn ligament in his left
ankle. As a result, doctors have suggested that
the quarterback sit out Sunday's game. He will be
replaced in the lineup by backup Tim Rattay. The
hope is that Garcia will only miss one game."
Guys, if you're OK with relying upon Tim Rattay to
get you into the playoffs, stop reading now . . .
if not, maybe we should talk Trent Green again.
```

The key phrase I make sure to end with is "The hope is that Garcia will only miss one game." Encourage doubt and your league-mates might be more inclined to deal.

Their response is not surprising.

```
Kevin: OK, but we won't be raped.
```

Grudgingly, I remove my Adebisi mask, my Fistmaster Super Turbo 2000™ strap-on dildo, and my assless leather chaps, and write back.

```
Me: Not looking to rape, but know that (a) a QB
like Green has far more value to you than he does
me; and (b) I'm getting fair value in return from
whomever I trade him to. I'm not just giving him
away for an Amos Zereoue-type player straight
up . . . but it won't be an irrational offer if
I make one.

Kevin: OK, make us an offer then . . .
```

And there you have it. I have them on the ropes, so to speak, because they know I don't *have* to give them anything, but they desperately need something that I've got. Not that I will capitalize on that desperation and make a ludicrious offer like "Duh . . . Green for Ricky and Horn" because, well, that says to them that I'm not serious about making an offer that will help them out, too. We've hit on this before, but it bears repeating because trades can sometimes make or break one's season. **Newbie Strategy Tip #11: Never make a lowball offer to start trade talks, as it ruins your credibility and makes future trades harder than necessary.**

But I *can* use their desperation to my advantage. I just have to take out the microscope, examine their roster down to its DNA, and see which of their players could benefit me based on my needs for this week and beyond, which are (a) an RB to fill in for Priest in his bye week and (b) a possible WR upgrade for Plaxico, whose useless ass I'm more inclined to trade now that I've acquired the *real* #1 in Pittsburgh, Ward. Note: This is a prime example of the trading "domino effect," with one deal making the next one possible, which makes the next one possible, and so on. You always have to think a couple deals down the line when making an offer. This is not to say that you *always* make an offer to Team A in order to then turn around and trade with Team B, because no matter how blustery they can be about wanting to trade, owners are skittish, paranoid, and/or fearful of change. What I'm saying is, always make the deal that benefits your team the most right off the bat, but if you have a second deal in the works—and by "in the works" I mean that Team B has more or less assured you, "If you make that trade with Team A, I will then trade you player X for player Y"—that's fine, too.

Wow. Listen to me with all the tips. It's almost impressive.

Week 9 is looming. I have a new stud WR in tow. And I'm up against my longtime fantasy nemesis, Shergul. It's not just a huge game due to the smack-talk potential and bragging rights, it's a key game standings-wise. I'm 5-3 and second in total points, he's 5-3 and sixth in total points. If I win, I will be in sole possession of third place with a 6-3 record, and cruising in total points, a combination that, barring some unforeseeable collapse or—FF gods forbid!—a serious injury, will virtually assure me of a playoff spot.

My nemesis awaits . . .

26

Matt Lauer Intervenes

Throughout the long, often entertaining history of the world, there have been some big-time rivalries—in sports, politics, and otherwise—fueled by hatred, fear, jealously, greed, or just your run-of-the-mill thirst for competition. Athens vs. Sparta. Mozart vs. Salieri. Russell vs. Chamberlain. Kennedy vs. Khrushchev. Ali vs. Frazier. Godzilla vs. Mothra. Eminem vs. Christina. The list goes on.

And fantasy football is no different. Rivalries abound. Especially when two hundred grand is on the line, as Chris Schussman, our WCOFF champ, is currently taking a beating on the message boards for his perceived sour grapes and excuse-offering for his bad season thus far. Thanks in part to injuries to Portis and Culpepper, he sits at 2-6 with virtually no chance to repeat as champ save a miracle. "I now understand what it's like for the injured teams at the bottom of the pack," he writes to his fellow WCOFF participants. "By the end of the first month this season, I had already doubled time lost to injury compared to *all* of last season. Good luck with the injury bugs the rest of the way!" When I spoke to him a while back, he made clear that his intention in this post was not to pass blame or make excuses, but to say that he sympathizes and understands the plight of owners with injuries. Still, his WCOFF rivals let him have it.

"After Portis your running backs are dreadful," one poster digs, "your wide receivers are average to bad, and you have virtually no depth. You can't blame this on injuries." Another chimes in with "Chris is tearing himself down with the endless blather about injuries to his team when the truth is it's not a very good team. Stop blaming the f'n injury gods.

Whenever you point your finger at someone else, you have three fingers pointed back at you." Not backing down, Chris tries in vain to defend himself from the onslaught: "I stand by what I said. When you lose your first- and second-round pick to injury, you are going to get crushed. *Give up* isn't even in my language. Losers give up. I will fight to the death with every last [free agent] bid dollar I have!" But his rally cries have no effect on the rabble looking to pile onto his misery, especially from the owner who still believes that Chris "stole" his Travis Henry pick, one of the key draft choices that led to his victory. "I think if you didn't sit next to us at the draft and hear us talking about Travis Henry in the third round, you win nothing," this owner claims, "so don't cry about your first two picks this year. Be happy with the money you cashed."

These attacks go on and on, back and forth, Chris volleying and rushing the net, and fending off bullets down the line, only to see someone lob an insult over his head that he has to chase down at the baseline. (OK, that's the last tennis analogy I'll use, I promise.) But as real as they are, rivalries like Chris vs. WCOFF are between strangers on a message board and, in my opinion, pale in comparison to the verbal battles between two friends. Because even though I'd like to destroy *all* my Felon Fantasy League competition this season every chance I get—I pride myself on being an equal-opportunity combatant—one particular owner, and friend, remains at the top of my annual nemesis list.

Shergul.

It's weird. Shergul and I are good friends. Used to work together at the ad agency. Our wives like each other. He's a genuinely good guy, and a family man who adores his wife and sons. We've spent summer weekends together in Maine and even broke bread in Siena, Italy, of all places. He's one of those guys who can somehow, some way, weasel tickets to any major, sold-out sporting event you want to attend and is always glad to share the wealth of a center-court Final Four or fifty-yard-line Super Bowl seat. (I cannot reveal his Shergulian tactics here, but, for now, suffice it to say that he once conned his way into a Super Bowl by telling security that he'd flown all the way from Moscow to take his son to his first football game, only to discover that his ticket broker had sold them stolen tickets. Moved, empathetic, on the verge of tears, and totally scammed, they gave him three freebies right on the fifty.) Born in Florence, Italy, he's also one hell of a soccer player with a competitive streak a mile long. In short, he's someone you always want on your side when it comes to all things sports, the ideal ally, a guy who would do anything for his friends.

But, when it comes to fantasy football, he's also a guy who would do anything *to* his friends if it gained him a victory. Shergul is quite simply the devil. He conjures up the mystical powers of darkness to benefit his team, usually at the expense of your own, and usually in the form of some flukish, how-the-hell-did-that-just-happen? play that makes you shake your fists at the heavens above when you should really be looking down below. So, as good friends as we are, there's nothing I'd like more than to reach down his throat, pull out his spine, and wrap it around his neck. He flat out drives me insane.

Exhibit A: Minutes after my Hines Ward trade, he announces a trade of his own—he sends Chad Pennington and Ashley Lelie to Karl's NH Hillbillies (the FFL's That Guy strikes again!) in exchange for Donald Driver and Tommy Maddox. Worse, he gloats about his strategy to the whole league. "Now I can start Maddox to 'neutralize' St. Amant's WR tandem of Ward and Plaxico!" In other words, he's screaming "Aren't I a genius?" in front of everyone and, worse, doing so at my expense.

My reaction? *That mother$#!*ing son of a bitch!* I'm shorthanded as it is without Priest, and now, by using Maddox to nullify Plax and Ward, he's virtually taking away any real points advantage I can get from my WRs. If Ward and Plax catch a TD each, for example, it's 20 points for me, 14 for Shergul, not a huge advantage when all's said and done. And if Maddox tanks, it means two of my key guys have probably tanked, too, while only *one* of his guys has.

And he didn't even need Maddox! He had already picked up Raiders rookie QB Marques Tuiasosopo, who, with Gannon hurt, was *the* hot free agent QB this past week. And Oakland's opponent this week, the Lions, downright suck, so if there's any defense that even a backup rookie QB might shred, it's Detroit. But it clearly didn't matter to Shergul; he's just one of those crafty guys who's always looking for an edge, an angle, a way in the back door, not to mention free beers and a luxury box seat. And this little Maddox "preemptive strike" of his will probably end up costing me a win! Plus, he also got Driver in the deal, an upgrade from Jerry Rice. (Note to self: send mail bomb to Karl.)

You can't blame Shergul for doing whatever he can to give his Funk Soul Brothers team a better chance of winning each week. But when he does it *against me*, it's infuriating! This turn of events, combined with Priest's bye week, means I'm screwed in Week 9. 5-4 here we come. No *way* do I recover from a 5-4 start. I'm *so* done. And to have my fate sealed by my ultimate nemesis is just salt in my wounds. But just as panic starts to set in—*poof!*—the Voice of Fantasy Football Reason suddenly appears right next to me, causing me to jump out of my skin and almost knock a cup of coffee all over my keyboard. And even more bizarre, he appears in the form of Matt Lauer.

Um . . . okayyyyyy . . .

Now, I might have expected Vince Lombardi, Chuck Knoll, Knute Rockne, Tom Landry, Bill Walsh. Hell, Tony Robbins wouldn't have surprised me much. But *Matt Lauer*? Why on earth is *he* my Voice of FF Reason? "That's easy," he answers, settling into the couch and casually crossing one leg over a knee. "You secretly admire me for not fighting my baldness and just letting nature take its course and therefore believe that I must be a rational, down-to-earth kind of guy." He's right; I do. But still, I gotta stop starting my days with the *Today* show.

"Feel free," I mutter, as he helps himself to the cofee mug on my desk and takes a long, satisfying swig.

"Goddamn, Mark," Matt says, "this is some serious gourmet shit! I would have been satisfied with some freeze-dried Taster's Choice and you spring this serious gourmet shit on me. What flavor is this?"

I just stare at him.

"Come on, come on, I never get to swear on the *Today* show. Throw me a bone here. Let's do Tarantino and Sam Jackson from *Pulp Fiction*. I know you know how the rest goes."

Of course I do. It's one of my all-time favorite movie scenes, just a notch below the following exchange between Max Fischer (Jason Schwartzmann) and Dr. Flynn (Luke Wilson) in *Rushmore*.

Max: I like your nurse's uniform, guy.
Flynn: These are OR scrubs.
Max: Oh, are they?

Classic. Anyway, reluctantly, I figure Matt won't offer any insight into my little Week 9 Shergul dilemma unless I play along and recite Tarantino's next line, from that scene where Vincent (Travolta) accidentally blows the kid's head off and he and Jules (Jackson) have to go to Jimmie's (Tarantino) house to clean it up under the watchful eye of the Wolf (Harvey Keitel). So, I do. "I don't need you to tell me how good my coffee is, OK?" I say with a monotone delivery. "I'm the one who buys it. When Celia—"

"'Bonnie,'" Matt interrupts. "Do it right, now. Jimmie's wife's name is 'Bonnie.'"

I roll my eyes. This can't be happening. "When *Bonnie* goes shopping she buys shit. I buy the expensive gourmet stuff 'cause when I drink it, I want to taste it. But you know what's on my mind right now? It ain't the coffee in my kitchen. It's the game with Shergul coming up this weekend."

Matt nods appreciatively and claps. "Well done, De Niro. And very nice improv at the end to bring it back to football."

"Well," I admit, "I'm just trying to figure out why I'm hallucinating that Matt Lauer is in my living room about to counsel me on fantasy football, that's all."

"Any chance a figment of your imagination can get a cup of that Lavazza? Some frothed milk and a couple of sugars would be great. And if you have any cookies or anything . . ."

Jesus, imaginary Matt is pretty demanding.

"OK, let's get to the point here," Matt says, settling back into the couch after I hook him up with a latte and some Milano cookies. "You need to stop obsessing about Shergul's trade and worrying about what he's up to and, instead, manipulate him to do one simple thing: bench Maddox."

"I do?"

"Yes, knucklehead," Matt says, rolling his eyes, "you do. We want to keep Maddox as far away from this game as possible. Christ almighty, you've been knee-deep in fantasy football for, what, three months now? Have you learned nothing so far? Christ."

"Sorry, Matt," I say sheepishly. He seems much nicer on TV.

"Everyone says that. Truth is, I can be a real prick when I want to be. I never get to explore that side of me." He lights a cigarette, takes a long drag, and blows perfect smoke rings. *Matt Lauer can be a prick* and *he smokes?* "Yeah, don't tell my wife. Anyway, here's what we do: Shergul's trying to get cute with his lineup, making rash trades that indicate he's worrying about who his opponent—you—is starting instead of just starting his best team. This never works in FF, trust me. Those dopes who think, 'Duhhhh, my opponent has David Boston so I'll start Drew Brees over Peyton' . . . that's a smart move, right?" Matt belts out an obnoxious game-show buzzer: "*EHHHHHHHH! Wrong! No, idiot, it's a dumb move. You start Manning every time.*" He pauses dramatically, lights another cigarette, shakes out the match, and flicks it at me. It misses my head but lands in my coffee with a little hiss.

"Sorry, man," he says with no remorse whatsoever. "Were you still drinking that?"

"Not anymore." Jesus, who invited this guy?! "You know," I tell him, "I think I like the TV Matt much better than the acting-like-a-jackass-in-my-apartment Matt."

He shrugs and kicks off his loafers. Argyle socks. At least *that's* not a total shock. "Oh, quit your bitching. Now where was I? Oh, yeah, Shergul's gut instinct to trade for Maddox was right because Tuiasowhatever (Marques Tuiasosopo, he means) is still a rookie, and *both* of your WRs are Steelers, so if they have a monster game, Maddox will, too, as you pointed out. But his Achilles' heel is that Harvard undergrad/Michigan MBA brain of his. He's a sharp guy, but he wants to look like the 'master strategist' in front of the whole league. And he wants to seem like the lone FF wolf, rolling the dice like a rebel. He wants to show how big his brain *and* his balls are. So he's vulnerable to a little psychology experiment. Meaning, it's up to us to goad him into the absolute wrong decision: starting Tuiasothingamajiggy. And how do we get him to do this? Agree with him that starting Maddox is a great idea on his part. You follow?"

"Yes," I respond weakly, having no idea what Matt's talking about.

"Were you kicked in the head by a mule as a baby? Fuck, man." Matt sighs and sits up, looking me directly in the eyes and blowing cancer-ridden smoke at me. "Look, we don't want him to follow his gut and start Maddox. So we use the most transparent, FF 101 reverse psychology, an obvious ploy which a fantasy veteran like Shergul won't fall for. We tell him that starting Maddox against Seattle's revamped defense in miserable weather conditions instead of Tuiasosopo against the woeful Lions is the best thing he can do for you. Hearing this, he'll first think you're trying to use basic reverse psychology on him and you really want him to start Tuiasosopo. But here's the kicker: being smart, he also knows you're no dummy either and knows that you wouldn't be stupid enough to think that *he'd* fall for basic reverse psychology. So he'll stick with Maddox.

"But then?" Matt chuckles, takes another long drag, and flicks ashes right on our parquet floor. "Then his Ivy League brain will kick in and he'll start overanalyzing, wondering if Tuiasosopo was the right move. And by that point, we've gotten him so twisted up inside he'll make a panicked game-time decision, and as we all know, those rarely work out. I'm not really a betting man, but my money's on him starting Tuiasosopo. And that's a victory for us, my friend. I just don't see a big day for the rookie. He's being pimped hard right now all over the FF kingdom, but he's still a rookie backup, and rookie backups don't typically do well whether they're playing the Lions, Tigers, Bears, or Sisters of the Poor. Maddox *will* have the better game. Send that e-mail. Now."

My *God*, Matt Lauer is an FF genius! Who knew? I would never have guessed that so much thought would have gone into such a relatively small lineup decision.

"Wow, thanks, Matt. That was—" I say, standing up to shake his hand. But he's gone. Damn, there were so many questions I wanted to ask him: Will Priest make it through a full season? Should I trade Davis before he gets hurt? Is Katie Couric meaner than she looks on TV, too?

I then remember Matt's marching orders: get Shergul to start thinking about starting Tuiasosopo again. So I quickly send the following e-mail and make sure to copy the whole league.

Me: Maddox in the rain and wind against Ray
Rhodes' Seahawks D, in Seattle, or future stud
Tuiasosopo at home against the pitiful Lions? By
all means start Maddox! You're wayyyyyy
overthinking this, my friend, and I thank you in
advance for making the wrong QB decision.

Yes, it was kind of obnoxious, but I didn't want Evil Imaginary Matt to come back and put his cigarette out on my forehead, so I did exactly what he said. Will it work? That remains to be seen—lineups don't have to be in until game time on Sunday—but knowing Shergul, I know one thing: he won't want to publicly agree with me.

I think he starts Tuiasosopo.

The Next Day . . .

Damned if Psycho Matt Lauer wasn't 100 percent right! At 11:49 A.M., an hour or so before game time yesterday, Shergul left a message to let me know that he'd be starting . . . drumroll please . . . Tuiasosopo!

Shergul sounded confident, proudly declaring that he was going with the rookie's "great matchup." And trust me, he thought he was being a genius. No one calls his opponent to confirm a lineup change unless he thinks that it's something he can gloat about later. But no Maddox would mean that after all his preemptive trade strikes, and all my reverse psychology e-mails, my WRs were no longer nullified.

And how did this work out for him? Just like Matt predicted, Shergul overanalyzed himself right into a defeat. Tuiasosopo was a rookie disaster. He threw an interception in his first series (-3 FFL points) and proceeded to be knocked out of the game with a torn ACL. Final stats: 65 yards, 1 INT, for *minus* 1 total points. "Damn right I'm bitter," Shergul admits after it becomes clear that I'll win this week. "If I keep Pennington or start Maddox, at least I'd have a shot heading into tonight. I overmanaged myself into a loss, plain and simple."

Sure, had he never traded Pennington at all he might have beaten me. Pennington threw for 281 yards and 4 TDs—for Shergul's trading partner, Karl, that is. But that's the chance Shergul took by overthinking his way into a new quarterback and worrying more about *my* lineup than his own. In here somewhere there's a **Newbie Strategy Tip #12: Always run your best lineup out there regardless of whom your opponent is starting.** Unless you're dealing with stud vs. stud (e.g., you have Randy Moss and your opponent has Daunte Culpepper), you should resist the temptation to "neutralize" your opponent's players. That's overcoaching.

In Shergul's case, he was clearly punished for thinking he knew too much by acquiring Maddox. Executing the perfect trade is like Man discovering fire—the FF gods just don't like us getting too high and mighty in their domain, and like Prometheus, we usually end up chained to a rock having our livers pecked out by eagles. Not that Maddox had a great day (226 yards, 1 TD, 14 FFL points), but that TD went to Ward, and Burress racked up 75 yards, all in all a decent day from my WRs (24 FFL points), who had been awful. Best of all, they got those points without giving *any* to Shergul via Maddox. Combine that with another monster effort from Stephen Davis (153 yards) and a huge game from Todd Heap (a 33-yard TD, 53 yards, and a 2-point conversion for 27 FFL points) and our beloved Acme squad fell into the win column once again with a 97–49 victory. This was Shergul's worst outing of the year. And let me tell you, I couldn't have enjoyed it any more.

Project Kick My League's Ass is now 6-3.

27

Stalking Joe Horn, Part II

Anyone who has had CBS SportsLine as their league host knows that you can create fun polls throughout the season, you know, like "Who had the worst draft?" or "Who is this season's fantasy MVP so far?" or "How long before Randy Moss runs over another rent-a-cop in his Bentley?" All that kind of stuff.

Well, the following hateful poll appeared on our CBS SportsLine home page today:

```
Which ACME star will tear ACL?
   A. Stephen Davis
   B. Peyton Manning
   C. Priest Holmes
   D. Todd Heap
   E. Celia, running from FFL-obsessed husband
```

Ha-ha, very funny. Apparently, the ghost of Henny Youngman, fresh off a gig in the Catskills, has joined our league and I didn't even know it. What an honor.

OK, look fellas—I know I'm obsessed. Celia, er, St. Cecilia knows all too well that I'm obsessed. But is it *that* obvious to the outside world that I've gone totally around the bend? I guess so. And normally, this public home-page humiliation would be one of those rock-bottom wake-up calls, sort of like an alcoholic waking up in a pool of his own urine outside the apartment he was just evicted from just in time to watch his wife and kids drive off in a U-Haul. But I'm not phased; I think this poll is just my league-mates' fear talking. They *know* I'm going to win this league, and they hide their fear behind a tired, old joke.

Yup, their fear . . . not the fact that I'm a total lunatic. That's gotta be it.

As the playoffs loom, I scan my roster to see whom on my bench I can turn into an upgrade at a starting position. The place I need to upgrade is #2 WR, where Plaxico has been inconsistent at best, downright drunk at worst. The guy who stands out like a sore thumb to get me that new stud WR is, once again, Trent Green.

Reasons to trade Trent: (1) I'll never start him over Peyton; (2) he's got value as the signal caller of the mighty Chiefs and is coming off a few above-average points weeks (the big 59-point game against the Pack and Week 8 versus Buffalo, when he racked up a respectable 31 FFL points; (3) I just don't like having a guy named Trent on my team. Then again I'm fine with guys named Priest and Plaxico, so go figure.

Anyway, I will next scan the other Felon rosters to see who needs a QB. But before I can even start doing any homework, my old friends the Bonesky Crushers come a'callin'. They have a little QB dilemma this week: both the injured Jeff Garcia and his backup Tim Rattay are on bye, and the fifty-seven-year-old Rich Gannon is still hurt. If they don't get a QB right now, they're facing the frightening possibility of starting the immortal Jeff Blake if, *and only if*, they're able to get him off waivers, which is no sure thing.

And the WR they have who is wearing a big, neon TRADE FOR ME NOW!! sign around his neck like a gaudy Flavor Flav clock is, once again, Joe Horn. If I could pair Horn with Ward, I'd immediately have the best WR duo this side of the Big Dogs' Harrison and Moss. Making Horn possibly more attainable is the fact that he's on bye this week, and Bonesky needs to win *now*, so they might be tempted by the prospect of acquiring Plaxico along with Green, and starting him against the lowly Cards in Week 10, when they'd have to sit Horn anyway.

So I make the offers to the Brothers Bonesky and quickly receive the following repsonse:

```
Jason: I will wait for my brother to respond . . .
if he does. Fair offer, but I am not going to pull
any drastic moves.
```

AAAAAAARGH!!! MOTHERF%#*ING two-owner teams! Fighting the urge to take the yelling, ranting approach and napalm the trade negotiations before they even start, I instead go the calm route.

```
Me: Totally understandable . . . but you guys
have to win NOW, and Blake ain't gonna cut it.
This offer is on the table for a while, but
please don't take forever. I'm definitely
shopping Green. . . .
```

And Jason's smug reply to my semihardball e-mail is:

```
Jason: Go ahead and shop Green. Don't let us hold
you up.
```

Wow, by that response you'd think they *aren't* facing the horrifying possibility of starting Jeff Blake in a must-win week. But am I really shopping Trent Green? Yes and no. Yes, I'd trade him if the right offer came around, but let's be honest here—I want Horn. Again. But it never hurts to let them know that they can't take their sweet time and play me like a fool while courting other, possibly more attractive, suitors. **Newbie Strategy Tip #13: Don't be pushy during trade negotiations, because that'll make the other owner think you're trying to sneak something by him.** But, you also can't be so laid-back that you end up being the loser boyfriend in the bar, either. You've seen the loser boyfriend—the one who sits at the bar alone watching *SportsCenter*, sipping a Zima, trying not to notice his hot girlfriend dancing with some dude who looks like Fabio, and yet, always caves and hands her another $20 bill whenever she sidles up and, in her sexiest, most endearing voice, says she needs another drink. You always wish the loser boyfriend would start hitting on some other broad in the bar, if anything, to regain some self-respect. But he never does. He just sits there like the doormat he is, pretending it all doesn't bother him, waiting for the hot girlfriend to toss him whatever scraps are left once Fabio's done with her. You feel for the loser boyfriend, you really do—but you would never, ever want to be him and, honestly, feel like punching him in the face.

Don't be the loser boyfriend! I remind myself, and scan the other rosters to "hit on another broad in the bar" and scare up some competition for Green's services that the Brothers Bonesky will have to contend with. Still, I want to keep them on the leash so I send a kinder, gentler e-mail to keep the trade doors open.

Me: Let me know if you talk to Kevin.

Letting them play pool might be all right. I just don't want to see any dirty dancing.

Jason: Will do.

Moments later, right in the middle of our little bonding session here, he sends me a final response to my trade offer. Apparently he went behind the iron curtain, conferred with his brother/co-owner, and reemerged with some bad news:

Jason: I spoke with my brother, he feels okay with the Rattay/Garcia combo, so I guess we will hold off for now.

Great. Just *fucking* great! Joe Horn Trade Attempt #2: failed! All those dreams of pairing Hines Ward and Horn for the playoff stretch are dashed on the rocks below! Granted, this trade negotiation wasn't anything nearly as torturous as that Bataan Death March we endured a couple weeks ago during Joe Horn Trade Attempt #1. Still, why do I bother to try to trade with two-ower teams? It's like trying to reason with Two Face from *Batman*—one of the personalities wants to do the deal and then—*whoooooop!*—the head spins and the other *less reasonable* personality spits at you and kills the deal.

But OK. Fine. Let them start Jeff Blake. It's their funeral. Sure, it would have been nice for them to be a little stronger as they play my competitors, but that's fine by me if they don't want a QB upgrade. I'll still win this week while they'll drop to 4-6. Am I tempting fate here? I mean, Karl's previously flatlined NH Hillbillies team (my 2-7 opponent this week) is looking a little stronger now with Pennington and Santana Moss, and is coming off a 143-point week. But fuck 'em—I'm Acme, dammit! I've worked my ass off assembling a team to be reckoned with! I'm tired of being afraid of the FF gods and their petty whims! I'm tired of being led around by the nose on fair trade offers and losing in the end! So that's it, folks . . . the Felon League has officially awakened the beast. It's time to go for the throat!

But wait, am I falling victim to the Seven Deadly FF Sins?

1. Pride in one's team.
2. Lust for a championship.
3. Envy of other teams' stud players.
4. Greed to acquire all those stud players.
5. Anger at failing to do so.
6. Gluttony for points, points, and more Felon League points.

OK, Six Deadly Sins anyway. (At least I haven't been slothlike this season.) But, by displaying these loathsome traits, am I brazenly challenging the almighty power of the FF gods by pulling a Joe Namath and guaranteeing victory this week? You bet your ass I am! So piss off, Bonesky Crushers . . . I don't need Joe Horn, I have the resurgent Plaxico against the sorry Cardinals at home! I have Priest at home against Cleveland! I have Davis, Peyton, Ward, Heap, the Bucs D! BRING IT ON, YOU SORRY-ASS NH HILLBILLIES! BRING IT ON, FF GODS! *I'm ready for whatever you're dishing out, you miserable, vindictive sonsabitches!*

> (Sincerely, your humble, ever-repentant servant,
> Mark St. Amant)

28

The Gods Must Be Crazy

I *had* to go and talk smack to the FF gods, didn't I? For the first time this year my guys are showing signs of breaking down and threatening to truly derail Project Kick My League's Ass. Priest is banged up. Plaxico is banged up. Davis is banged up. Ward has some weird eye infection that you can only catch from spitting tree frogs in certain parts of Tanzania, yet has mysteriously traveled to Pittsburgh and attacked *him specifically*. Figures.

What a jackass I am, poking my finger into the chests of the one group of "people" who can decide my fate. I bet you that mere seconds after reading the previous "BRING IT ON!" diatribe, the FF gods gathered in their Hall of Injustice or wherever the hell they live, lit up cigars, poured some single-malt Scotch, and said, "Gentlemen, we have a 'situation'—it seems St. Amant is getting a little uppity again down there in Boston, dissing us. How should we punish him?"

I can see it now.

"We could chain his wife to a rock and expose her to a Cyclops," one of them suggests. They all pause and glare at him. "Whaaaat? What'd I say?" he asks. "Too harsh?"

"Uh, yeah," the head FF god says, rolling his eyes, "just a tad harsh. And a little too Homer's *Odyssey* for my tastes. I'm thinking more along the lines of a worrisome injury to one of his stars."

Murmurs of agreement all around.

"Which star?" another God asks, swirling his Glenfiddich and ice. "Priest? We could zap him on the hip again like last season. Man, that screwed a lot of owners."

"Yeah, that was fun, wasn't it?" the head god replies, and they all laugh and high-five. "But Priest would be too obvious. St. Amant's half-expecting Priest to break down. I'm thinking someone more subtle, yet equally as devastating . . . someone like . . . Stephen Davis."

Murmurs. A few enthusiastic nods.

"Davis," another FF god says. "I like it. I like it a lot. He's good for one major breakdown every season, and even though Davis has looked pretty damn solid this year, St. Amant's fooled himself into thinking that the guy is indestructible. Yes, if we hit Davis with the injury whammy, it'll drive St. Amant freaking nuts! He'll be second-guessing himself till the cows come home, kicking himself for not trading Davis before he got hurt. It's brilliant!"

"Aw, shucks," the head FF god says, waving him off. "It was nothing, really."

"So what kind of injury are we talking here," another god asks. "Torn ACL, shoulder, hit over the head with a stool in a nightclub fight . . . ?"

The head FF god polishes off his Scotch, kicks back in his Barcalounger, and chews on an ice cube. "Nah. I'm thinking one of those annoying injuries that pops up out of nowhere in the middle of the week. Like a mildly sprained ankle that just gets worse, and worse, and worse as the week wears on, until it's totally unclear whether Davis can even play against the Bucs on Sunday. We'll make Davis owners everywhere worry right up until game time, make them scour the injury reports and message boards, pull their hair out wondering, 'Davis or Foster? Davis or Foster?'" The head FF god tips his head back and laughs. "Shit, it'll be priceless."

"Yes, yes!" One of them stands up and claps. "FF players hate nothing more than the words *game-time decision*. If St. Amant starts Davis, he might wind up playing one series and limping off the field. And if he starts Foster, Davis could make a miraculous recovery and stampede over the Bucs for 130 yards and a TD again, just like he did in Week 2. It's the FF owner's worst mightmare! I love it!"

The head FF god stands up, raises his glass in the air, and says, "So it is hereby agreed—we will make Stephen Davis a game-time decision! All in favor say yea!"

A rousing "YEA!" fills the room.

"All opposed say nay."

One of them, the one who originally suggested they make Celia pay for my transgressions, blurts out a weak "Nay." All heads turn. "Whaaat?" He shrugs. "What'd I say? I still like my Cyclops idea, but maybe instead we can give Hines Ward pinkeye, Plaxico a shoulder injury, and—oh, I don't know, just thinking out loud here—maybe bring some distracting sexual-harrassment charges against Peyton Manning, too? Can we, please?"

The head FF god considers it for a moment, then pats the dissenter on the shoulder. "Sure, we can be a little more harsh. All in favor of pink-eye for Ward, a shoulder injury for Plaxico, and sexual-harrassment charges for Peyton say yea."

A second rousing "YEA!" fills the room.

"Good. Now let's go have some lunch," the head FF god says. "Ted's made some wonderful egg-salad sandwiches."

And from the FF gods' mouths to the ears of the Internet, today I read:

```
Nov. 7. Priest Holmes was held out of practice
Wednesday with a sore rib cage.
```

```
Nov. 7. Plaxico Burress was held out of practice
Wednesday because of a sore shoulder.
```

```
Nov. 7. Hines Ward practiced Thursday despite
having pinkeye.
```

```
Nov. 7. Stephen Davis missed his second day of
practice with a sprained ankle and he has been
getting eight hours of treatment a day. There is
a chance he may have to sit out Sunday against the
visiting Buccaneers.
```

As for Peyton, a former Tennessee trainer just accused Manning of placing his "naked butt" on her face while in the Volunteers' locker room. According to reports, Manning was not personally accused of sexual harassment, and a university investigation characterized it as "horseplay." Still, this comes at the exact wrong time not only for the Colts, but, more important, for our beloved Acme squad. If Peyton is distracted, possibly thinking about putting his butt in a girl's face during college—but, c'mon, who hasn't thought about doing that at some point?—then he might not perform at his typical high level. I don't need this. Not at all.

Week 10 here we come. Pinkeye, bare butts, and all . . .

12:55:57 . . . 12:55:58 . . . 12:59:59 . . . Sweaty brow. Clammy hands. Mouse. Finger. Davis? Foster? Davis? Foster? (Please let me not screw this up, please let me not screw this up, please let me not screw this—)

Click.

Start DeShaun Foster. Let the games begin . . .

The early part of the day pretty much goes par for the course. Priest, sore ribs and all, scores two rushing TDs in about the first five minutes of the game. Peyton hits Harrison for a 30-yard TD. Ward catches a TD from Maddox. Bang-bang-bang, I'm up big right off the bat. Of course, Plaxico is doing his usual mannequin impression and doesn't even appear in the box score yet. Still, I'm up big early, 65–10.

But even though the NH Hillbillies team I'm playing against isn't particulary imposing—Chad Pennington, Michael Pittman, Duce Staley, Santana Moss, Steve Smith, Marcus Pollard, Olindo Mare, Dolphins D—I have this nagging little worry growing tumorlike in the back of my mind. Pennington and Moss, probably the hottest QB-WR combo in the league over the past four weeks, play against the Raiders, who couldn't stop most Pop Warner teams right now. And they play the late game, 4:15, meaning I'll probably have a huge lead and a false sense of security after the early games. I have a bad feeling about Moss and Pennington. It just seems like the kind of situation that will explode in my face.

After the early games, I'm up by about 60 points. Problem is, all my top "skill" guys are finished for the day, except Heap (sure, I have Wilkins going tonight against Heap's Ravens actually, but I hate to rely on a kicker and a TE). Karl, on the other hand, still has Pennington, Moss, and Staley left in his holster. And he's already chipping away at my lead. As the final guns sound on the early games, we have Acme 120, NH Hillbillies 48.

On paper, it seems like a safe lead. But I just have this bad feeling. So bad, in fact, that I decide that I can't wait around helplessly in the apartment and watch them destroy my team firsthand. So Celia and I meet our friends Ben and Holly and go see *Elf*, the Will Ferrell movie. Now, I would pay good money to watch Will Ferrell cut his toenails for two hours, so it's not as if I mind getting out of the house to watch him in action as a six-foot-three-inch Christmas elf in yellow tights. And it's a nice way to get my mind off the powder keg about to explode in my face on the West Coast.

After the Movie

When Celia and I get home a couple hours after the late games have finished up, I eagerly rush over to the computer, expecting to see a nice, comfortable score like Acme 120, NH Hillbillies 85. Instead, as I refresh the CBS SportsLine website, to my shock and horror I see the following inconceivable score staring back at me:

    NH Hillbillies 126, Acme 120.

The disbelief and rage well up inside me and finally manifest in a blinding, mental mushroom cloud. I'm going to lose to a 2-7 team! Karl has averaged, what, 75 points per game so far this year? I hear an angry siren go off in my head—a shrill, piping-hot whistle, like when Fred Flintstone used to get mad and *literally* blow his top—and I say a very bad word. Then another. Then a third. Then, knowing full well what happened but wanting to torture myself nonetheless, I go to Rotoworld and read the following:

Santana Moss—WR New York Jets *11/09/03*
Moss leads all receivers today, pulling in six passes for 146 yards, one being a 65-yard first-quarter touchdown. He also added a single rush for 25 yards.

And then I black out.

When I come to, I'm lying under my desk. And though still incredibly pissed off, I take a few deep breaths and realize that it's not over quite yet. Karl is going to have to work *a lot* harder than that to knock off our mighty Acme squad. Then again, this *is* me we're talking about here, and the FF gods and I sometimes—how do I put this delicately?—hate each other's fucking guts, so you just never know. Losing to That Guy might not be too much of a stretch.

Later, the ESPN game is absolutely painful to watch, from both a fantasy standpoint and as an NFL fan. The Ravens and Rams seem to be trying *not* to win—fumbling, committing stupid penalties, turning the ball over repeatedly—and I watch in horror as, over the first half, Heap drops an easy 30-yard pass from Kyle Boller; gets interfered with on another 30-yard pass; gets overthrown by Boller in the end zone. *Finally,* in the red zone, Boller play-actions, lets it fly, and hits a wide-open Heap, right? No, silly, of course not! Instead, Boller connects with eligible lineman Jonathan freaking Ogden. And to top it all off, at the end of the half, Boller floats another long one up that Heap momentarily catches, but then he gets drilled by his former Arizona State teammate Adam Archuleta, which dislodges the ball and sends Heap to the turf in a mangled—forgive the pun—heap. As ESPN cuts to a commercial with Heap lying motionless on the turf, I swear I hear Joe Theismann tell me to go screw myself.

AAAARGGHHH! I can't take it anymore. Angrily, as if it's all the remote's fault, I slam it with my fist and the game flicks off. Wilkins has two piddly extra points, so it's now 126–122 Hillbillies. But Heap should have had about 75 yards and a TD already. Instead, he's got 10 yards and a possible fractured skull. I want to stick a shish-kebab skewer into my own eye. FF is going to be the death of me.

I go to bed knowing that the score heading into tomorrow night's *MNF* game will be something utterly painful along the lines of NH 126, Acme 125.999999, with Wilkins missing an extra point.

All hope is lost. I hate kickers. 6-4 here we come . . .

Did I ever mention how much I love kickers? They're the best!

All right, I'm full of shit . . . I've called kickers the redheaded stepchildren of FF on more than one occasion. But all that's over now because after I went to bed, convinced the FF gods had given a celestial hosing to both me *and* Heap, Jeff Wilkins put on one of the greatest single-quarter kicking shows in FF history: 4 field goals and an extra point for 15 FFL points. Add Heap's 4 points (45 yards)—he wasn't killed on the Archuleta hit, after all—and lo and behold, I'm back on top.

```
Acme 141, NH Hillbillies 126.
```

But this is a precarious 15 points thanks to the impending presence of Duce Staley on *MNF.* And if my past luck is any indication, Duce will absolutely go off tonight. You can bet on it. Duce will probably get exactly 16 points to defeat me 142–141, and he and Karl will then come to my apartment, defecate in my living room, eat all our food, drink all my beer, and then take turns having sex with Celia.

Maybe the FF gods have just beaten me down, but despite the brief window of hope provided by Jeff Wilkins, I'm not feeling good. Stay tuned . . .

As I predicted, Duce almost beat me last night. *Almost.*

He got a lot of those anoying little dump-off passes into the flat from McNabb, each time causing bile to rise up into my throat. In fact, after one particularly gut-wrenching 30-yard reception, I had to simply turn the game off. I couldn't take it. I *knew* Duce would get the necessary points to send me to my most bitter loss of the year (me losing to a 2-7 team would be like Halle Berry losing a wet T-shirt contest to Henry Kissinger). So, wisely, I just went to bed, taking my piddly 141–132 lead with me, fully expecting to wake up and find out that Staley had scored a last-second TD in the final seconds of the game to stick the dagger into my heart.

But to my shock and delight, I logged onto CBS SportsLine to discover that when all was said and done, Staley fell short! He only scored 9 points. Karl needed 16 for a win.

Game over. Final score: Acme 141, NH Hillbillies 135. Can you say "skin of my teeth"?

Maybe this season will be different after all? Maybe, if I just ride out the ups and downs, the FF gods will finally reward me for all my hard work? Last year I would have lost this game, no doubt, but maybe having Priest on my team *is* the good-luck charm I needed all along? Who knows why, and I don't care. Project Kick My League's Ass sits safely at 7-3, good for third place.

While the Felon League is still very much up in the air, I check in with the fellas in the Hershey Highway League, and they have all but conceded the title to Phil Kwan. "It's over," says Steve Oh. "Kwan is now nine and one, and anyone with any hope at this point is simply wallowing in delusional fantasyland. We all said he couldn't possibly win with Deuce McAllister out. His victory is impossible? No, it's inevitable."

But Kwan isn't so sure that his march to the HH championship will go unimpeded and they should start measuring his hat size for the league crown quite yet. Standing in his way? Russo, aka the White Monkey.

"Russo's starting RBs are Shaun Alexander, Stephen Davis, Domanick Davis, and Rudi Johnson," Kwan reports warily, "and from what he tells me, they have a cake schedule over the last seven games. So all of you, including myself, beware: White Monkey is back. Someone will need to sacrifice themselves over the last seven games to stop Russo from spreading through our entire system. Who will be this hero sacrificing himself? Who will be Neo?"

"The secret that is not so secret," adds Samip, "is that people would not mind Kwan winning if they themselves don't win. That said, nobody who is anybody wants Russo to win. A repeat honky would be too much to stomach."

Ah, nothing like a little reverse discrimination to spice up league politics.

Now, I've seen two of the *Matrix* movies, and still, I absolutely have no idea what any of that computer-code, alternate-universe gibberish means, so the whole Neo/system reference is lost on me. Does he mean that Keanu Reeves has to somehow stop Russo from winning? And what about Morpheus and Trinity? Do they play FF, too, and if so, can they stop Russo and Phil Kwan? Thankfully, Steve Oh attempts to explain the *Matrix* analogies floating around the e-mails today:

```
Steve: Kwan is Neo. We all hate him because we are
jealous losers. Russo is Agent Smith. He has
infected the hapless Wong, who basically became
another Russo, thereby giving the real Russo all
of his good players. Russo is on a rampage to
infect the rest of the league and steal all the
good players from everyone else. Impossible? No,
INEVITABLE. [Steve loves that turn of phrase.]
None of this matters, though, because Keanu Kwan
is The One.
```

And with that bit of cryptic Korean/*Matrix* wisdom in mind, we head off into Week 11, armed and dangerous, but still cautious and full of questions. Do I bench Plaxico once and for all? Do I keep trying to parlay Trent Green, who had yet another big game while Krazy-Glued to my bench, into that elusive #2 WR upgrade via trade? After all, he's an asset, a valuable player who will never see the starting lineup with Peyton in front of him, so I might as well see if I can parlay him into something of use. **Newbie Strategy Tip #14: Late in the season, depth doesn't matter as much. If you have valuable bench depth that you can parlay into an upgrade to your starting team, do it.** Granted, this is only my personal philosophy, and you might not be as naturally reckless. But this late in the season, I always figure it's time to lay all your cards on the table and go for broke.

This is our last week for trading—like many leagues out there, our trade deadline is Week 11, timing that, in theory at least, prevents collusion in the later playoff weeks—so it's now or never. Which leads us right to another quick **Newbie Strategy Tip #15: Know your league rules inside and out.** Know when your trade deadline is. Know when (or if) your free agency periods end. Know every rule there is to know, because you don't want to be caught off guard by anything. Luckily, in the Felon League, we're allowed to pick up players through the Super Bowl if need be, which helps reduce the risk of being decimated by injury in the late weeks. But is there one more free agent pickup that might make a difference in my season? Maybe the flashy Titans wide receiver, Tyrone Calico, whom I snagged off the waiver wire recently. But can I risk benching Plaxico's lazy, bad-route-running ass for Calico, an unproven rookie? We'll see, but two out of my last three games are against the first and fourth top scorers in FFL, so it's not exactly a cakewalk into the playoffs for yours truly. I have to consider all options.

That said, while owners around the country like me are trying to improve their teams any way they can at this point in the season, some take the exact opposite tack: they flat out quit. And when an owner quits, it can have a disastrous ripple effect upon the remaining teams still trying to win. Case in point, this e-mail I receive from Kevin (of Bonesky Crushers fame), who is the commish of another league:

```
Kevin: The idiocy in my other league is
ridiculous. One of the guys dropped his ENTIRE
TEAM last night! Even worse, all of the playoff
```

teams picked up his good players. Here's the
Transaction report. What a f*cking joke!

In other words, some loser who is out of playoff contention decided to completely give up and drop all his good players and replace them with players who are on NFL practice squads, IR, whatever. And worse, the remaining playoff teams—showing no FF ethics whatsoever and trying to gain any edge possible—frantically scrambled to grab the discarded stud players as if they were $100 bills accidentally spilling out of an open Brinks truck.

I won't list the entire transaction report, because it's about as long as the Vietnam Memorial Wall in D.C., but I will list a few notables on this utterly shameful, sour-grapes move by a gutless, weak-ass owner:

Dixin Herholes Drop WR Anquan Boldin

Dixin Herholes Pickup WR Onomo Ojo (Who?)

Dixin Herholes Drop Def Buccaneers

Dixin Herholes Pickup Def Texans (Huh?)

Dixin Herholes Drop RB Rudi Johnson

Dixin Herholes Pickup RB Ron Dayne (Ugly.)

Dixin Herholes Drop RB Travis Henry

Dixin Herholes Pickup RB Tim Biakabutuka (*Very Ugly.*)

I've heard of non-playoff teams playing out the string and lazily going through the motions, maybe forgetting to turn in a fresh lineup one week . . . but I've never seen anything like *this*! He dropped all of his good players! But it just goes to show you: you never know how people—we're humans after all, and therefore flawed to the hilt—are going to react to losing. Whether it's dumping an entire roster like this nimrod here, or—and this is another all-too-common "trick" of weasel owners who aren't going to finish in the money—colluding with a winning team in exchange for a share of the profits (i.e., Bad Team trades his studs to Good Team in exchange for all of Good Team's crap players; Good Team wins using Bad Team's studs; Good Team slips Bad Team some cash). While any commish worth his/her salt will overturn obvious collusion trades, weasel moves like this still add up to one thing: winning illegally. Trust me, I hate losing. That I'm jobless right now because I want to win so badly is testimony to that. But, to drop your whole roster out of anger, or to take advantage of a team that pulls that kind of lame stunt, rails against all that is good and true about fantasy football. Maybe there should be some sort of nationwide "FF war crimes" tribunal that could hand down punishment in such egregious cases? Maybe make them play fantasy figure skating for a year? That would make 'em think twice.

29

Plight of the FF Widow

Let's look at one of the subjects I've pushed out of bounds, but haven't fully tackled quite yet: the fantasy football widow. (Note: yes, there are FF widowers as well, but most often if a wife plays FF, chances are her husband does, too.)

You've no doubt seen the FF widow. She's usually a sad, beaten-down and/or angry-looking woman, typically with a few children hanging from various parts of her body in Baby Bjorns as she reshingles the house, cleans the gutters, changes diapers, pays the bills, buys the groceries, changes the oil in the car, spays the cat, unloads the groceries—all while her FF-playing husband sits at the computer and manages his team. Or, if there are no children, she can be found next to an empty seat at movies, in restaurants, or at her beloved grandmother's funeral.

It's really a cruel fate. I pity them. Yet I am powerless to change their unfortunate circumstances. After all, I am close to creating my own FF widow in poor Celia. That is, I *would*, if I knew that she wouldn't divorce or kill me first.

Maybe you even *are* one of these fantasy widows yourself. If so, God have mercy on your soul. (Maybe you and Celia should start some kind of nationwide support network?) Every late summer, you must resign yourself to the fact that right before the season begins, your husband will disappear into the basement, his office, wherever, and six months later will reemerge from his self-induced exile like some kind of mole person, blinking, shielding his eyes from the sunlight, and asking who that young woman at the dinner table is (your daughter, who was an infant when he left) and who that older man beside her is (your new husband, whom you married after you had the FF-playing husband declared legally deceased).

It was this past July, during preseason, that I first realized there were more FF widows out there like poor Celia. A guy going by the name of Atlanta Cracker posted the following question in the Huddle forums: "How do I get my wife to like football?"

"The season hasn't even started yet," he wrote, "and we already had a fight about how much time I spend doing football stuff and ignoring her." Apparently, this had been a degenerative problem for Mrs. Cracker, downshifting from "not really concerned" while they were dating, to "mildly concerned" while they were engaged, to "totally fed-up" now that they both had rings on their fingers. "And now the gloves are coming off," Atlanta Cracker sadly reported. So, not wanting this battle of the sexes to last for the subsequent six months, he came to the Huddle in the pre-season for help, advice, prayers—anything to help start his 2003 fantasy football wife-management off on the right foot.

Some offered less-than-practical advice, saying she should have known that he was a football fan before she married him, and that if she now suddenly wants to change him into some kind of *Oprah*-watching, Sarah McLachlan–listening, quiche-eating wussy, then he should tell her to hit the bricks. One guy simply said, "Divorce her." Another suggested having more sex with her on Sunday mornings so she'll be more relaxed during the day, but as any man knows, offering to have *more* sex with a woman is like a four-hundred-pound glutton offering to eat more Twinkies. One helpful gent threw out an even more drastic solution. "You could just have her killed," he kidded. "I hear Jeff Gilooley is looking for work." Another guy, guessing Cracker was from Atlanta, suggested he visit the famous Gold Club strip joint and find a brand-new wife who doesn't complain so much. And yet another suggested that Cracker introduce his wife to his *other* passionate hobby—hard-core porn—and tell her to "pick her poison."

Fortunately for Cracker, other Huddlers soon chimed in with more useful tidbits. One advised him to "clear the minefield early by making Saturday hers." In other words, no matter what hellish, estrogen-packed activity she wants him to do with her on Saturday, he should just smile, nod, and jump in with both feet. She wants them to go visit her mother and massage her aching bunions? Perfect! She wants to attack the dust-ruffle sale at Bed Bath & Beyond? Can't think of anything he'd rather do! She wants him to join her for a movie marathon of *Beaches*, *Fried Green Tomatoes*, and *Thelma and Louise*? Not only should he eagerly accept, he should suggest they add *Boys on the Side* and *Pretty Woman* just to make the day complete! A second helpful soul suggested Cracker use the "reward" approach. "I take all my profits from winning leagues and use it to take my girlfriend on a trip in the winter," he said. "All it took was one trip to Aruba and now all she cares about is how I am doing in my leagues." Ah, I know this one all too well, mostly because it's always back-fired when I try it on my own wife. Whenever I tell her that I'll use any fantasy winnings to buy her something nice or take her to dinner, she tells me that she'd pay me double the prize money for me *not* to play. (Advantage: Celia.) My pal CJ, however, who owns the Felon League's Charlemagnes team, has successfully employed this money-dangling strategy. "The year I won, I just gave all the cash to [wife] Lisa and I still have no idea what she did with it," he confesses without an ounce of shame. "Something about a fireplace cover."

Another Huddler soon threw out an interesting approach: start a league for the wives/girlfriends so they could start understanding what the men in their lives get so riled up about. While this assumes that the women *actually want to learn about football*—a huge leap for many females—it seems to have worked for this particular fella. "The ladies have learned a lot more about football and actually watch most of the games now. Talk about twenty very lucky and happy husbands/boyfriends!"

What it finally came down to, however, was what it always comes down to in any marital issue: compromise. If he did most of his fantasy research at work, people advised Cracker, he'd have more time to spend with the missus at home. Never make her ask him twice to do something, just do it the first time. If he showed an interest in some of her hobbies, maybe she'd be more willing to show an interest in football? On and on it went, until Cracker, loaded up with plenty of ammunition, went off to battle.

And now, a couple months into the season, how is it all working out down in the Cracker household?

"A total success!" he reports excitedly. He compromised until the cows came home (or, more fittingly, until the mother-in-law came home, which she did on more than one occasion, all to Cracker's utmost joy). He's made every Saturday the sole property of Mrs. Cracker. And he even went so far as to get his wife to play a "wife's fantasy game," in which she picks a few players and, based on their Sunday performances, gets rewarded with a buck per fantasy point. "That lasted a couple of weeks before she got bored with it," Atlanta Cracker admits, "but went a long way toward helping her understand my addiction." Bottom line, as we head toward the fantasy playoffs, he's proud to report that every Sunday is smooth sailing and he's received official permission to "belly up on my buddy's couch to take it all in on the Sunday Ticket!"

Not surprisingly, this subject attracts male Huddlers as if it came flowing out of a frosty keg, and soon many are chipping in with their own stories of wife/girlfriend/kid management.

Some, sadly, are unsuccessful. "We took a cruise in September with another couple—a buddy from my league—and our wives got pretty pissed when we'd visit the Internet cafe to check scores and set rosters during the week," one Huddler says. "But the funniest part was that there were about eight other guys in there setting lineups for their games that week. I think every husband there got in deep shit that day." But other strategies have worked out. "We were working on the Christmas budget and I told her I was in the running for about a thousand bucks if I win my league. She now supports my hobby."

But don't be fooled into thinking that FF is *only* for men. On the contrary, more women are playing now than ever, anywhere between 3 and 6 million by some estimates. David Dorey says that while he used to get maybe a few e-mails per month from women, that number is now in the hundreds, mostly because many women coming into the hobby now are brand-new to it, and as any man will tell you, they are not afraid to ask for directions. "It always amazes me how many women play nowadays," Dorey says. "And there are a lot more coming into it as it becomes more mainstream. In many ways, they like to prove to the men in their office or wherever that it's not a strength thing, it's a mental thing." Regular Huddler Lisa from New Hampshire tells me, "I enjoy showing up the guys who think that it takes testosterone to play the game. I started playing several years ago when my husband got tired of me looking over his shoulder all the time, so I got my own team. I enjoy whipping him whenever I get the chance. We don't really argue about it, but we get a little testy on draft day." She also says she's noticed more and more women playing and, hopefully next season, will start an all-women's league. "I think that would be fun," she says. "Of course, there wouldn't be much trading or trash-talking for fear of hurting people's feelings."

When I read this last quote to Celia, she agrees, but adds, "Women can be catty, though. It might be more cutthroat than an all-men's league."

"You think?" I ask.

"Definitely." She nods. "It would be a bloodbath."

Now that I have her attention on the matter, I decide to go straight to the source once and for all. I ask Celia what she likes least about my FF obsession (or, I should say, what she dislikes most, as "likes least" implies that she likes anything at all). "Oh, there are just so many things. First, by far, is the sheer amount of time it takes—on the computer, in front of the TV, making us listen to staticky sports radio on car trips. The money doesn't bother me because it's not all *that* much. But the time . . ."

Uh-oh, I've just opened Pandora's box.

"And I hate the fact that your mood can be determined by what has or hasn't happened in a stupid football game," she continues, "and your inability to be anywhere but near a computer or a TV on Sunday around lunchtime. And I hate when we're out somewhere, and you excuse yourself to 'go to the bathroom' and disappear for fifteen minutes, and I find out that you were checking scores. And I *really* hate your burning need to discuss how your team is doing with me when you know that I honestly just don't care. You know, when you say stuff like"—she puts on her best, testosterone-filled "dumb guy" voice—" '. . . Tonight's game is *huuuuge* because so-and-so scored this many points today and I need so-and-so to score this many.' My friend, the list goes on and on."

My wife is no girly girl by any means. She was an all-state swimmer as a kid and can flat out kick my ass in a race. She doesn't particularly care for baby showers, bridal showers, or, as she puts it, "any event where women ooh and aah over stupid things." And it takes a serious overflow of emotion to make her cry. But, despite being exposed to more fantasy football—and, through osmosis from her idiot husband, learning far more *about* fantasy football— than she's ever wanted to over the past few years, Celia's feminine sensibility still can't allow her to fathom why the game is so appealing to so many people. But this has as much to do with her being a non-sports-fan in general, rather than just being anti-fantasy-football. "I like *going to* games, the whole live atmosphere, the people-watching," she concedes. "But, fundamentally, I just don't understand why people love to watch sports on TV, so, naturally, I can't understand why people take it a step further into *fantasy* sports." I see her point: going to a game is much more fun than watching it on the tube. But what is it about having double-X chromosomes that makes it impossible for one to understand that it's the game-watching (and accompanying stat-accumulating) that's the linchpin to the entire FF hobby? I guess this—along with the mysterious toilet seat cover and sex in the morning—will remain one of life's greatest gender battles.

With the exception of Shergul's wife, Alison, none of Celia's girl-friends' husbands or boyfriends are into FF to the degree that I am, so she has to suffer in relative silence. That said, she's not so anti-fantasy-football that she'd ever dream of asking me to stop. "Because I know you love it," she tells me.

But that's where her goodwill ends. There is nothing at all that would ever make her get into fantasy football. Nothing. Even just plain football itself is a tough sell. I've often tried to lure her into football-watching by preying upon her most base instinct: attraction to rich, strong-jawed, ath-letic men. "Aw, c'mon," I begged once, when a Pats game was cutting into some wifely activity that she wanted us to enjoy as a couple. "Don't you want to watch your boy Tom Brady? He's a handsome man."

"Nah," she replied matter-of-factly. "He's all covered up."

Damn her and her estrogenical supremacy! She's too smart for me! I should know that the only time she ever really tunes into football is dur-ing Brady's postgame press conferences on *Patriots 5th Quarter*, and even then it's nothing more than a cursory glance.

And if players wearing pants tight enough to make David Lee Roth blush aren't doing the trick for the ladies, we FF-playing husbands have little hope of ever luring our FF widows to the dark side.

It's a sad state of affairs.

30

Fight Club, Philadelphia Chapter

I'm on special assignment, writing to you live from a smoke-filled lounge in the Philadelphia International Airport.

I've been down here since Friday for my friend Bill's bachelor party. We played paintball, which was more fun than I ever imagined, but also kind of painful. I have welts on my legs and arms, and my knees are all banged up from sliding and rolling like some kind of spastic infantryman. I could have saved the fifty bucks and just had someone beat me with a tire iron for free.

Still, despite my pain, I managed to pull a last-minute blockbuster trade this morning: Peyton (and throw-in Calico) for Marvin Harrison and Bengals QB Jon Kitna. My WRs have been my Achilles' all season long, so I need a Marvin-type stud; and Kitna has been hot, so it'll offset the Peyton loss a bit. We'll see how it works out. Fingers crossed.

Until this very second, here in the Sky Asian Bistro, Terminal C, I've never really appreciated the smoking ban that we have in bars and restaurants up in Boston. But having spent the majority of last night drinking gallons of beer in McGillins Ale House (aka the Burning Smoke Eyes and Seared Smoke Throat Ale House), and having spent the past half hour sitting here in the direct line of fire of a Newport Lights jet stream courtesy of two vampy, husky-voiced, heavily made-up kiosk workers on their break at the next table, I have never missed that smoking ban more in my life. These ladies seem to be purposely blowing their smoke directly at me just for sport.

Now that I look around, I am literally the only person in here not smoking. Jesus, am I in Philly or Prague!? Well, there *are* some people not smoking at the moment, but it's only because they've just finished a cigarette and haven't lit another one up yet and are gearing up to add to my misery by pounding the bottoms of their packs into their palms or onto the bar, grinning at me and thinking, "Oh, yeah, Mr. Nicotine Prude, we're coming for you!" My eyes are tinged red. (Yes, I'm a little hungover, and achy from being shot at with hard plastic pain pellets, too.) And my voice is crackly, weak, raspy, totally shot. I was just on the phone with Celia, as a matter of fact, and if she didn't know any better, she might have thought she was either chatting with a midpubescent teenage boy or Harvey Fierstein.

But risking lung cancer is the price I have to pay to put myself into the epicenter of the *Fight Club* Theory—the airport lounge.

Aside from being at the actual football stadiums or sports bars, nowhere else on earth am I more likely to run into FF nuts than in an airport bar. Especially on a Sunday, when men and women coming from and going to all parts of the country see the flickering of the lounge televisions, stop in their tracks, and, even if they're rushing to make a connection, come inside, drawn to the daylong football coverage like proverbial moths to a flame. Whether they sit down for drinks and some food or just stay through one set of game updates scrolling on the bottom of the screen, this is the place to get their fix.

That's really why I'm here—to throw myself into their natural habitat. I want to give them the secret *Fight Club* nod or handshake and, assuming they don't think I'm some total lounge creep trying to pick them up, drug them, and harvest their kidneys for sale on the black market, perhaps get their FF stories while I'm at it.

As if on cue, a stout, early-thirtyish-looking guy sporting a bushy blond hairdo and wearing a Donovan McNabb jersey with a white turtleneck underneath comes in with his girlfriend (or wife). She's also wearing a McNabb jersey. They clearly came straight from the game, and they both emit a slightly panicked sense of urgency. I half expect him to say, "Do you have a phone? We need to call a doctor!" but instead he points to the three TVs suspended over the bartender's head and asks, "Quick . . . which games are on?"

"Let's see," the goateed bartender casually responds, leaning forward and twisting his body so he can see each screen. "We got Minnesota-Oakland, Bucs-Pack, and—"

"Two TDs for Sharpe. *Nice!*" blond McNabb suddenly yells, referring to the Fox halftime highlights and excitedly pumping his fist. Clearly, he's not so worried anymore. "*Nice!* The Eagles win, the Skins lose, the Pats will beat Dallas tonight, and Sharpe has two TDs. *Nice!*"

Apparently, this is all very *Nice!* and to prove just how *Nice!* it is, he high-fives his girlfriend/wife and kisses her on the cheek. They then choose two open seats in front of the Vikings-Raiders TV and order two glasses of merlot, an odd choice. I'd have bet my life savings that a fist-pumper in a Donovan McNabb jersey would be a Coors Light kinda guy.

"*Nice!*" he yells once again upon seeing Peyton's stats, and doles out another round of starch-crisp high fives for his wife, the bartender, and the frightened businessman next to him, who then quietly gathers his *Philadelphia Inquirer* and moves one seat farther away.

Soon, I deem it safe to approach without being whacked in the head with an errant palm-slap and introduce myself to blond McNabb, who turns out to be named Brian, and his wife, Karen, a pleasant, gregarious brunette. He's an insurance claims adjuster and she's a high school teacher. They live in Westport, Connecticut, now but grew up outside of Philly in Haverford, hence the Eagles jerseys and the preppy bushy-blond-hair-and-turtleneck combo, as Haverford is a town that has spawned scores of preppy blond guys with turtlenecks over the years.

After making clear that I'm not here to pick up strange couples in air-port lounges and swing with them at the nearby Ramada, I learn that Brian plays in four leagues, three online with total strangers just for kicks, and one big-money local league with eleven of his work buddies.

This is the serious one. This is the one with the bragging rights, and the trophy.

"It's more like a plaque-type thing with all our names etched onto it," he says between sips of merlot. "I've never won in six years. Came in last place twice, though. And we have this league tradition that whoever comes in last place has to sneak in late at night and mount the championship plaque right in our office reception area. It's a small company— about twelve people—but the CEO has no idea we hang our fantasy football trophy in the company lobby. He probably thinks it's some kind of insurance industry award we've won. He'd freak out if he knew clients of ours were waiting in the lobby right under a fantasy football trophy!" This is the league that's causing all the fist-pumping and high-fiving, as he's playing the league leader today and is absolutely kicking ass. Like me, he's in third place overall and second in total points. This is his best year yet. And, again, he's never won in six years.

It hits me—Brian might just be my slightly bigger, slightly blonder, slightly bushier alter ego. I am suddenly rooting for Brian to win his league more than anyone I've met so far. If Brian wins . . . I win!

We spend the next half hour or so talking our *Fight Club* talk. Karen, while not playing in any leagues, says that a ton of her students—mostly tenth-graders—play, so she hears a lot of FF talk in the hallways. "One time on a Friday afternoon, I caught a kid passing a piece of paper to another kid during a quiz," she says laughing, an infectious giggle that makes the businessman look up from his *Inquirer,* smile, and tune into her story. "I figured they were cheating. But when I confiscated the paper, it was their fantasy lineup. They were trying to decide between starting Marc Bulger from St. Louis, I think it was, or Jake Plummer." She shakes her head in amazement as both her husband and the businessman listen. "Of course, I had to play the hard-ass teacher and told them to knock it off during quizzes, but inside I was *dying*. I couldn't wait to tell Brian that my school is growing a whole new crop of 'Brians' to unleash on the world."

While teachers might not want their students passing fantasy football notes in class—especially when said notes are about Jake Plummer, of all the third-tier fantasy impact players—not everyone believes FF is necessarily a bad thing for our country's admittedly shaky educational system. Pat Kirwan, former New York Jets player personnel director and current writer for both NFL.com and CBSSportsLine.com, argues that fantasy football is, in fact, doing its part to create a *more* educated youth. "My wife is a teacher," Kirwan says, "and like every schoolteacher she's frustrated with kids who don't read. So about two years ago I told her that a kid reading about fantasy football on a website for two hours a day because he or she is in a fantasy league is better than not reading at all." He's got a point, to which I'd add that a fantasy football website is probably a lot safer than some of the other sites out there that kids might be attracted to in their downtime. Pat agrees: "It's a wholesome activity, it's not porn, it's not X-rated—it's football. So basically, you can drive these kids who wouldn't necessarily be reading to a site that interests them." But one can see why teachers, especially, might be skeptical of fantasy football websites as an educational tool, primarily because the stereotype is that they're written by dumb lunkhead jocks ranting and raving about Manning's inability to win the Big Game, Warren Sapp's "slavery" comments, or Brenda Warner's meddling with her husband's career via the media. But Kirwan, who teaches sports business at NYU grad school and has taught at virtually every level of school in his "pre-NFL" life, argues that FF sites are extremely useful tools to teach everything from grammar to vocabulary to math. "I said to her, go on a fantasy football website and just extract the vocabulary list. Then tell your students, 'Okay, we're going to set up a fantasy football league in class, but first, here's a list of vocabulary for homework tonight.' I think that progressive people looking for an edge to make learning fun have already figured that out." And what of the math and history angles? "Elementary school and junior high math teachers can make a mathematical experience out of fantasy leagues, due to the sheer number of statistics involved. It'd be the ultimate way to get kids excited about math. And you could do a history lesson, matching up events in the National Football League with simultaneous events in world history."

Bottom line, Kirwan believes teachers should start incorporating fantasy football into their lesson plans. "Look, I listen to, know, and have experienced the frustrations in education firsthand, but I see fantasy football and say, 'Are you kidding me? This reaches every level of where education needs to be taken . . . learning needs to be fun.'"

Suppressing the urge to belt out the first line of Whitney Houston's "Greatest Love of All"—*I believe the children are our future / Teach them well and let them lead the way*—I mention Kirwan's comments to Karen, and she agrees wholeheartedly. "He's got a point. Some of my kids hate reading, and most of them despise math. But, like he said, I'd rather see them reading about football than not reading at all, and if it takes fantasy football to get them excited about learning, then I'm all for it. Tell him [Kirwan] I'll start drawing up my new lesson plan tomorrow."

Being an NFL fan herself but not an FF player, Karen follows Brian's work league with the fervor of any junkie. "I think it's great," she says. "It makes work so much more fun for him. I mean—let's face it—insurance isn't the most exciting industry in the world, so it makes it more enjoyable for him to go to work every day. And from what he says, it doesn't prevent them from getting their work done."

"Actually," Brian interjects, "if anything, I think fantasy football makes our office *more* productive because we all get along better, we know each other better, we communicate more and hang out more after hours, talking trades, all that. I think it's great for morale overall, especially in a small company."

He adds, chuckling, "One of these days we'll have the balls to let our CEO know that the plaque in the lobby that appears in mid-December every year isn't a J.D. Power award."

Their flight to La Guardia is soon announced and we all shake hands. I wait another few hours for my own flight, drinking water with lemon to purge Harvey Fierstein's smoky voice from my throat and wondering if, by trading Peyton, I have just officially sabotaged any chance I have of winning this year, just as I did last year when I traded Marvin to All-American Angus down the stretch for that broken-down bastard, Marshall Faulk. Dammit . . . didn't I learn my lesson? Stupid, stupid move.

When I arrive back in Boston—still feeling incredibly stupid, I'm glad to report—I find myself in a long cab line, odd for ten o'clock on a Sunday night. But this gives me time to check the final scores and stats on my cell phone so I don't have to do it when I get home, which would infuriate Celia, considering I just spent the previous forty-eight hours running around the woods shooting my friends and drinking beer. Quality husband-and-wife time will be a must.

So where does our beloved Acme squad stand in the Week 11 game? I'm up 18 points thanks mostly to Trent Green's 300-plus yards and another solid outing by the workhorse, Stephen Davis, who logged 90-something yards and a TD against his former team, the Skins. So, tomorrow on *Monday Night Football*, it'll be CJ's Terrell Owens against my Plaxico Burress, Hines Ward, and 18 cushion points.

I can't help but think that 18 points just isn't enough.

Turns out, I was right: 18 points wasn't even close to being enough.

At exactly 9:32 P.M. EST last night, Terrell Owens caught the first ball thrown to him by Tim Rattay and took it about 60 yards to the house, immediately erasing my 18 point cushion and putting CJ up by 6. And Owens never looked back, in the end racking up 155 yards and that long score for a total of 45 Felon League points. And Plaxico and Ward? They just couldn't keep up, and in the end CJ's Charlemagnes, led by T.O., overtook me to win by 14 points, 113–99.

As expected, *Monday Night Football* bites me in the ass again! It's gotten to the point that, like one of Pavlov's dogs, whenever I hear John Madden's and Al Michaels's voices, I immediately fall onto the floor, curl into the fetal position, start crying, and soil myself. If the FF gods have any mercy whatsoever in their souls, they will not make me suffer the indignity of having to endure another *MNF* matchup. Which, of course, means that I'll be sweating out another one next week.

After eleven roller-coaster FF weeks, our beloved Acme squad is now 7-4, good for third place. Two more regular-season games to go. A win next week against the Dream Team *might* seal a playoff bid, but as I've learned all too well, a lot can happen in this crazy game. And when it *does* happen, it usually happens to me. And it usually hurts, in a proctology exam kinda way.

31

FF Rehab

It's the Saturday before the Week 12 games and something is dreadfully wrong. Well, let me amend that—lots of things are dreadfully wrong, but one in particular.

Depsite that we're less than a week from one of football's highest holy days— Thanksgiving, second only to the playoffs and the Super Bowl for pure pro football gluttony—outside it's a balmy, humid seventy-two degrees. Don't be alarmed. Global warming hasn't finally struck with a polar-ice-cap-melting vengeance and turned the planet's climatic infrastructure upside down. It's only this hot outside because, right now, I'm writing my FF diatribes while firmly planted in the Cordillera Central mountain chain on the island of Puerto Rico.

But of course, you're thinking. *Football. Puerto Rico. It's the classic combination!*

Trust me, I'm as confused and bewildered as you are about my being in the rural boonies of the Guajataca Forest, this time of year, so far from civilization. *Edgy* is more like it. After all, no civilization means no instant access to the Internet, no cell phone service, no ESPN, no last-minute Huddle injury updates, no nothing. The FF information umbilical cord has been severed. I'm adrift on an island—literally. We've been here since Thursday morning, two days now.

Please, don't get me wrong: being on one of the more beautiful islands in the Caribbean isn't what I would call a bad thing, especially considering it's probably twenty-five degrees and drizzling slush up in Boston. And, it's nice being so far away from everything with the woman I love. But, as Week 12 draws near, it's also a little too far from the Acme team I love.

With the playoffs hanging in the balance and some potentially season-making lineup decisions to be made, I feel like Steve McQueen in *Papillon*, the classic flick about France's infamous, inescapable island penal colony, Devil's Island. It's as if Celia has staged her own one-woman FF intervention. Under the guise of telling me it's a Thanksgiving vacation—kind of like telling the dog he's going to the park to play ball with the other dogs when in fact he's being taken to the vet to be neutered—she's whisked me off to an FF rehab facility of sorts, high up in the mountains away from all FF temptations. I'm surprised she didn't confiscate my belt and shoelaces when we checked in.

But I shouldn't complain. This is a beautiful place. And after the three-night stint up here in Che Guevara's mountain hideaway, it'll be off to the west coast of the island, first to the surfing/resort town of Rincón for two days of beachside fun, followed by three more days in the city of Mayagüez, where Hugo, Celia's mom's husband, grew up. We'll be spending Thanksgiving with his large and, from what I hear, loud, friendly, fun family, enjoying some turkey, stuffing, cranberry . . . and rice and beans: the traditional Thanksgiving feast. And if you think I'm *not* already wondering whether they have DirecTV for the Packers-Lions and Cowboys-Dolphins games, you're nuts.

(Oh, and I must stress one thing: while this little Caribbean excursion might make you say, "Heyyyy, now wait one goddamn minute . . . you said you were unemployed and scraping by on your meager savings, you lying son of a bitch!" please don't think I've conned you here and that Celia and I are independently wealthy, globe-trotting trust-fund babies. Fact is, we had planned this Thanksgiving trip more than a year ago, long before I decided to quit my job to play FF full-time and had already paid for the *nonrefundable* plane tickets and hotels with the money we *used to have*, so we figured, what the hell?)

As the torrential rain beats down on our little glorified camping cabin, I'm tormented, thinking about my corp of WRs who have sucked donkey butt pretty much all year long. Was Plaxico's 92-yard performance last week a mirage, or is he (and the woeful Steelers offense) finally ready to snap out of his season-long funk, and therefore should I start him at Cleveland tomorrow (oddly enough, Plax is averaging about 70 more yards on the road this year than within the "friendly" confines of Pittsburgh's Heinz Field)? Is Marvin going to get enough playing time on that fragile hamstring to warrant me starting him, or should I just play it safe and go with Ward and Plaxico one more week and wait until Marvin is back at full strength? (But the reason you traded for Marvin in the first place, I tell myself, was to run him and Ward out there until the cows come home, Marvin and Ward, Marvin and Ward, Marvin and Ward, every week until you bring home the FFL title, knock on wood, so why wouldn't you start him even if he's only 75 percent healthy?)

But what to do now? Sounds strange, but now would be the worst possible time for Plaxico to start acting like *last year's* Plaxico and reel off a string of monster games, mostly because our trade deadline has passed, meaning all he'd be is another great WR on my bench. Dammit, I hate lineup conundrums!

Of course, I'm assuming here that this little jungle getaway spot will allow me to use the office computer. Celia, intentionally or not (I'm betting intentionally) has chosen a location that more or less resembles *Gilligan's Island* on the modern-amenity scale. There's one ancient-looking, communal pay phone that might as well be two coconuts held together with a vine or one of the Professor's other useless, wacky inventions. And even if it *does* work, it's not like there's a twenty-four-hour FF hotline I can call to make lineup changes. (Yes, that's a free business idea should one of you want to run with it; just give me some credit, OK?)

In other words, unless a miracle happens by game time tomorrow and I find computer and/or cell-phone access all the way out here, I might have to just blindly throw myself on the mercy of the FF gods and trust that they, in all their glorious benevolence (he said, shamelessly kissing their asses), will help a poor, helpless fool like myself win this week's game using *last week's* lineup.

I might have to trust that going with Ward and Plaxico for one more week will be the right move (or nonmove, as the case may be), and that I should ignore the burning urge to hop into our rented Toyota Corolla and make the treacherous, twisting, turning half-hour drive back to Utuado (the closest thing resembling a town), hope my cell phone works, call Shergul, and have him check on Marvin's status for me.

But who knows, maybe for once I can go a day without *any* fantasy football interaction whatsoever? Maybe I should give this whole FF rehab thing an honest try, just to test myself? I mean, it's supposed to be just a game, right? Something to make the NFL season a little more interesting, as opposed to something that—and this is just a hypothetical here—has you so bent out of shape that you're actually considering selling your wife to the locals in exchange for directions to the nearest Internet cafe?

Maybe this will be good for me. I admit I've been taking this whole FF thing very seriously this year, too seriously, perhaps.

It's all starting to wear on Celia, I can tell. On the eve of her birthday—the *Monday Night Football* game that featured Terrell Owens (of CJ's Charlemagnes team) single-handedly kicking my ass—we had a rockin' argument that stemmed from my shitty mood after I realized I'd lost my game. You heard me . . . on the eve of Celia's birthday. You *never* mess with a woman's birthday (something I learned the hard way a few years back when I stupidly gave her the romantic gift of stationery). I let a stupid FF game ruin my mood and start her birthday off on a shitty note, something I still feel horrible about.

Is it possible that I can make it up to her by going cold turkey, at least for this short time? Can I give her the brief respite from my obsession she so deserves?

I'll try. I swear I'll try. But between you and me, I'm already starting to shake and hallucinate, seeing Internet-ready computers in the bushes. FF message boards scrolling up and down the bark of palm trees. And the pool guy? He eerily resembles Priest Holmes. Not good. But, I somehow last until Sunday morning.

Creeping out on my tiptoes in search of a merciful FF fix while Celia sleeps, I walk up to the main office and ask the humorless woman at the desk if there's Internet access anywhere nearby, and if so, can she possibly—

"No," she answers before the words are even all the way out of my mouth, this despite her blatantly sitting in front of a PC with an Internet Explorer home page on the screen, taunting me.

"No?" OK, Mark, ignore overwhelming evidence to the contrary. Regroup. Play the polite card. "I'm sorry to bother you, but I can't help but notice that the computer right there—"

"No Eeenternet," she says, covertly rolling her swivel chair a few inches to the left and now blocking out the whole PC with her body, as if

I'll believe the computer has disappeared if I can't *actually see it*, like a kid covering his eyes and playing peekaboo.

"What about in Utuado?" I ask. "Is there maybe an Internet cafe or something there?"

"No, ees not." Still looking right at me—she clearly believes that if she takes her eyes off me for one second, I'll put her in a sleeper hold, jab her in the neck with a syringe KGB-style, and commandeer the computer while she lies slumped in the corner—she covertly reaches back behind her and with a deft swoop of the mouse puts the computer to "sleep."

The polite card is slipping out of my grasp. I mean, for Christ's sake it's not as if I've asked how I can score some roofies and a few underage local girls. "So you're saying no Internet, huh? What if I said it was an emergenc—"

"You hafa talka to dee owner," she interrupts again, sighing and glaring at me through untrusting eyes.

"OK, no problem. When is he back? *When can I talka to him?*"

"Martes. Toos-day." She says this proudly, as if she *knows* I need to set my lineup in just a few hours. And worse, I *know* she knows, and now she's screwing with me because I'm in a weakened, helpless state of FF detox. I officially loathe her.

Thwarted once and for all, I walk back to our bungalow wondering how I can get my hands on a syringe and a KGB training manual.

So now, here I am back on the porch of our bungalow, swaying nervously in a hammock—helpless, scared, twitchy, biting a nail (for more good luck?), eyes darting left and right, hallucinating Priest skimming the pool while Trent Green chops mangoes in the kitchen. Yes, folks, whether I like it or not, I *have to* go cold turkey today. Either that or I'll go completely bonkers and pull a full-on Colonel Kurtz out here in the heart of FF darkness. I mean it, I'm about to snap. Going cold turkey means that for this all-important Week 12 our beloved Acme squad will have to go rudderless, drifting through the FF waters without a captain at the helm, hopefully not running aground on a reef and tearing a gaping hole in the hull through which Priest, Davis, Green, Plaxico, Marvin, Ward, Heap, the Bucs D, and Wilkins will be sucked out into the freezing-cold water and devoured by circling sharks.

The horror . . . the horror . . .

• • •

As expected, FF cold turkey sucked. On more than one occasion I considered taking the total Robert Downey Jr. route and leaping the walls to freedom in the middle of the night.

But, I have to admit, there's something kind of cool about arriving in Rincón (on the west coast of the island) and having no idea whatsoever how my team did yesterday. I feel as if this were the beginning of a whole new season, the first day of the rest of my life, as the twelve-steppers say. After all, these next two weeks—NFL Weeks 12 and 13—are the most important of the season. They will determine whether our beloved Acme squad will storm the playoffs for the first time since 2000 or suffer a monumental collapse and find ourselves on the outside looking in. Again,

Yes, I've made it through an entire Sunday of football without having a single clue how my FF team did. None. Zero. Zip. And as Celia and I twist and wind our way into the palm-tree-covered surfing town of Rincón, I realize something odd—I don't care!

Can you believe that? I, the most obsessed FF player I know, just don't care whether I won or lost yesterday! Seems that in just two nights of remote-mountain FF rehab, the FF toxins have been purged from my bloodstream. I'm clean. It didn't take any therapy, not the conventional kind anyway. It didn't take any walking over coals or snake-handling to oust the evil FF spirits who've been possessing me. No, it only took a couple of days alone with my wife in a place where Priest, Marvin, and even my erstwhile FF man-crush Stephen Davis just weren't invited. It took a night out at a quaint shack-of-a-bar down the street with live music, a chatty owner, and ice-cold Medalla beers (the Budweiser of Puerto Rico). And best of all, it didn't even involve any shaking, vomiting, or hearing suicidal voices!

The usual angst and worry of game day has been replaced by an overwhelming feeling of—what's this strange sensation? . . . Can it be? . . . No, it can't be, can it? . . . Yes, it is—optimism! Hope! Trust that all will work out in the end! This is the beginning of a "new way."

I just *know* I've won. Who needs the stinking Internet? Who needs to follow CBS SportsLine all afternoon, cringing and sweating out every screen refreshment? I don't even need to go watch those ESPN highlights playing on the TV hanging over the bar, showing the Dallas-Carolina game and—

—WAIT, ESPN HIGHLIGHTS?! HOLY MONKEY, GET ME OVER
THERE!

Like Carl Lewis on amphetamines, I leap over two, three umbrella
tables at once and land directly on a barstool right in front of the bartender, who, from the startled look on his face, might be reaching for a can
of Mace or a baseball bat. Behind me, I don't even have to look at Celia
to know that she's shaking her head, watching her carefully crafted plans
of rehab go right down the toilet. One look at ESPN—the pipe that deliv-
ers my crack, the needle that injects my heroin—is all it takes to send me
right back down the dangerous, self-abusive path of FF destruction. I'm
a junkie again. And I'm loving it! Ah, sweet, sweeeeeeeet football. It's
good to have you back in my bloodstream!

But as quickly as the euphoria comes, I feel hollow, empty, wanting
more but not sure when or where I'll get it. Since *SportsCenter* is mixing
in NFL highlights with annoying NHL and NBA game recaps, I turn to
my cell phone for answers, but there's no Web service. So, I'm at the
mercy of the highlights, and I immediately revert to my old ways: brood-
ing, wringing my hands, worrying about my team, sure that the Dream
Team's studs have all had career days while my guys went in the tank.

I'm losing it again, and there's nothing I can do about it. As the highlights continue, I see that at least my stud RBs didn't let me down.
Priest, bless his heart, had 191 total yards (100 receiving! Hello FFL bonus
points!) and a TD for 39 FFL points. Stephen Davis had 59 hard-earned
yards and a TD against the stingy Dallas run defense for a serviceable 15
FFL points. And Trent Green, my starter now that I've traded Peyton, had
a halfway decent day, threw no INTs and had 244 yards and a TD for 15
FFL points. So, I know I at least have 69 points, which isn't great, but
depending on how Ward and Plaxico did, I could be in good shape.

But then, as it reveals the team leaders in each stat category, ESPN's
bottom-line scroll more or less picks up my drink and tosses it in my face.
How bad were my WRs? I'd say that Ward and Plaxico sucked, but that
would be giving them *far* too much credit, and my eyes widen in horror
as I learn that Plaxico led the entire Pittsburgh receiving corps with 16
yards. Yes . . . 16 total yards . . . for an entire game . . . four quarters of football, folks. Ward didn't even get 10 yards. Their total FFL points? One,
count 'em, 1 point. And Marvin, who I was going to start had I had cell
phone access up there in the mountains? He didn't go off, but managed

47 yards while running around on one gimpy hammy—not a good day for a stud like Marvin Harrison, but 3 points better than sad sacks Ward and Plaxico *combined*!

And the cherry on the sundae? The always-run-oriented Ravens had 344 yards passing and 4 TDs and none of them went to Heap. I didn't even know the Ravens *had* wide receivers before today, but apparently former Chicago Bears one-year-fantasy-wonder Marcus Robinson, who I believe has been refilling water cups on the Ravens' sidelines all year, chose this weekend to catch *all* 4 TDs from backup QB Anthony Wright, not even leaving any scraps for my boy Heap. This is inexplicable. So now with my TE and WRs basically having shit the bed, it's up to my kicker and my defense to get me even a few measly points if I'm going to have any hope of winning. I soon learn that my robo-kicker Jeff Wilkins had a very good day, with 4 FGs and an XP, for 13 FFL points. So, once again, it'll come down to *Monday Night Football* where my Bucs D takes on the Giants.

As for the Dream Team's players, if memory of their usual lineup serves, the only guys I'm sure they started are Marc Bulger and Clinton Portis, both of whom had good days, with Portis rushing for 165 yards and Bulger throwing for 329 and a TD. Of course. Why wouldn't they? After all . . . *they're playing against me.* Thankfully, however, Portis never found the end zone and Bulger threw 4 picks (at minus 3 points per), so they only totaled 41 FFL points.

But thanks to our self-imposed exile down here in paradise, I have no idea who the Dream Team's #2 WR is, nor their TE, kicker, or defense. There are just too many blanks to fill. I just have to assume that those slots are filled with players who racked up huge points because . . . well, because they're playing against our beloved Acme squad and that's what players have been doing to us all year long.

OK, screw this. I can't take the suspense anymore. I've tried my damnedest to play it cool down here and just let the chips fall where they may without knowing the specifics about my game, but I just . . . can't . . . do . . . it . . . anymore! I *have* to know the *exact* score going into *MNF,* and who *exactly* the Dream Team started.

Time to send the Shergul signal.

Moments later, Celia (whom I've dragged with me under the pretense of grabbing an authentic Puerto Rican lunch) and I are sitting in our sporty Toyota Corolla in the dirt parking lot of a no-frills seafood taco joint—I'm dialing Shergul, she's looking at me with a mix of pity, worry, and frustration, perhaps wondering where her FF rehab project went wrong. Can she sit idly by while I relapse and return to obsessing about my team while on vacation? Should she have taken me farther away than Puerto Rico? Somewhere more primitive, remote, and cell-phone free? I can see these and countless other questions racing through her mind as Shergul answers.

"I knew you'd be calling sooner or later," he says smugly before I can even speak, and I can almost see him grinning on the other end of the crackly line. "Just can't stay away, can you?"

"Actually, I have no idea how my players did," I blatantly lie. "I don't even know who Steve and Joe started." I'm trying to sound cool and casual, as if FF is the last thing on my mind as I go with the tropical flow down here. *Hakuna matata.* Don't worry, be happy. All that shit. Shergul, I don't have a care in the world, my friend—I'm on vacation! And he's not buying it for one second.

"Whatever," he says. "Anyway, you're up eighty-six to sixty-one, I think." *Yes!* I internally pump my fists and do the wave, which isn't nearly as impactful with one person, let me tell you. "But," Shergul continues with a tone of dread, "he's got McCardell and Barber going tonight against your Bucs D. Doesn't look good." *Shit!* I internally stop doing the wave and give the finger to Steve and Joe. Even though I already knew in the back of my mind that they'd start the *MNF* players, I was holding out a sick hope that they'd somehow started Henry and his modest 77-yard/no-TD game, over Tiki.

"The only reason I know your score is that I need you to beat the Dream Team, so I was checking your game, too," he adds in the same phony casual tone that I gave him not thirty seconds earlier. "Looks like we're both losing out this week. Oh, well."

"Whatever," I volley right back to him, knowing full well that no matter how much we try to bullshit each other with this stilted, pathetic laissez-faire attitude toward Week 12, he knows that I've been absolutely *dying* to know my score, and *I* know that *he* was checking my score because he was checking every score in the league, all day long, minute after minute, every time there was a scoring change in the little upper-right-hand corner of the Fox or CBS games. And I guarantee you that every time something good happened for one of the Dream Team's players, Shergul swore or cringed just as I would have had I been able to watch the games and follow the Felon League matchups with my usual zest and concentration. Shergul is pulling for me this week, big-time. His own playoff chances depend on it. As much as he probably doesn't want to see me—his mortal FF nemesis—succeed, he needs me to beat the Dream Team.

But, sadly, as he said, it looks as if we'll both be done in by a mutual enemy this week. He would be all but knocked out of playoff contention, and my chances would become a little slimmer (though better than his, thanks to my points total).

Don't worry, Mark, the warm Caribbean breeze sings to me (in a Jamaican accent, of course) as we get out of the Corolla and walk into the rustic little roadside cantina where we'll eat our 1,256th meal of rice, beans, and fish . . . *be happy.*

Easy for you to say, I snap back to the meddling breeze. *You're not the one going against Tiki and McCardell tonight. You're not the one who was held hostage in an FF rehab facility up in the mountains, unable to make a possible game-saving lineup decision to start Marvin over one of those two useless Steelers. You're not the one who might not even make the damn play-offs.* Oh, I add, *and that Bobby McFerrin song sucked!*

The breeze tells me that last one was a low blow.

That evening, despite that the Bucs-Giants game is on TV and would be my first live NFL fix in the past ten days (aka a fucking eternity), I just can't bring myself to watch it. Nope. Can't do it.

It's one thing to know that you're going to lose an important game; it's quite another to see it with your very own eyes. Why should I subject myself to that kind of frustration? I saw what it did to me when Terrell Owens kicked my ass a week ago. It turned me into a bitter, mean old curmudgeon—on Celia's birthday eve, no less! I'm not going to do that to her again. Look, I *know* McCardell will blow up. I *know* Tiki will blow up. I know that my Bucs D can't make up that difference. I know Acme is falling to 7-5. As Agent Smith of *The Matrix*—or Steve Oh from the Hershey Highway League—would say, it is the "sound of inevitability." Why make myself suffer more than I have to? I'll just wake up tomorrow, grab a paper at some point, check out the box score, see Keenan and Tiki's huge games, sigh, and look toward next week (Week 13), when my entire season will be on the line.

So as game time rolls around and the raucous cheers and shouts of my fellow guests pour into our second-floor room from the tiki bar below, Celia and I watch the furthest possible thing from NFL football: the *American Idol* Christmas special.

Yeah, yeah, I know—admitting to watching Clay Aiken sing "Holly Jolly Christmas" instead of watching a crucial MNF/FF game is like announcing that you're a child molester on your first day in a new prison. But, it accomplishes two things: (1) it saves me from a certain coronary and, by extension, prevents Celia from being a young widow; and (2) it makes Celia think that her rehab plan has maybe worked in some small way, and honestly, scary as this may sound, my wife's happiness is more important to me than fantasy football.

Now, if you'll excuse me, Clay's launching into "Winter Wonderland."

Walking in a Winter Wonderland indeed!

Why am I so excited? Well, I drove down the street— where for some reason our cell-phone Web access works, even though it *doesn't* work one hundred yards away back in our room—and discovered that despite all my bitching and moaning . . .

. . . we freaking WON last night! When all was said and done, Tiki Barber and Keenan McCardell only combined for 16 measly points, and my Bucs D racked up 11 more. Translation: Acme 97, Dream Team 77.

The Dream Team had been scoring in droves all year, but this week, they racked up a paltry 77, while Priest and Davis—my most reliable studs—got me through. FF, just like the real NFL, is a game of inches. Every point counts. **Newbie Strategy Tip #16: The schedule always finds a way to even out over a season, so don't panic if you're getting hammered by high scores early on.** I was the poster boy for bad schedule luck out of the gates, but eventually I caught some teams on their down weeks. So, don't panic and make dumb trades early on if you believe that you have the players (read: studs) to get you through the tough patches. Week 12's game is a prime example of that.

So, heading into Week 13, the final week of the regular season, Project Kick My League's Ass and our beloved Acme squad are 8-4. But that's not the only good news. I just got off the phone with Shergul again, and he informed me that . . . drumroll please . . . we've clinched a playoff spot!

That's right, folks, you heard me: Acme is in the Big Dance, baby! The Felon League Playoffs! I can't believe it, I've actually accomplished a goal I set out to accomplish! No more C-plus/B-minus! No more "whatever," Mr. Briggs! First playoffs in three years, baby! I feel like singing! Where's Clay Aiken when you need him?

The next day, to celebrate Acme's playoff berth, Celia and I go on a scuba-diving excursion to the tiny island of Desecheo, thirteen miles off the coast. Well, I was celebrating the playoffs, anyway; Celia, while happy for me, just wasn't *as* excited.

Thanksgiving

Ah, there's nothing like not having any FF pressure on you for the Thanksgiving games! I don't have any Lions, Packers, Cowboys, or Dolphins on my roster, so I can just sit back and enjoy today's games the old-fashioned way. In the past, I've been known to hurl wedges of pumpkin pie at the TV screen if things aren't going my way fantasy-wise on Turkey Day. Or, I've been seen clapping and giggling like a schoolgirl if they *are* going well (e.g., Randy Moss's Thanksgiving Day massacre of Dallas back in '98). Either reaction is embarrassing. I wouldn't wish it on anyone.

But this year, not having to worry about any players today means one relaxing afternoon of food and football-watching. Yes, I said "football-watching." Even though we're still in Puerto Rico, I don't have to worry about whether I'll be able to see today's NFL games. Until we came to this wonderful island, I'd never seen so many satellite dishes in my entire life. Seriously, they're everywhere: Hotels have them. Gas stations have them. Restaurants, bars, hair salons. But it's mostly in the various neighborhoods we've visited that we've seen this utter dominance of the Comcast empire. Even the tiniest, most ramshackle tin shacks have satellite dishes. They're sometimes bigger than the houses themselves, making me wonder whether the occupants of said shacks should just put a few cots up in the dishes themselves and save on the rent.

So, of course, Hugo's mom, Divina, has a big, fat satellite dish dominating her roof. Hence, while I'm filling up on that traditional Thanksgiving dinner of turkey, stuffing, rice, beans, and fried plantains, I will not have to starve myself of NFL football, a key staple of Thanksgiving ever since 1621 when the Pilgrims defeated the Wampanoag Indians, 14–13, on a controversial last-second touchdown by early Plymouth Plantation resident Tobias Cooke. (The Wampanoag claimed Cooke's knee was down on the 1-yard-line but Governor William Bradford—no shock here—overturned their challenge. Though not widely reported, this was just the first of many total screwings we colonists would give our Native American predecessors over the centuries.)

Hugo's mom, and sister, Divi, live in a modest, four-room ranch house in Mayagüez, a lively, crowded, working-class port city of just over a hundred thousand people where music blares, neighbors chat, traffic honks, and the heat beats down from above. And what a day they give us! Hugo's family and friends—about thirty people stop in and out over the day—are warm, welcoming, fun, and eager to help me speak my *niño*-(baby)-level Spanish while I help them with their English. The games, especially the Lions upsetting the Packers, are exciting, and I feel closer to home just watching them. I'm full of beans—literally—as I sit on the couch next to Mama, who has kindly allowed me to watch football in place of her favorite *novelas* (soap operas). I occasionally try my best to explain some of the rules to her in my broken Spanish, which I can tell she appreciates, smiling often, nodding, laughing, in part because she clearly enjoys having her oldest son and his new family here, but also because while trying to say things like "It's a touchdown when the man carrying the football crosses that white line," I'm actually saying, "Man crosses the line when he touches his balls with his foot."

Despite all this contentment—new extended family, new friends, great food, an FFL playoff berth firmly in my grasp—somewhere in the back of my mind, lurking like a stalker, ready to pounce out of the bushes when I get home, is Week 13. See, when we fly home on Saturday, we have to stop at my friend Bill's wedding that night in Philly, and then, assuming I can find computer access the next day—which shouldn't be hard in a hotel—I have to get back to work on my team. Already the questions are mounting: will Marvin be healthy enough to start? Should I sit Green in place of the red-hot Jon Kitna? (Kitna was an under-the-rader component of the Peyton-Marvin trade with Big Dogs, but one I secretly counted on bearing fruit at some point. He was money down the stretch last year for those same Big Dogs, when they took home the 2002 FFL title.)

Most important, I find myself wondering whether, with a victory over the mighty, high-scoring Rat Bastards, I will leapfrog into second place overall, which would mean a first-round playoff bye. Huge. I've already beaten Josh once head-to-head this year (remember my improbable victory against Jamal Lewis's 295-yard, 2 TD game back in Week 2?), and if we both finish at 9-4, I'll pass him into second place. But not having had access to our CBS website this past week, I haven't been able to assess all of the possible playoff scenarios. But you can bet your ass that once we get to the DoubleTree Hotel in Philly, I'm making a beeline to the business center and some sweet, sweeeeet Internet access.

32

Messenger of the Gods

Adam Duritz of Counting Crows once sang, "A long December and there's reason to believe maybe this year will be better than the last." (And to give credit where credit's due, the great ESPN.com columnist Bill Simmons eventually used this same line in a funny piece about Red Sox Nation's optimism after the early-December Curt Schilling signing . . . but, Bill, I swear, I already had this chapter written!) Anyway, that melancholy yet optimistic song, "A Long December," plays over and over in my head as I—just as I knew I would—sit here in the business center of the DoubleTree Hotel in downtown Philly as November gives way to December, and my playoff seeding hangs in the balance. Yes, we've clinched a playoff spot, but a win today and we could snag a first-round playoff bye.

It's 9:20 A.M. Celia is sleeping off a possible hangover sixteen floors above. I'm fighting a bit of booze-fueled grogginess myself (my college buddies and I were all drinking those unnecessary "last beers" at 2:30 A.M. as the sleepy, overworked bartender flicked the lights on and off in the Ritz lobby in a vain attempt to tell us that while we didn't have to go home, we couldn't stay there). I figure I have at least an hour before she wakes up and wants to hit the road, a daunting task on this, the Sunday after Thanksgiving, the biggest travel day of the year. Like morons, we've rented a car and will be joining the fray on I-95. But not before I get my team squared away. Being back on a computer—alone, with no distractions (read: Celia hovering over my shoulder wanting to leave), no time or money restrictions, no cell-phone limitations—is pure, unadulterated heaven. I spend almost an hour and a half getting caught up on everything I've missed over the past ten days. I read about twenty stories on the Curt Schilling trade to the Red Sox (I love the image of Stein-brenner throwing a hissy fit; maybe spilling cocktail sauce on his nice, white turtleneck). I digest all the latest Pats news and read about their big game on the road today against the mighty Colts.

Most important, I'm back in touch with my Acme team. I scour injury reports and news. I spend time in the Huddle checking Dorey and Whit-ney's start/bench lists and game predictions, reading posts in the forums, all the stuff that is the FF equivilant of reentering earth's atmosphere after floating isolated in deep space. Marvin is good to go today. Priest and Davis are healthy. Ward, despite his 13-yard day last weekend, seems ready to bust out against Cincinnati. Plaxico? Screw Plaxico, that mutt. He's benched as I officially usher in the Marvin Harrison era. The only tough decision I have to make is whether to go with Green against the sorry Chargers or Kitna against division rival Pittsburgh. My gut says Kitna, but the easy matchup favors Green. Literally, I go back and forth, clicking "Active . . . Reserve . . . Active . . . Reserve" about ten different times, swap-ping Green and Kitna in and out.

Finally, at about 10:55 A.M., I realize that we have to check out in a mat-ter of minutes and hit the road if we're going to have any chance in the traditionally horrific post–Thanksgiving traffic. I have to make a decision, pronto. Green's in there now. Yes, I think Kitna will have a big day against the equally woeful Steelers D, but division games are tricky, and that AFC North tends to feature grind-it-out, low-scoring affairs that are fantasy killers. Green is the safer bet. But Kitna has been on fire lately, his receivers (Chad Johnson, Peter Warrick, rookie Kelley Washington) are becomg a studly trio, and he'll at least match Green. Kitna's the right call here. No wait—Green is. OK, Kitna it is, go with Kitna. But Green was your original draft pick, you must have liked him for some reason . . . where's your loyalty? Fuck loyalty, FF is all business. Aww, screw it, I say to myself, go with your initial gut instinct—Kitna.

So, that's that. Done deal. I'm going with Kit—

Poof!

What? What happened? Just as I'm about to activate Kitna and bench Green once and for all, the computer crashes. In the blink of an eye, CBS SportsLine disappears, replaced by a black screen and a binking cursor, at which point a bespectacled face suddenly peers around the little cubicle wall.

"Oh, God. Shit. I'm sorry."

It's the clean-cut, fortysomething-looking guy who's been working on his laptop next to me this whole time. Poor guy. He looks truly worried—downright frantic—that he's messed something up for me. "I'm so sorry," he says again. "I was trying to plug in my CD burner and I accidentally hit the power strip down there. Shit, I hope I didn't make you lose anything important. Man, I'm really sorry. Shit."

"No problem," I say, standing up and putting on my coat, wishing I had a .38 in my pocket. "I wasn't writing my manifesto. Just doing some fantasy football stuff." *(I was only deciding a key component of the game that could get me a first-round playoff bye, no big deal!)*

"Yeah, I saw your CBS league home page when I came in," he says. "My league uses CBS, too."

Ah, the *Fight Club* Theory makes yet another cameo. We're everywhere. Plain and simple.

"I'm getting my ass kicked this year," he sighs, clearly forgetting about my computer problems now that his FF problems have the floor. "I took McNabb in the first round and it was all downhill from there. I'm a huge Eagles fan and I just couldn't resist. Should have taken Ahman Green, that was my gut feeling, but I'm such a pathetic homer I had to go with Donovan, the fat bastard. Then I took Boston too early and Tiki hasn't been too great, either. "How are you doing?" He means my team, of course—not me personally. He probably couldn't give a shit how I'm doing personally. We met thirty seconds ago. I tell him that I'm 8-4, third overall, second in points, and am totally torn between Green and Kitna this week. "Go with Trent," he says confidently. "He's my backup and I've benched him every week thinking that Jabba McNabb will snap out of it, and every week I've regretted it. And KC plays San Diego this week. Kitna's been hot, but I have a feeling that Pittsburgh will shut down Cincy at home. Green's your man."

"Funny you say that," I say, pointing to my dormant computer. "I was just about to start Kitna when the thing shut down. Maybe you were trying to tell me something. But I'm OK with Green."

But the truth is, deep down I'm *not* OK with Green. My gut says Kitna. That's why I was about to activate him and be on my way. **Newbie Strategy Tip #17: Gather as much information as possible, weigh the options carefully, compare defenses, weather conditions, whatever you have to** do . . . but in the end always, *always* go with your gut. I think he senses my apprehension. "Don't worry, Green's going to tear San Diego apart. Good luck. And sorry about the computer thing." With that he disappears back into his cubicle and begins click-clacking on his laptop once again.

I walk out of the business center, wondering what just happened in there. Who was this messenger of the FF gods, this wing-footed, laptop-wielding Mercury? Was this their crafty, celestial way of telling me that I should stick with Green, by sending a bespectacled, plug-pulling messenger boy to sabotage my computer and prevent me from making a last-minute blunder? Or, my more suspicious side chimes in, maybe it's their way of saying, "We know you were going with Kitna, and he *is* going to have a huge day against the shitty Steelers just as your gut told you. But we're going to make you start Green anyway . . . and why? Because we're the mother-effing FF gods and that's what we do." Maybe my cubicle-mate in there was not a messenger at all, but rather an assassin sent to kill my chances of beating the Rat Bastards, finishing the Felon League regular season in second place overall, and attaining that precious first-round bye.

Whom can I trust? The *Fight Club* Theory has taken an unexpected turn. To this point it has always been for the powers of good—for information-sharing, support, a nationwide brothers-and-sisters-in-arms network of FF fanatics all working together in the spirit of friendship, aid, comfort, help, understanding. But have the FF Gods now infiltrated my precious *Fight Club* and, through meddling counter agents like computer boy in there, begun to use it for the forces of evil to sabotage my season? And, in turn, ruin my life?

Perhaps . . . perhaps. Time will tell. A few hours, in fact. That's when Celia and I—traffic willing—will be at my brother Doug's house in Summit, New Jersey, reclining on his couch, watching today's games, and recuperating from the hangover that's beginning to grow larger, right along with my suspicion that I've been the victim of a covert, celestial FF screwing of unprecedented proportions.

Later, at Doug's

Trust no one . . . trust no one . . .

This is the phrase I keep thinking over and over as I watch the stats pile up that afternoon. Apparently, *Fight Club* has turned into the *X-Files*.

Green struggles against the lowly Chargers, throwing for only 200-something yards, 2 scores, and 2 INTs, good for 14 points—making him a pitiful twenty-first on the Felon League QB rankings this week behind such bottom-feeding QBs as Anthony Wright, Kordell Stewart, and Jake Delhomme. And Kitna? Well, the man I *was* going to start—until the FF gods' ham-fisted hit man rubbed out my computer, that is—put up 270 yards and 3 TDs (one long one) for 41 FFL points, good for the second-best QB performance of the week. Better than my former stud starter, Peyton. Better than Culpepper, McNair, Hasselbeck, all of 'em.

That's the bad news. The good news? Unlike his lame-ass teammate, Green, Priest tore up the Chargers for 48 FFL points, Davis had a solid 21 points, Ward had a fantastic game with 150 yards and a TD for 35 points, Marvin had a decent 80-yard, 1 TD game for 18 points, Wilkins (quietly the number one kicker in football, I might add) chipped in his usual 12 points. Bottom line, despite the meddling of the FF Gods . . . *I won!* Granted, it was close, with Blaz's Rat Bastards team putting up a valiant fight with Tomlinson nearly matching Priest, Anthony Wright (in for the injured McNair) coming out of nowhere for a big game, Holt going over 100 yards for the millionth time this year, and Jamal Lewis doing his normal thing and putting up nice numbers. But, our beloved Acme squad prevailed 154–130, meaning I've beaten Blaz twice this year, meaning that despite our identical 9-4 records and his higher points total, thanks to my two head-to-head wins (which is the first tiebreaker in our league; highest points is second), I leapfrog him into second place and grab that precious first-round bye.

Now *that's* more like it, guys! Back to my roots—winning high-scoring games. *That's* the Acme team I built out of the gates and improved with trades and pickups! *That's* the team that now has a nice, relaxing rest in Week 14 to prepare for our Week 15 playoff matchup, whoever that poor soul might be!

So with that, here we have the final Felon League regular-season standings:

Team	W	L	PF	PA
Account Guys	10	3	1,552	1,297
Acme FF, Inc.	9	4	1,693	1,560
Rat Bastards	9	4	1,754	1,321
Bonesky Crushers	8	5	1,291	1,147
Funk Soul Bros.	8	5	1,330	1,341
All-American Angus	7	6	1,610	1,426
The Pound Dawgs	6	7	1,107	1,146
Big Dogs	5	8	1,359	1,476
Charlemagnes	5	8	1,146	1,401
The Dream Team	4	9	1,464	1,491
SoCo	4	9	1,223	1,434
NH Hillbillies	3	10	1,139	1,628

The Dream Team is the poster child for our new playoff format (adding two extra playoff spots for high-scoring teams to counter the "luck factor"). Imagine that, a 4-9 team making the playoffs! But in their defense, they scored the fifth-most points in the FFL. At least the other "wild-card" entry, All-American Angus, was over .500 for Christ's sake. And poor Shergul . . . he finished with more points than the painfully average Bonesky Crushers (who sport the fifth-lowest points *for*, but benefited all season from the second-lowest points *against*). However, with both of them at 8-5, he lost out on the head-to-head tiebreaker, hence he's ousted from playoff contention. Them's the breaks. But Erik, co-owner of the Big Dogs, can't help but rejoice in Shergul's misery.

Erik: Am I the only one who's happy Shergul didn't get in?

To which Shergul responds:

Shergul: F*ck you all. I am extremely bitter. I'm out fair and square, but I played each matchup brilliantly with a crappy team. I started QBs

```
just to win a game, never once throwing up crazy
numbers. Oh well, at least the Big Dogs can blow me.
```

Kids, kids . . . come on now, play nice. Just because you've both been eliminated is no reason to start a catfight. Although I know I would have done the same thing had I been eliminated after all this time and hard work. Yes, unlike my fantasy nemesis, Shergul, I survived the wrath of the FF gods and overcame their giving me the second-highest points against. I survived the ups and downs of an average regular season. Project Kick My League's Ass is back in business and ready to bring home the title starting Week 15!

As for the Hershey Highway, Phil Kwan, who has been running away with the league to date, is now being stalked by both Samip (aka Teddy KGB) and Russo (aka White Monkey), with Sly and Cenk a couple games behind.

Team	W	L	PF
Kwan	10	3	1,041
KGB	9	4	949
Russo	9	4	840
Sly	7	6	955
Cenk	7	6	866
Tolga	6	7	975
Steve	6	7	899
Sujay	6	7	855
Kaan	6	7	782
T.K.	5	8	784
David	4	9	816
Wong	3	10	636

This league is still very much up for grabs because unlike many leagues who have the top four or six teams enter a single-elimination playoff tournament like the real NFL, the HH doesn't have playoffs, per se; rather, in rotisserie fashion, their champion is determined by overall record for *all* seventeen weeks. Many believe this is a good system as it eliminates the one-week luck factor that comes with a traditional playoff format, but foes say that the season-long rotisserie total record/points style eliminates that "any given Sunday" excitement that can come with a single-elimination playoff system, *and* that it allows Week 17, when most NFL playoff teams are resting their studs (or at least reducing their playing time), to play a role in the final standings. The HH guys wholeheartedly believe in their rules, however. "[The one-week luck factor] is why you can't have *just* a playoff system," Cenk tells me. "Based on head-to-head luck, our playoff final is likely to be me and Kaan, yet the *real* champion this year should definitely not be either one of us. Kaan is under .500, and yet in a playoff system he would be the champion of the league? That's just dumb. People who do [one-week, single-elimination] playoff systems need to realize how silly that is."

As for me, here I sit, trying to come to grips with having no game this weekend. Yes, I'm happy to have a bye week during which, hopefully, Marvin and Ward will heal up (hammy and glute injury, respectively). And I won't have to start Kitna against the Ravens, whose defense has been known to send even the best QBs crashing back to earth. But, still, with nothing riding on the games, I'm a little bored. So, to keep things interesting, I make a side bet with Shergul for ten bucks. ("Of course you did" was Celia's dry reaction when I told her about my extracurricular FF activity.) For the last few years, when knocked out of playoff contention, side bets were the only way I'd keep interested in FF after the season ended. Even though it inevitably ended in heartbreak, I just never wanted to admit that the season was over and it was time to move on. It was kind of like having a girlfriend who eventually cheated on me, and yet I wanted to keep trying to make it work with her. Pathetic, yes, but also endearing and loyal in a weird way. (Okay, maybe *just* pathetic.)

Anyway, this year's no exception. I need to make a side bet, but with one beautiful difference: I'm actually in the playoffs this year, so thankfully I only have to do so to pass the time for one, single weekend until my *real* postseason begins. It's just a way to keep my head in the game, not get complacent, keep my guys fresh, and give them something to play for on their "off week." After all, I don't want them getting stale while they lounge around in the plush Acme fantasy clubhouse—there's a fantasy flat-screen TV, fantasy pool table, fantasy Nintendo Gamecube, fantasy hot tub, I spare no imagination for my guys—and wait to see whom we'll be playing next week. Who knows, maybe we'll have some light no-pads workouts to prepare for the different defensive schemes we might face, whether it's All-American Angus, Rat Bastards, or Bonesky Crushers? Now if you'll excuse me, I have to go confer with my imaginary offensive coordinator and prepare for Week 15.

The FFL playoffs have begun. Week 14 is in the books.

While it's a shame to see the high-points team for the season, the Rat Bastards, get knocked out in the quarterfinals, that's exactly what happened. Yesterday, Josh's third-seeded team was vanquished by the sixth-seeded Dream Team, who lucked out behind an absolutely insane 5 touchdown day from their stud RB, Clinton Portis. That's the unpredictable side of fantasy football at work.

And, in the second quarterfinal matchup, my trading nemesis, the fourth-seeded Bonesky Crushers, dispatched fifth-seeded All-American Angus (the other high-points wild-card team), leading to the official semifinal pairings.

#6 Dream Team @ #1 Account Guys
#4 Bonesky Crushers @ #2 Acme Fantasy Football, Inc.

Both games project to be slugfests. Dream Team's Clinton Portis/Mike Vick combo could be scary. The Account Guys' Ahman Green could win their game all by himself against the woeful Chargers. Priest/Davis vs. Detroit/Arizona is nice for me. The resurgent Michael Bennett at Chicago and Ricky Williams vs. the porous Eagles run defense could be huge in Bonesky's backfield. Scary schedules all around. I'm not making hotel and rental-car reservations for Week 16 quite yet.

Because, first, I have to survive Week 15, the Felon League Playoff semifinals.

33

The Revenge of Joe Horn

At last, sweet God in heaven at last, playoff Sunday is here! Everything I've worked for, all the hours of interviewing, e-mailing, writing, researching, message-board-surfing—all of it has led to this moment. Our beloved Acme squad versus the Bonesky Crushers, just a few hours away!

Meanwhile, there's other relatively unimportant news today: they finally captured Saddam Hussein. On the videotape, his "spider hole" looks like Jame Gumb's basement in *Silence of the Lambs*. I personally like to imagine that, for the last eight months, Saddam has been held prisoner in a dank hole while some homicidal lunatic tells him, "It puts the lotion on its skin or it gets the hose again."

Regardless, I think his capture is a good omen for our beloved Acme squad, a sure sign that today will be a day of Good (Acme/Democracy) defeating Evil (Bonesky Crushers/Saddam)! Of liberation! Of freedom from the chains of FF failure that have bound me all these years! I am going to find that spider hole that the Felon League Championship has been hiding in all these years and, with great force, root it out and drag it into the light kicking and screaming if I have to. That said, when I win, I don't plan on firing a rifle into the air to celebrate, like the Iraqis. It's against condo rules.

Despite these good omens, I'm a little edgy about one crucial lineup decision today. It's the same dilemma I faced in Week 13 when I sat in the Philly DoubleTree business center flip-flopping and hemming and hawing—and that dilemma is, do I start Kitna or Green? Green or Kitna?

The argument for Green is simple: he's playing Detroit. The Lions secondary can't stop most Pop Warner teams. Plus, the Chiefs are coming off an embarrassing blowout at the hands of division rival Denver, so they might want to make a statement today with a points explosion. But the argument *against* Green is pretty sound, too: if the Chiefs go up big in the first half, they're bound to stop passing, which is good for Priest, but bad for Green, obviously. So the question is, are the numbers Green is likely to put up *before* KC downshifts into the running game going to be as good/better than the numbers Kitna will put up for an *entire game*? And then there's the "pro-Kitna" argument. The Bengals are fighting for their playoff lives, as is their opponent (the Niners), so it could be a shoot-out in Cincinnati today with both teams playing anything-you-can-do-I-can-do-better. And aside from a tough day against Baltimore last week, Kitna has been a stud Felon League QB all year. Plus, his WRs (Chad Johnson, Peter Warrick) are far better than the invisible stiffs in KC. They're usually good for a long TD or two per game, beefing up Kitna's FFL bonus points.

Translation? I'm already freaking out here, and it's only 8:30 A.M. I'm a wreck. I look worse than Hussein, who looks like someone beat him with a bicycle chain and then glued a fake beard to his face.

My gut first said, "Go with Kitna, you dolt," because Green exploded for 50 FFL points in week 14 and Kitna sucked (8 points), and I'm always skeptical of guys repeating monster performances two weeks in a row, whether they're monster-good or monster-bad. But then I started thinking about Detroit's secondary, which last time I checked included Stephen Hawking at strong safety, Howard Stern's "Beetlejuice" at free safety, my three-year-old nephew, Drew, at one corner, and the exhumed corpse of Eleanor Roosevelt at the other. "What are you waiting for?" I shouted at myself, "Green should tear them apart! Start Green!" But then I thought, "What if he only tears them apart for two quarters before the game gets out of hand and—God forbid!—Weepy Vermeil decides to bench him (or Priest!) to save him for the *real NFL* playoffs?" That would suck. Suck badly. And the Kitna-to-Johnson combo could be huge . . . big FFL points! Kitna could get more on two long TDs than Green might get all afternoon. Green? Kitna? Green? Dammit, why can't the FF gods send their DoubleTree Hotel assassin to make my decision for me *today*?

But then, just as I'm placing the paper bag to my mouth to stave off hyperventilation, I remind myself that I have an ace in the hole just for decisions like this. Or "aces," as the case may be.

Unlike past seasons, this year I've built an "FF Thinktank" of sorts over the past five months—all my interviewees—whom I can turn to in desperate moments like this. So like Batman to the Bat-pole, I rush over to the computer and fire off a group e-mail to my "ringers."

```
Me: Hi, guys, we're coming down to the wire in this
2003 FF season, and I'm in the playoffs for the
first time in three years. It's crunch time, so I
thought I'd ask a crucial lineup question for
today. (After all, you guys are the brains I've
picked over the course of the season, my "FF
Thinktank" of sorts, so who better to help me solve
this do-or-die QB dilemma?) Based on the majority
opinion combined with my sometimes-unreliable gut,
I'll go with that player. Anyway, here goes: KITNA
vs. SF or GREEN vs. DET? One-word answer or
detailed analysis . . . any input would be great.
```

The responses come in almost as quickly as the e-mail went out. All the helpful Ghosts of Interviews Past start appearing with advice. Hell, I even hear back from the now dormant Shergul, who is always glad to help me out with an opinion when it doesn't directly affect him. (Hey, you can't blame him; he's a competitor. But that's the beauty of being FF nemeses . . . when we're not competing *against* one another our fantasy rivalry often turns into something of an alliance. A shaky alliance—like Seinfeld and Newman—but an alliance nonetheless.)

```
Shergul: Tough call, BOTH have good matchups. They
also both lost and are mad and desperate. I'd go
Kitna on a hunch that KC can win games with Priest
alone AND it minimizes risk for you if KC is in a
funk. Plus, Kitna has Warrick/Chad . . .
```

(1–0, Kitna.)

Chris Schussman: HI, MARK, I WOULD GO WITH GREEN.
S.F. IS GOING TO BLITZ THE SHIT OUT OF KITNA. GOOD
LUCK!!!

(Tied 1–1.)

Cenk: Kitna vs. SF looks tempting, there have been
many games that the 49ers let up a lot of points
and Green might not pass much if KC starts beating
up on Detroit. All that being said, I STILL go with
Green. The reason—you always go with your better
player. You don't want to get cute and have it wind
up costing you. Green is still a better rotiss
player than Kitna, and he's had great numbers for
the last 6–8 weeks. If I were in your position, I
would put Green in and sleep well at night.

(2–1, Green.)
I soon hear back from some more.

Mark (a big air dog trainer from San Diego): Green
at DET . . . no-brainer. KC has a MUCH better
offense, Kitna's good fortune is running out. He
has shown marked improvement this year of course,
but since their midseason run, the Bengals have
only been average. Green has 20 TDs to 9 INTs this
season . . . plus, Holmes is WAY overdue for a
couple receiving touchdowns this season, as he has
none to date (hard to believe!) no-brainer here . . .

(3–1, Green.)

Max (Mark's roommate, a New Zealander turned
California FF freak): Green—no-brainer.

(4–1, Green.)

```
Jay (a surfer dude/restaurant manager from
Daytona): I like Kitna here. I firmly believe that
KC opens up a lead early and will pound the ball
with that Holmes guy. Even in bad weather it could
be somewhat of a shoot-out, which helps Kitna a
lot. Either way, I just don't see Green throwing a
lot. I have Green and I'm leaving him on the bench
for Hasselbeck. Good luck.
```

(4–2, Green.)

OK. Green's in the lead. I take a break to see what the guys in the Huddle might think and discover, to my relief, that I'm not the only one consumed with a silly little playoff lineup decision even on this historic day in U.S. military history, as the following post indicates:

```
Poster 1: Just announced . . . Hussein captured!!!!
Poster 2: Big deal. Should I start A-Train or
Domanick Davis?
```

I think that says it all. The war on terror has taken an unprecedented turn for the better, one of history's most diabolical despots has been captured and humiliated, and yet FF *still* marches on without skipping a beat. We're all looking for league championship trophies hidden in spider holes all across America, so there's no such thing as a "silly little lineup decision."

After weighing all the advice, and most important, following my gut, I finally go to CBS SportsLine and—hands trembling, eye twitching—make my QB decision: Green.

No turning back now.

Later that evening . . . the day games have ended and I'm neither happy nor sad. I'm just . . . neutral. Waiting. In a holding pattern. That's all I can do right now as the Saints and Giants prepare to take the field on the ESPN Sunday-night game. Too many things have to happen (or not happen as the case may be) for me to advance to the Felon League Super Bowl next weekend. I'll get to those in a second because, for now, I'm afraid to even move, for even the slightest motion might upset the precarious balance of my temporary lead, like Tiger lumbering into the *Brady Bunch* living room and knocking over the house of cards.

Instead, I'm just going to sit here quietly, all alone, barely breathing, in complete darkness aside from the eerie glow of the TV, and just . . . wait.

For now, I *will* tell you that it was probably a good thing Celia and I just spent the entire afternoon at our friend Scott and Colleen Madden's house, watching the Pats game and playing with their three kids. After all, FF junkies like myself have a couple of ways to spend a tense playoff afternoon:

(1) Sitting at home in front of multiple TVs with a computer nearby, agonizing over *every single* play of *every single* game, screaming, swearing, keeping track of *every single* point, minute by minute as clumps of your hair fall out and your wife starts programming Dr. Kevorkian on the speed dial.

(2) Out at a sports bar or some other public setting doing the exact same thing, but with two hundred other lunatics just like you sitting nearby—and also drinking beer—which not only increases the possibility of FF-fueled violence, but also raises the odds of your ending the evening by calling your wife for bail money.

(3) In some "neutral" environment where football is present, allowing you to covertly keep track of your games, but not so present that it consumes you and turns you into a bug-eyed, raging, drooling beast. Preferably, an environment where kids are around so you'll not only have to put a lid on the swearing, but also stifle the urge to hurl large objects (and perhaps the children themselves) through windows if things go bad.

Wisely, I chose number three. Scott and Colleen's was an extremely football-friendly environment. They're both huge Pats fans like myself, and Scott is also a huge fan of such indoor tailgate products as beer, steak sandwiches, nachos, and Brigham's ice cream. And with the game constantly on and a computer upstairs, the home was FF-friendly as well, but not *so* FF-focused that I was unable to enjoy the afternoon. Yes, the Madden house struck the perfect balance between football enjoyment and fantasy obsession. This was the right call. I was edgy enough already, so I definitely didn't need to be at home, alone (Celia would have fled the premises), going nuts while following the Acme-Bonesky game. So I was perfectly content to watch the Pats game, get my occasional updates via the CBS ten-minute ticker, and just trust that our beloved Acme squad would do the job.

And as the afternoon wore on, boy were they doing their job! Every time CBS flashed an update it was either Priest bringing one to the house or Marvin catching a TD pass from Manning. Heap had some good yardage against Cleveland. The only downer was the Jets-Steelers game, which looked like a washout with about eight inches of snow on the ground by midafternoon (something the Steelers would file an official league complaint about later), and Hines had a big, fat goose egg next to his name with every CBS update, so I had already written him off as a no-show. But hopefully that wouldn't come back to haunt me if Priest and Marvin continued their rampage. Plus, I had Davis going against the lowly Cards in the late game.

Oh, yeah. I'd be fine.

As for Bonesky, I was able to keep an eye on Jimmy Smith all afternoon since he was playing the Pats. He didn't do much . . . well, except for catching a 60-something-yard bomb on like the third play of the game, which made me stand up and *start* to yell "Fuck!" but then I paused, looked down at the kids coloring quietly on the floor, and quickly audibled at the line, changing the play call to a more toddler-friendly, "Fu*dge!*" But Bonesky's other players seemed to be doing well. Jeff Garcia was throwing TDs left and right. And the Bucs' Thomas Jones (*a lousy, no-good free agent, rent-a-player pickup Kevin made just a few days ago, the motherf$#!er!!*) was having a huge game against the Texans, already racking up a TD and over 100 yards. I swore right then and there, I was going to go nuclear if I lost a playoff game to a freaking free-agent pickup.

Bottom line, it was still way too close to call. And to top it all off, I'd have to wait until Tuesday morning—yet again! Why do the FF gods taunt me with *Monday Night Football* stress?!—to find out the final verdict. Bonesky had Joe Horn going in the late ESPN game against the weak-ass Giants secondary, and Ricky Williams and David Akers going in tomorrow's Dolphins-Eagles *MNF* matchup. Meanwhile, my guys would be done by late Sunday afternoon, meaning I'd just have to pray that my lead would be big enough.

When Celia and I got back to our place, and I performed my Carl Lewis–dash/Mary Lou Retton–somersault combo over to the computer, I discovered that Heap had caught a TD during our trip home and was pushing toward 100 yards receiving. Davis had been banged up but had 40-something yards rushing and would surely top 100 against the Swiss-cheese Cards D, right? Things were moving for Acme.

But then they stopped. Cold.

Priest finished with 94 rushing yards (6 measley yards short of the magical 100), and while he had 3 TDs, Weepy Vermeil rested him late in the game for Derrick Blaylock and screwed me on all kinds of bonus points. Heap ended with 93 yards and that lone TD (7 yards short of 100!). Davis pulled a Lara Flynn Boyle with a positively bulemic 47-yards rushing and 30-something receiving for a lame 7 FFL points (while his backup, Foster, scored 26 on my bench! Fucking running back by committee! It's the most evil coaching virus set loose upon fantasy football!). Not good. The only good bit of news was that my QB decision (with the help of my advisers) was the right one: Green blew up, with 341 yards, 3 TDs, completing 20 of 25 passes for the highest possible QB rating of 158.3, tallying 53 FFL points to Kitna's solid 30. So at the conclusion of the Sunday *day* games, our beloved Acme squad was leading by a comfortable but not too comfortable score of 185–120.

That was the good news. The bad news was that I *only* had a 65-point lead heading into the ESPN and *MNF* games thanks mostly to Jeff Garcia's absolute torching of the Bengals for 70 FFL points! That's right, Garcia pulled a Clinton-Portis-in-Week-14 and went *off* against the Bengals for 340 yards, 2 *long* TDs, and 1 rushing TD for—I'll repeat it just to torture myself again—70 FFL points! (I can't take the luck factor anymore, the week-to-week uncertainty of it all, the fact that one unlikely player [Garcia] on a fluke day can single-handedly destroy an entire season's worth of hard work, dedication, preparation.) Add in Thomas Jones's 34 points and a few more from the Bonesky TE and defense, and we suddenly have a game, folks. Plus, they still had Horn, Ricky, and Akers to make up those 65 points. Better than no lead, yes, and I've seen 65 points hold up before . . . but I just didn't have a good feeling about this one.

Anyway, so that's where we stand as the Saints and Giants take the field. Good God, Joe Theismann is already clinging to Aaron Brooks's nut-sack like a three-dollar hooker, touting the guy's skill, saying how he and Joe Horn had a private "sit-down" this week to smooth out their differences and get back on the same page—meaning, Theismann says that he expects Horn to have a *big* night. Then, if I'm not mistaken, just as during the Rams-Ravens game a few weeks back, *I swear* I hear him mutter, "And go fuck yourself, Mark."

I stand up and point an accusatory finger at the TV. "Hey, I have an idea, Joe . . . why don't you stand in the pocket one more time so LT can snap your leg in half like a frozen Charleston chew! How's that sound? Huh?"

"Who are you talking to?" Celia calls from the bedroom.

"Um, the TV," I say meekly, and sit back down.

I hear her sigh and turn a page of her book. "Of course you are."

And that bastard Theismann was right. On the third play of the game Brooks heaves a backyard, Nerf football rocket toward the end zone and—big shocker here!—Horn catches it for a 50-yard TD! My eyes nearly pop right out of my head. Just like that, 25 points for Bonesky . . . and the game's not even two *fucking* minutes old! This has *got* to be a joke? Seriously, am I on *Punk'd* right now? Where's Ashton Kutcher? Is he hiding in the pantry?

And then, before I can process the disturbing thought of Ashton Kutcher hiding amongst our canned goods—boom!—Horn catches *another* touchdown. There are no other Saints on the field, apparently! Brooks is *only* throwing to Horn! They're just playing catch. And get this . . . on the second TD Horn grabs a cell phone from underneath the goalpost padding (where all NFL players keep their cell phones), picks it up, and starts dialing! I think he's calling me to tell me my season's over. Seriously, if the phone rings, I'm pulling a Rodney Dangerfield triple Lindy down onto Beacon Street!

I throw the remote across the living room, thankfully hitting a pillow instead of, say, our wedding picture. Sure, technically, I'm still ahead by 20-something points, but let's face it—even if I *do* manage to survive Joe Horn is rampaging through the Superdome end zone, I still have to face Ricky and Akers tomorrow night.

It's over.

Five months of preparation, dedication, work . . . down the drain.

It's over.

Just like that. Our beloved Acme squad has been vanquished by an undeserving foe.

It's . . . over . . .

Project Kick My League's Ass has officially failed.

34

Postgame

Lying in bed the next morning, I have only have one thought: *What do I do now?*

I feel like Jack Nicholson in *About Schmidt* the day after he retired from Woodman of the World Insurance. I'm paralyzed, at a complete and total loss. Seriously, what *do* I do now? Buy an RV and go on a cross-country trip? Start putting little model ships into bottles? Good Lord, do I have to get an actual *job* now?

Normally, on a Monday morning I'd already be getting prepared—up with the sun, strong coffee in hand, staring at the computer, scouring that weekend's injury reports, reading articles, getting geared up for next week's game, and, in this case, for what would have been the most important game of my FF life: the Felon League Super Bowl. But *now?* There's nothing to do. It doesn't matter who got hurt yesterday, who didn't, who is playing whom tonight, tomorrow, or next weekend—my season's *over!* (Sure, OK, next week I play in the Consolation Bowl against the Dream Team, losers of the other semifinal game yesterday. Whoop-de-fucking-do. That's only about money—$200 for third place as opposed to $100 for fourth. There's no pride on the line there. No league-wide respect. Honestly, I couldn't care less about the Consolation Bowl; no one ever remembers who came in third.) I cover my head with my pillow, wondering how much pressure it'd take to suffocate myself.

"That's it. I'm not playing next year," I call in to Celia, who's brushing her teeth in the bathroom. "I hate this game. I'm done."

The little swish-swish-swish of the toothbrush stops. My exceedingly patient wife, who's heard me say virtually the same thing at the end of the last three seasons, doesn't respond for a moment. She's been about as supportive as a wife can possibly be over the past five months. As much as it probably worried her, she put her misgivings aside and *actually encouraged me* to quit a perfectly good job in the middle of a horrible recession to devote all my free time to FF. Best of all, she didn't think twice when I said that I thought it'd make a good subject for a book, she didn't even hesitate—she just grinned and said, "Do it." But this—the moaning, the groaning, the I'm-never-playing-ever-again stuff—is too much. She simply isn't buying it. She knows me too well.

"Wha-ever," she finally says through a mouthful of toothpaste, spits, then resumes her brushing. Swish-swish-swish. And while she does, I can hear her laughing to herself.

She knows that my quitting fantasy football is like Cher quitting plastic surgery . . . it just can't be done! So, painful as it is, I take a look at the bright side: I had quite possibly the best five months of FF I'll ever have. With a job (I'll have to get one sooner or later) and possibly kids on the way in the near future, Project Kick My League's Ass was my last hurrah in total FF immersion.

Celia's simple, Crest-garbled response—"wha-ever"—was her understated way of saying, "Look, don't lose sight of the fact that, above everything else, it was a fun season, and that's what it's all about, isn't it?" When you peel away the layers of strategy, smack talk, message boards, rankings, FF is about taking my already strong love of NFL football and making the season *that much more enjoyable*. And enjoyable it was. I had some classy, talented players to root for—Priest, Marvin, Peyton, Davis, Ward, Green—and I can be proud that I finished 9-4, second overall (my best finish in four years), and scored the second-most points. Sure, I might feel like sucking on the tailpipe of my Jeep *now*, but in time I'll forget about the Bonesky Crushers, Joe bleeping Horn, all of it, and just look ahead to next year.

Celia emerges from the bathroom and climbs into bed next to me. "I'm sorry you lost," she says without the slightest trace of her normal cynicism or sarcasm toward my beloved FF, and plants a minty-fresh kiss on my forehead. "You OK?"

I nod. I feel a little silly for being so down about something so relatively insignificant, and for her feeling that she has to console me. I mean, it's not as if I lost a relative here. Still . . . I should have won. "Yeah, I'm OK," I finally answer. "I just hate losing to teams I should have killed."

She runs her fingers through my matted hair, which I *swear* I had more of five months ago. "Who's Joe Horn?"

"What?"

"You were mumbling about someone named Joe Horn in your sleep this morning. I think you even said 'motherfucker' at one point. Is he a guy on your team?"

I can't help but laugh. "No, but he almost was. Twice. I tried to trade for that bastard all year long but frigging Kevin and Jason kept dicking around with—" I pause, feeling myself getting worked up again—blood rising into my face, hands curling into fists—so I stop, take a deep breath, and let it out evenly, smoothly. "You know what? Never mind. Joe Horn's nobody, but thanks." I sit up and give Celia a big kiss. And while a nasty morning-breath smooch isn't exactly a just reward for everything she's done for me this season, it's a start. I owe her more than she'll ever know.

"Well," she says, shrugging, "whoever he is, he was making you grind your teeth."

"Really?" Jesus.

"Speaking of," she adds before leaving the room, "you might want to brush those fangs of yours."

After showering, I don't even have to check our CBS home page to know I was Adebisi'ed by Horn last night. But, being a glutton for punishment, I finally drag my gloomy ass out of bed and check anyway. His final stats? One hundred thirty-one yards. *Four* touchdowns. *Seventy-three* FFL points! Ricky and Akers could sit out tonight's game and it wouldn't even matter if they chip in more salt-in-the-wound points. Final score: Bonesky 233, Acme 185. While I can take some solace in that I didn't outcoach myself or do anything moronic that directly caused my loss—I made the right lineup moves (e.g., Green at QB) and put the best team out there I possibly could, and yesterday it was the best team on the field, make no mistake—but it still pisses me off that, once again, I fell victim to the FF player's greatest nemesis: the petty whims of the FF gods.

Fitting that I'm ultimately euthanized by the trend I battled all year long: teams having their best days of the season against me. Bonesky had been averaging a Calista Flockhart–thin 102 points per game until Week 15, but they went Chernobyl on me and put up 233. Amazing, just amazing. Despite feeling like a bass that's been gutted, filleted, and thrown onto a George Foreman grill, I know that all my "I'm never playing FF again, waaah waaah waaah" griping doesn't mean anything. I *will* be back next year, just like all the other die-hard FF lunatics around the world whose seasons didn't turn out as they'd planned. I'll be right there at the 2004 Felon League draft, opening my latest "Christmas presents" right alongside Shergul, the Rat Bastards, All-American Angus, the Bonesky Crushers, the Big Dogs—all of my enemies/brothers-in-arms—to see which "toys" we'll get to play with for the next five months. I'll have my Huddle mock drafts and cheat sheets in one hand, a beer in the other, and I'll be grinning from ear to ear as I say, "And with their first pick of the 2004 Felon League season, Acme Fantasy Football, Inc., selects . . ."

After all, I'm a fantasy football junkie and that's what we do.

Epilogue

Season Highlight Reel

In my Felon Fantasy League, the "Anti-Acme"—the Account Guys—behind Ahman Green and Daunte Culpepper, took home the coveted 2004 Felon League Super Bowl title, knocking off the Bonesky Crushers. It was a dark day for me. A team starting Curtis Martin, Isaac Bruce, and Justin McCareins won a championship while a team starting Priest Holmes, Stephen Davis, Marvin Harrison, and Hines Ward *didn't*. Amazing. At least Shergul didn't win. That would have been more pain than I could possibly bear.

Final standings (for the six playoff teams):

Team
1. Account Guys
2. Bonesky Crushers
3. Acme FF, Inc.
4. The Dream Team
5. Rat Bastards
6. All-American Angus

Shergul's Funk Soul Brothers.finished seventh, a startling fall for my FF nemesis (though, in his defense, he lost out on tiebreakers). Big Dogs, Pound Dawgs, SoCo, and the Charlemagnes rounded out the middle. And bringing up the rear, we have Karl ("That Guy") and his NH Hillbillies. Remains to be seen if he'll be back next year. Nice guy, and every league needs a That Guy, but it's clear that he just doesn't have the time anymore. Might be time for the Big Dogs to split up and Erik to get his own squad. One less two-owner team would be fine by me.

As for the Hershey Highway, as Phil "Neo" Kwan predicted way back in Week 10, his greatest challenge would come from Greg "White Monkey" Russo. And lo and behold, Russo overtook "Teddy KGB" Samip *and* Kwan to win the 2004 HH title and become the first repeat champ ever. And the league is pissed. Kwan, sounding exactly like me, reels off the reasons why, if all were right with the universe, he should have won. "I scored *the most points* this season; I am the *only one* to have a winning record against *all* eleven opponents; I have won nineteen of twenty-four games dating back to last season; I had the week's high score more often than anyone else this season, and more than anyone else over the span of two seasons; I've spent more time on this mind-numbing HH e-mail list than any other business, college, or friends lists; and finally, I've watched hours of meaningless games, ESPN *SportsCenter*, and *NFL Matchup*, etc.—time that could have been spent preserving family wealth, providing for my family, raising my children. Please remove me off all fantasy football mailers." But despite the anger and second-guessing, Dave "Reckless Guy" Koller puts a positive spin on it when he says, "If anything, the establishment of a dynasty that now has to be toppled makes the league better, stronger, and more interesting. Unless he [Russo] wins three in a row. Then it's a catastrophe."

And what of the biggest, richest league in the world, the WCOFF? Huddle head honcho David Dorey had a decent showing, finishing 7-5, good for third place in his league, which landed him five hundred bucks. But, when the smoke cleared, the title of 2003–4 FF World Champion went to two regular guys from Hoboken, New Jersey, Alex and Jed. In fact, they were one of the teams originally drafting in my very own League #47! In a weird way, I feel like a proud parent (and, hell, I should get a cut of the action for sticking their players' names on the board straight!). Of the incredible $200,000 victory, Alex says, "I've been doing this for around ten years, and the biggest fantasy pot I've ever won is probably thirty-five hundred. We had the lead heading into the final weekend, and somehow, everyone at work, all my friends, family, everyone knew we were so close. I almost felt like we would have let people down had we not won." So what does one do when he wins two hundred grand playing FF? "I'm looking to put in a pool, pay down some of my mortgage, and, with whatever is left, maybe go on a nice tropical vacation." Does the champ have any advice for people entering in 2004? "Follow your gut. There are so many different opinions out there, but in the end you gotta make the moves you believe in. And be flexible—you may have a strategy heading into draft day, like taking two running backs in the first three rounds, but if the guys aren't there, you have to adjust and take the best guys available. And keep the ego in check. If you were high on a guy and he just isn't panning out, don't be afraid to cut him loose and start over."

What a win. But, I'm not jealous of the money; I'm jealous that, at the awards ceremony in Houston just prior to the Super Bowl, they got to put their arms around Suzy Kolber's sexy little waist during the post-trophy-presentation photo op.

But, really, it's not about the money (or even Suzy Kolber's sexy little waist). It's about having an outlet to keep in touch with friends old and new, to enhance relationships with coworkers, and to enjoy watching NFL football even more than you already did. "Anyone who's in it for the money is in it for the wrong reasons," David Dorey told me all those weeks ago. "You *have* to do it for the pure love of football. That's why I started. I loved football, loved playing around with spreadsheets, and soon learned that I love talking smack, the league camaraderie, all that. Anyone who plays it for money will eventually stop and sure as hell won't enjoy it."

Amen. Just enjoy it, everyone. I know it's a bit of a stretch to take that particular advice from someone who just quit his job to win his league (or not win, as the case may be) and nearly lost his mind in reckless pursuit of a Holy Grail he may not ever find, but I'm learning how to take it all in stride. I'm trying. It's just a game. Have fun. No need for tantrums or smashed TV screens or alienated wives and girlfriends. Your blood pressure will thank you later.

Deep-breathing "serenity now" exercises aside, another thing that FF players often do to help counter the sting of defeat in their favorite/primary league is to hedge their bets, if you will, by playing in multiple leagues. Take Joe from the plane to Vegas. He loses one league? Hell, who cares—he's got eight more to go. In fact, most FF players rarely play in only one league. I'm an exception, I guess. I'm just not a multiple-league kind of guy—that lame-ass, seven-team Yahoo! league I joined doesn't count. But I still managed to find a way to be involved in other leagues this season without any heavy financial, emotional, or time investment: I took a few newbie "protégés" under my wing.

First, there was my college/WCOFF-Vegas-weekend buddy Craig, an avid fantasy baseball player who had just joined his first FF league as co-owner of a team called Turf Toes with his brother, Vincent. And second, remember the groom who cornered me in the bathroom to discuss Marty Booker during his wedding reception? That, a I told you before, was Celia's cousin Wick, who had also joined his first FF league with some coworkers and owned a team called the Stool Pigeons. Since I was the most obsessed FF player Wick and Craig knew, they naturally came to me to find out how to get started. After warning them that I haven't exactly been an FF dynasty over the years, I gladly agreed to help them out. And I had my work cut out for me. While both had played fantasy sports before, they were total FF newbies and, as early as August, were already taking shit from their cocky league-mates for being the designated sacrificial lambs, just a couple of clueless human ATMs. Craig and Vince, who had drawn the number one overall draft pick, were already receiving oh-so-helpful tips from the weasels in their league like "You guys have to take the best tight end available with your first pick, because the position is so thin." What a bunch of douche bags. What fun is it to take advantage of a couple of newbies? It pissed me off, actually, and I therefore made it my mission to help the newbies crush the weasels. After all, I'd been there. I knew what it felt like to be That Guy at his inaugural draft, taking the Chiefs defense too early and dodging beer-can missiles. I didn't want that to happen to them, so I would do everything I could to make sure they kicked ass. For starters, I told them that LaDainian might be the best choice at number one overall. Not Tony Gonzalez, thank you very much.

As for Wick, back in preseason—man, does that feel like decades ago, or what?—I helped him rank his players for the automated draft (blecch!) that would take place in late August. Looking at his league's scoring system, I noticed that, while most leagues award more points for rushing and receiving touchdowns than passing, in Wick's league, *all* touchdowns were six points. Translation? With top-tier stud quarterbacks likely to throw anywhere between thirty and forty touchdowns (while even the best running backs, unless it's an extremely rare Marshall Faulk/Priest Holmes twenty-five-plus TD season, "only" rush for fifteen or twenty per season), the value of said stud quarterbacks shoots through the roof. Hence, while Wick's league-mates automatically went with the stud running back theory, I ranked Peyton Manning and Daunte Culpepper one-two, followed by all the usual running-back suspects.

Throughout the season, I advised both teams on which players to start and bench, which players might make buy-low or sell-high trade candidates, who the hot free agents were, et cetera. Craig and Vincent started calling me the Puppetmaster. Wick reported that his league-mates were confused and angry at his strategic moves, sending him bile-filled e-mails whenever he scooped them on hot free agents or started a sleeper who blew up that week. Secretly, I relished the idea that I was pulling the strings behind the scenes. And the results? Using my occasional input and their own growing FF acumen, both teams steamrolled to their respective league titles. It wasn't even close. Wick rode the magical arms of Daunte and Peyton—not to mention my suggested pickup newly emerged Houston Texans stud RB Domanick Davis—to his championship. Picking Daunte and Peyton one-two leads to our last, but important **Newbie Strategy Tip #18: Always know your league's scoring system.** Too many times, FF players will look at mock drafts and cheat sheets in the preseason and automatically apply those rankings to their own draft in almost cut-and-paste fashion. Bad move. Why? As Wick's league proves, different scoring systems can affect rankings in a huge way. Luckily, Wick had me, the Puppetmaster, watching his back.

As for the Turf Toes, they hopped on LaDainian Tomlinson's back and rode the Chargers' stud RB to the championship of the Langhorne, Pennsylvania–based XFL, a league formed at Vincent's environmental-consulting company. I felt like a proud father, watching my sons not only taking their first steps, but suddenly break into a full forty-yard dash and leap hurdles like Edwin Moses. At the start of the season, Craig actually asked me who Clinton Portis was. By the middle he was saying less newbie-ish things like "A satellite dish and DirecTV Sunday Ticket are mandatory for all men." Then, by season's end, he was making start/bench moves and trades worthy of a ten-year FF vet, eventually upgrading from Aaron Brooks to Matt Hasselbeck for their championship run.

Yes, folks, even though I never did encounter that one, true Yoda-like Jedi master who would help me crank up *my own* FF Force and roll to a league championship, it turns out that I, of all people, was a poor man's Yoda—and Craig and Wick, my two young Paduan apprentices, just might have the FF Force in them after all. But I feel a little sorry for Craig's lovely fiancée, Renda. At this rate, she might not see him again until their tenth anniversary, when my advice will be for him to honor the "diamond" anniversary tradition, or else . . .

While the loss to Bonesky still stings, it makes me feel good knowing that I've helped spread the gospel of FF to three new converts. And more than that, that they both won their league championships. Most of all, I'm glad that I was able to keep in touch with these guys throughout the season and share the common bond of FF with a couple of good friends. (Oh, and that we stuck it to the weasels in their leagues didn't hurt, either. Revenge, I have to admit, was sweet.)

Another way I deflected the pain of the FFL loss was to get back into *real* football full swing. Not that I ever got off the Patriots bandwagon. Again, my true allegiance has been and always will be to my beloved Patriots, not Acme Fantasy Football, Inc. But you know how it is: it's just harder to pay *complete* attention to real football when a fantasy title is at stake. But, the second that Bonesky and Joe Horn put a slug in the back of my skull Mafia-style and knocked me out of the championship hunt, I was riveted to the Patriots' glorious playoff and Super Bowl run. I actually got to go to the Pats AFC Championship win against the Colts at Gillette Stadium. Man, what a night! Snow, beer, good friends, and an ass-kicking from start to finish. As in 2001, there was just something . . . magical . . . in the air that told all sixty-five thousand spectators, and everyone watching on national TV, that there was no way these New England Patriots were going to lose again this season—and they didn't, finally upending the scrappy, gutty Carolina Panthers in one of the best Super Bowls in recent mammary . . . um, I mean memory. Sorry, Janet Jackson Boobgate is still fresh in my mind. ("Wardrobe malfunction" my ass.)

Another interesting note from the Super Bowl: aside from my season-long man-crush, Stephen Davis (who ultimately let me down in Week 15), and *maybe* his Panther teammate WR Steve Smith, who had a good season (when he wasn't beating the shit out of his own teammates in team meetings, that is), there was not one, single fantasy stud on either Super Bowl team. Not a one. Just goes to show you once again: there's a big difference between what leads to success in *real* football, and what makes a winner in fantasy football. And in case there's any confusion (are you listening, Norman Chad?), I'd trade a Felon League Super Bowl title for a Patriots Super Bowl championship every single time!

Speaking of yours truly, what are my plans for the 2004 season? Well, I'll be back for another shot at the Felon League title; that goes without saying. But I'll also be adding a new wrinkle to my FF career. In January, I received the following voice mail: "Hi, Mark, this is Larry calling from the World Championship of Fantasy Football. We received your hunderd-dollar deposit check and you are confirmed as a participant for 2004." And not just as a facilitator, folks—as a team owner.

Vegas? An unholy alliance of Felon League enemies (Me, Shergul, Big Dog, "Rat Bastard" Blaz, CJ) joining forces to buy a team and make a run at the prestigious WCOFF title and the $200,000 pot? Yikes. To use one of my favorite athlete-interview clichés, it sounds as if I'm about to take my FF obsession to the "next level."

And, who knows, maybe when next season rolls around, I'll have another perfectly good job to quit.

Epilogue

One Year Later

When my editor and I first discussed my writing an epilogue for the paperback version of *Committed*, I was a little hesitant.

Don't get me wrong, I love the book to death. But as you just read, my tale ended in less-than-heroic fashion. I knew that jumping back into that world again would be painful, and, honestly, I just didn't feel like reliving the now infamous 2003 "Joe Horn incident"—he quickly became Joe *Effing* Horn, much in the same way that Bucky Dent became Bucky *Effing* Dent—especially after so much time has passed, the wounds have started to at least scab, and the nice doctors and nurses at the institution worked so hard in those therapy sessions to make me forget all about my Felon League failures and, instead, just picture cute little kitties . . . do you see the pretty little kitties, Markie? . . . sure you do . . . just look at the cute little kitties playing with their widdle iddy biddy balls of string and forget allllll about Joe Horn kicking your ass in the semifinals . . . thaaaaat's it, nice kitties . . . good kitties . . .

Sorry. Where was I? Oh yeah—look, it's been more than a year since that cell-phone game, and it still stings. Ask any Vietnam vet, or anyone who accidentally saw *Catwoman*: some atrocities just stick with you no matter how much time has passed. Do you think Joe Theismann can walk past Lawrence Taylor without flinching? Do you think Scott Norwood can hear the words "wide" or "right"—even independently of one another—and not develop a severe eye-twitch on the spot? And, most importantly, do you think Right Said Fred will ever get back together? (Answers: "No," "Uh-uh," and "A man can dream, can't he?") As such, I can never, *ever* forget or forgive the crimes against humanity that Joe Horn committed in 2003. And I figured that writing a stinking epilogue would just open old gnarly wounds. No thanks.

But I then realized that this reaction was not only irrational, immature, and quite possibly clinically insane, it was selfish. *Look at all the nice emails you've gotten from readers,* I admonished myself. *For whatever reason, people got attached to your 2003 Acme squad. They want to know how your 2004 team did. They want to know how your unholy alliance of Felon League mates did at the 2004 WCOFF in Vegas. They want to know who won the Jersey-based Hershey Highway League. They want to know if Celia finally smartened up and ran off with the cable guy.*

So, even if I might end up with my own Scott Norwood eye-twitch, I realized I *had to* write an epilogue and give readers the answers they deserved, this despite the urge to just get lost in my utopian world where little kitties play with string and Acme always, *always* wins the Felon League. Plus, if I refused, my editor threatened to leak to the press that *Committed* was in fact ghost-written by a highly trained chimpanzee named Bonkers, who, between you and me, was an arrogant sonofabitch . . . always hovering over me in his smoking jacket and ascot, blowing his nauseating pipe smoke in my face and reminding me that he had an MFA from Iowa State and his short fiction had been published in several esteemed literary journals, and disdainfully referring to me as "satire sports boy." Ooooh, yeah, we're all *so* impressed, Bonkers. Fine, you got me . . . I've never been published in fucking *Ploughshares*, but at least I don't throw my own feces against the wall.

Anyway, that's all I needed to hear. I'd be damned if I'd leave my kind readers hanging, or, worse, give that tire-swinging, Nietzsche-quoting poseur any credit for my hard work. An epilogue there would be . . .

The 2004 FF season began in Las Vegas at the WCOFF. The unholy Felon League alliance—myself, Shergul, Blaz, and CJ (our fifth co-owner, Big Dog, wasn't able to make it, so I'll say for the record that he chose to stay home and pick out window treatments)—arrived in Sin City the first weekend in September. Our wives came and hung out together, shopped, gambled. The boys strategized and plotted for draft day, and formulated a sound game plan knowing that we'd be drafting from the number two spot in League #8, and would no doubt land either Priest or LT, depending on who team #1 chose. Well, we got LT. Fine by us. Good start. He was good for an easy 1,600–1,800 total yards and 20 TDs. For the remaining nineteen rounds, Shergul and I huddled and called the shots at the draft table—even though our Felon League past made Liza Minelli and David Gest look like a more harmonious pairing—all with the considerable input of Blaz and CJ who lurked nearby via cell phone (and had the absentee Big Dog on *their* cell phones). Surprisingly, by the end of the marathon six-hour draft, the unholy alliance actually survived twenty-something rounds without getting into an Ultimate Fighting Championship-esque brawl. We snagged obvious studs like Daunte Culpepper, and nabbed some nice sleepers like Brandon Stokley, Willis McGahee, Keary Colbert, Michael Clayton, and Michael Pittman. Overall, a nice squad, albeit one with more than a few eventual busts (Travis Henry, Laverneus Coles, Peerless Price). But we were happy, and spent the remainder of the weekend going out for kick-ass dinners with the ladies and watching CJ's wife, Lisa, terrorize the blackjack tables like a rogue MIT student. Blaz and I even managed to squeeze in a ride on the "New York, New York" rollercoaster (and, as long as I'm disparaging Big Dog, I might as well reveal that Blaz screams like a little girl). As for the WCOFF regular season, we ran into bad luck in League #8, catching teams on their best weeks—sound familiar?—and finishing the eleven-week regular season at a pedestrian 6-5. Still, we had a shot at making the money round based on high points. But, alas, thanks mostly to starting the wrong shitty WRs on their most shitty days—damn you, Coles and Price—we fell a few points short on the final weekend. In the end, we finished 26th out of 100 in the consolation round. I have no idea what that means, but it sounds better than nothing. It was fun as hell, though, and we'll be making Vegas/WCOFF an annual migration . . . if only for the rollercoaster.

Next, we come to the Hershey Highway. Sirius radio host Cenk wrote: "[Computer] Kaan jumped out to an early lead with Culpepper, Dillon, and Tiki Barber. At one point, he proclaimed, 'I'm high-stepping now. This is my year.' I believe he was 7-0." Last year's *Matrix*-quoting Zen master, Phil Kwan started out miserably at 1-4 . . . then he traded for Peyton and proceeded to win ten in a row, catching Kaan and eventually passing him. But there was one problem, according to the Cenk. "Tolga, a.k.a. Dr. Strangelove, had cobbled together a potion of players that kept putting up magical numbers week after week," he reported. "Antonio Gates, Rudi Johnson, Muhsin Muhammed, Edgerrin James, et cetera. But he also started fifty-point Billy Volek at the right times." Soon, it became apparent that, down the stretch, it would be Tolga versus Kwan. "And neither one of these guys had ever won a HH championship before, so, finally, this would be someone's year of redemption." Meanwhile, in crucial Week 16, "Neo" Kwan ran into his old friend and new nemesis, 2002/2003 back-to-back HH champ, Greg "The White Monkey" Russo. Russo had payback on his mind: he's the one who foolishly traded Peyton to Kwan all those weeks ago; and Kwan had payback in mind for getting caught from behind *last season* by Russo. Battle royale. Hatfields versus McCoys. Suge Knight versus Dr. Dre. "And in yet another dagger in his best friend's back," Cenk reported, "Russo took Kwan down again! And it was over . . . Dr. Tolga cruised to his first ever championship and is still smiling as we speak. And Kwan, finishing second yet again, could only mutter to Russo as he lay bloodied on the ground, 'Et tu, Brute' and 'I shall return.'" Congrats to the good doctor, Tolga! And, Kwan, I feel your pain, my man. Trust me, I do.

And, finally, the one you've been waiting for, the 2004 Felon League. My season can be described in four words: same old, same old. After a 2-3 start, I roared down the stretch after pulling a Kwan and trading for Peyton right before he started stampeding toward Dan Marino-ville. I rolled in eight straight games, a streak that, in my league where parity—just like in the real NFL—runs rampant, was unprecedented. Fielding a juggernaut of Peyton at QB; Edge and (a tough but nice choice of) Domanick Davis, Michael Pittman and Julius Jones at RB; (falling stud) Andre Johnson at one WR; all-world Gonzo at TE; Kaeding at kicker; Redskins D/ST. And at the other WR? Get this—Joe Horn. Yes, *that* Joe Horn! He who drove me into a padded cell. I traded Mewelde Moore for him mid-season—Karl of the NH Hillbillies had *not one* healthy RB, Moore was starting for the injured Michael Bennett and the hooch-smoking Onterrio Smith, and Horn was playing horribly . . . buy low, sell high, baby! As karma would have it, Horn exploded for me down the stretch. Suddenly, in a very therapeutic turn of events, I loved Joe Horn! (But it was still a little weird having him on my team, kinda like seeing David Wells in a Sox uniform). Anyway, can you believe the squad I had in a competitive twelve-team league? Last year's team was good, but, man, this year I almost felt guilty running those guys out onto the field every week. In the end, I won my first regular season title outright with a best-ever FFL record of 10-3, snatching the #1 overall playoff seed and a coveted first-round bye in the process.

Coveted, my ass. I hate first-round byes. Hate 'em. Call me crazy, call me unable to distinguish fantasy from reality, but I just don't like having my guys sitting and watching for a week, getting stale, lazy, complacent, or hitting the cyber strip clubs, getting pinched for public cyber intoxication, resisting cyber arrest, or, worse, picking up a cyber STD from some cyber skank. Plus, like many sports fans, I'm insanely superstitious. After all, I had a first-round bye in 2003, too, and we all know how *that* turned out, with the erstwhile despised Horn picking up that goddamn cell phone and . . .

(Kitties . . . Markie, just envision the cute little kitties in their happy place . . .)

I just wanted to get right into the action in Week 14 . . . you know, keep that momentum going. But, alas, I once again had to wait an extra week to see whom I'd be battling in the Week 15 semi-finals. But I shouldn't have been worried, right? After all, our beloved Acme squad was once again a juggernaut, with total studs at every position. I was a menace just waiting to explode, right? I would cruise through Week 15 against the lowest-seeded remaining playoff team and land in the FFL Super Bowl, right? This was *finally*, finally going to be my year, right? *Right?* Wrong.

Any Peyton owner knows what happened in Week 15. He was our glorious *Titanic* all year long, majestically gliding across the ocean, unstoppable, his play-action passes as crisp as the roast duckling in the first-class dining room, his receivers flashing and sparkling like so many crystal chandeliers. But, next thing you know, I watched Peyton slammed into his iceberg—the Baltimore Ravens defense—and the *Titanic* was instantly reduced to the *S.S. Acme Is Cursed*, and began taking on water. Fast. Yes, with a positively James Hazlewood-esque performance, Peyton singlehandedly wrecked millions of fantasy teams across the land, their owners watching in horror as the NFL's most unsinkable creation went belly-up, sending their seasons, just like that poor, frozen Leo DiCaprio, down to a watery grave. Meanwhile—here's a little lemon juice for your paper cuts, sir—Pop Warner QBs like Billy Volek and Kerry Collins seemingly borrowed Peyton's arm for a day and exploded, carrying *their* lucky owners into the next round. Shit, I think Ryan Leaf threw for 350 and 4 TDs that weekend, and, last I heard, he was working at a Jiffy-Lube.

So, folks, after averaging a whopping 160 points per game over my wrecking ball eight-game win streak, our beloved Acme squad sank in Week 15 with a paltry 100. But it wasn't *all* Peyton's fault; Andre, Gonzo, and Edge didn't exactly carry their weight, either. And, as fate would have it, even if they all *had* exploded, I would have lost anyway because the meddling FF gods—oh how they taunt me!—decided to give my opponent, Big Dog, several utterly improbable explosions from bums/backups/busts like Jerry Porter, Larry Johnson and Chad Pennington. When I saw the CBS cut-away to Porter's not first, not second, but *third* TD of the day, I fell into some sort of trance, maybe even blacked out. Celia told me later that I'd zombie-walked into the kitchen and started to mix a Draino on the rocks with a twist of Murphy's Oil Soap. Thankfully, she knows by now to be on hand like an EMT during fantasy playoff games, and had wisely followed me in, slapped me once across the face—hard, with most of her palm and part of her wedding ring—and removed the cleaning supplies from my hands. I just stood there, blinking, nearly catatonic. I felt like Amber Frey. *Huh? What do you mean you weren't in Paris? What do you mean Peyton only got eight points? You were actually at Laci's candlelight vigil when you called me and said you were in Paris watching fireworks, you sick bastard? Larry Johnson and Jerry Porter defeated Peyton, Edge, Domanick, Horn, Andre, and Gonzo? But . . . I . . . what . . . this makes no sense . . . none of this makes any sense . . .*

When the smoke cleared, Big Dog's boys put up 226 points and my 2004 season crash-landed with a disappointing third-place finish. (Yeah, yeah, in the consolation game I soundly defeated last year's champs, the Account Guys, 135–60; woo-friggin'-hoo.) Bottom line, my studs crapped out when it counted in the playoffs. Hey, that sounds just like a certain Marino TD record-breaking quarterback I know! But, I should only complain so much. If I enjoyed the sweetness of Peyton's amazing 49-TD season, I'll take the sour Week 15 like a man, too. Problem is, I'm not a man; I'm a fantasy football player. We're unable to rationally break down proper psychological responses like that and be Dr. Phil-ized into submission and meek acceptance. We'd rather kick and curse and scream, *"Why did you have to crap out when it counted, Peyton?! If you weren't so*

*busy cheering on guys to 'cut that meat' maybe you'd have played better
against the Ravens! Damn you to Hades, foul FF gods!"*

And, now, the *real* painful part of this, the real reason I didn't want to
write this epilogue, the part that makes last season's Joe Horn knife-in-
the-back seem downright pleasant: my longtime fantasy sports nemesis,
Shergul, won his third Felon League championship, defeating Big Dog,
in Week 16. *Shergul!* Seeing him win it all was like watching the ball go
under Buckner's glove, Aaron Boone homering off of Wakefield, and Zed
sodomizing Marcellus Wallace all on a continuous loop. In the days following, I felt a bitterness I haven't felt since, well, ever. I seriously considered gouging my own eyes out, Oedipus-style, so as to never have to
witness such horrors ever again.

But, thanks to some of the illegal Mexican under-the-counter phar-
maceuticals left over from my aforementioned hospital stay, I can at least
take solace in knowing that I had a good draft, made some very smart free
agent moves and trades—I picked up both Pittman and Julius Jones off
waivers; traded Favre and Thomas Jones to another RB-starved team,
SoCo, when their values were at their peak in exchange for the thunder-
bolt-slinging Zeus of FF 2004, Peyton. And, for yet another season, I was
right in the hunt. Hell, I had my best regular season record ever. Yeah,
that's it . . . just keep telling yourself that, Mark . . . *kittens . . . cute kittens
playing with string . . .*

So, that's the 2004 wrap-up. Felon League and WCOFF. Oh-for-two. I
still remain one-hundred-percent championship-free. But I wouldn't trade
any of this for anything, win or lose. I love playing fantasy football. I love
writing about it. And I loved meeting and talking to an eclectic mix of FF
junkies out there, from our wunderkind Jeremy (who's still kicking ass at
Georgetown and preparing to rule the sports world, if not the actual
world) and the Chicago Bears' Patrick Mannelly (who's still one of the
NFL's best long snappers) to Dave Dorey and Whitney Walters (who are
still doing their thing at the Huddle) and Matt Lauer (though, looking
back, I now realize that might have just been a stress-related hallucination).

More than anything, though, I've really enjoyed hearing from so many
of you—my fellow *Fight Club* members—who also simply can't get
enough of this crazy, all-consuming passion every NFL season. I'm so
glad that you related so much to my Quixotic quest for Felon League
glory and got a few laughs along the way, so keep those emails comin' to

mark@markstamant.com. Bonky tries—er, *I* try—to answer each one in a timely, semi-coherent manner.

And, hell, all's not lost. If the Red Sox can *finally* win a World Series and erase that fabricated Curse of the Fat, Drunk Hot Dog Eater, then anything's possible. (Speaking of, I told Theo Epstein I was blind drunk when I wrote the infamous resignation letter, and he welcomed me back into the bosom of Red Sox Nation; he's nice like that . . . as is Celia, who, you'll be glad to know, hasn't divorced me yet). So trust me, I'll be back next year for another shot at that elusive Felon League title. I'll always come back.

What else am I going to do . . . *get a job?*

—Mark St. Amant
January 2004
Boston, Mass.

Appendix I

Newbie Strategy Tips

I know that you've already seen these little newbie strategy tips and other help-ful hints in the previous pages. Still, it's always nice to have a handy little crib sheet culled from experts and fellow FF players alike, advising you on everything from trade etiquette to draft strategy to team management—if you're a newbie, that is. If not, and you decide that you have no need for the remedial drivel below, I once again invite you to skip ahead. Or tear this whole section out to wrap some fish, line a birdcage, use as toilet paper, whatever. You already paid for the book (which I appreciate), so, please, do with it what you will. Except the toi-let paper thing. That'd be disturbing.

1. *Don't panic if your studs/top draft picks look sluggish out of the gates.* (Page 105.) As I wrote earlier, if healthy, nine out of ten studs will always rise to the top, so hold on to them, and certainly don't trade them while their value is lower than usual.
2. *When offering a trade, always make your first offer a good one, but never make it your best.* (Page 106.) Like in any game of chance involving bluffs and bartering, while you want to let the other "player" know you're serious and aren't wasting his time, you don't want to show all your cards right away.
3. *Always be as polite, sane, and respectful as possible when turning down a trade so as not to damage any future trade relationship.* (Page 107.) Even if the offer made is downright ludicrous, there's no need to alien-ate a fellow owner. You might need one of his players someday, and you don't want to be remembered as that jerk who berated him during trade talks.
4. *Always take what the draft gives you.* (Page 112.) In other words, never get so locked into a draft strategy—e.g., automatically taking two running backs first, even if there are better-value QBs or WRs available—that you're flustered or thrown off when the draft doesn't go as expected.
5. *Backups to other owners' injury-prone studs, especially running backs, make (a) great trade bait to those very same owners and (b) might turn*

into studs themselves if the starter gets hurt. (Page 117.) E.g., all of Marshall Faulk's backups over the years—Lamar Gordon, Trung Canidate, et al.—have been solid starters when Faulk inevitably missed some games. So, find out which players are injury-prone and play in a system catering to RB success (Denver, Carolina, St. Louis, etc.) and pounce on their backups late in your drafts.

6. *FF is all business. Whether it's in the draft or during trades, never let emotions dictate how you value a player.* (Page 136.) Other owners will often try to prey upon your home-team allegiances to trick you into giving up more than you should in a trade. E.g., if you're a Vikings fan, and you want Randy Moss, the Moss owner might say, "OK, I'll trade you Moss and Joey Harrington for Terrell Owens and Peyton Manning."

7. *The biggest names aren't always the best fantasy players.* (Page 142.) If you remember from the Jeremy Wien chapter, both Troy Aikman and Tom Brady are good examples of this axiom. Great NFL players? Hell, yes. They have the Super Bowl rings to prove it. Great fantasy players? Nope. Average at best. Don't be fooled by what you read in the papers.

8. *Someone trying to trade you more guys than they're getting back, claiming they're giving you "depth," is usually trying to Adebisi you.* (Page 178.) One of the oldest tricks in the trading book is the "I'll give you two guys for one" scam. Usually, what the other owner is saying is "I'll give you two slabs of meat rotting on my bench for one of your studs." Unless his two players are his Randy Moss and Peyton Manning, and your one player is Olandis Gary, study the lopsided deal long and hard before pulling the trigger. (Then again, if someone is offering you Moss and Manning for Gary, you're clearly playing in a league with your four-year-old brother, your pet hamster, and that crazy homeless guy around the corner who yells at mailboxes.)

9. *If you keep your ear to the ground and listen for even the most random information (such as a drug bust), you can parlay someone else's misery into a joyous upgrade for your team.* (Page 193.) This is a simple matter of research. If you don't have the time, *make* the time to scan other cities' sports pages, FF websites, anything you can read to get a handle on what's going on around the league.

10. *Always, always scan your fellow owners' rosters to spot weaknesses you can exploit in a trade.* (Page 196.) This is loosely connected to #9, but the same general thought applies: it's almost as important to know what's going on with your league-mates' players as it is with *your own* players. E.g., one of your league-mates' starting QB, Daunte Culpepper, is about to miss a few games. He only has, say, sixty-three-year-old Neil O'Donnell as a backup. He clearly needs a QB upgrade. You just happen to have both Matt Hasselbeck and Trent Green, and you need a running back upgrade. What's this? He just happens to have great running backs! I think you know where I'm heading with this.

11. *Never make a lowball offer to start trade talks, as it ruins your credibil-*

ity and makes future trades harder than necessary. (Page 198.) See tip
#2. This is the only NST that I hit on twice in the book. Why? Because I
think that trades can often make or break one's season, and you just
don't want to screw them up. And offering a pile of cow dung for solid-
gold bricks right off the bat is the fastest way to kill a trade.

12. *Always run your best lineup out there regardless of whom your opponent
    is starting.* (Page 206.) One of the most dangerous examples of "over-
    coaching" in FF typically involves starting a QB who might be throwing to
    your opponent's wide receivers, or WRs who will be catching passes from
    your opponent's QB, all in a lame attempt to poach some of your oppo-
    nent's points. Don't outsmart yourself. Anyone on any message board out
    there will tell you, always start your studs, regardless of whom the enemy
    is starting.

13. *Don't be pushy during trade negotiations, because that'll make the
    other owner think you're trying to sneak something by him.* (Page 210.)
    See tip #11. The second-fastest way to kill a trade? Acting like a used-
    car salesman. Nobody likes to feel strong-armed into making a deal, so,
    if you feel the urge to ask, "What do I have to do to put you into a brand-
    new player *today*?" . . . don't. Let him know you're eager to deal, and give
    him reasons why the deal helps both teams, but don't be too slick. That
    all but guarantees he'll think you're trying to disguise a Yugo as a
    Porsche Boxster.

14. *Late in the season, depth doesn't matter as much. If you have valuable
    bench depth that you can parlay into an upgrade to your starting team,
    do it.* (Page 221.) Self-explanatory. It's no use having Fred Taylor and
    Hines Ward on your bench if they can be packaged and turned into Priest
    Holmes or Marvin Harrison.

15. *Know your league rules inside and out.* (Page 221.) Speaking of late-
    season trades, you don't want to plan to upgrade your team sometime
    around Week 12, only to discover your league trade deadline is Week
    11. Every league website should have a link to a constitution and/or
    rules. Find them. Read them. Make flash cards if necessary. Just know
    them.

16. *The schedule always finds a way to even out over a season, so don't panic
    if you're getting hammered by high scores early on.* (Page 247.) The FF
    gods can be cruel, as you've just learned, but they're usually equal-oppor-
    tunity tormentors. So, if you're having an Acme-esque season early on
    (i.e., facing every f%#*ing team on its f%#*ing high-scoring week), don't
    let it get you down, especially if total points play any role in deciding your
    league's playoff teams. Then again, I wasn't exactly the poster boy for
    patience and tranquillity this season, so this is more of a "do as I say, not
    as I do" tip.

17. *Gather as much information as possible, weigh the options carefully,
    compare defenses, weather conditions, whatever you have to do . . . but,
    in the end, always, always go with your gut.* (Page 253.) In other words,

don't let articles on websites, message-board advice, or any other outside influences run your team for you. Use all the input you can to make an educated decision, but when it's time for a final call, even the greenest newbie has to trust his/her instincts.

18. *Always know your league's scoring system.* (Page 277.) This goes hand in hand with #15. As we learned with Wick, whose scoring system awarded equal points to passing, receiving, and rushing TDs (thus increasing the value of QBs), a scoring system can greatly affect how you rank players for your draft.

And because I believe you can never get too much advice, here are a few more gems from the folks in the Huddle forums who are as obsessed as I am—probably even more so—and think about this stuff constantly. Not all of the words of wisdom are foolproof (what in FF is?), and some advice hits upon past themes, but here are a few dos and don'ts for you newbies to consider anyway:

"Don't draft on name alone. When you're talking about players at the latter stages of their careers, it can be a problem. Big newbie error. And don't take rookies too high. Rooks are tough, especially QBs and WRs."

"Don't use magazines; they're usually out-of-date when they hit newsstands. Don't ask for advice at the draft from your fellow drafters. Don't draft like a homer. Just because you like the team doesn't mean that its players are FF studs. Get four or five 'cheat sheet' rankings from different websites and then compile your own. Finally, don't drink until the draft is over."

"Don't take a QB too early. Fourth, fifth round at the earliest. Load up on RBs and WRs, because after the top three or so QBs, they're all pretty much the same. For example, I got McNair and Brad Johnson last year in the ninth and eleventh rounds respectively."

"Don't take chances with your first-round pick. Take a solid, reliable producing stud. Avoid injury-prone players (e.g., Marshall Faulk) or inconsistent performers (e.g., Corey Dillon). You do not win your league in the first round, but you sure as hell can lose it."

"Avoid RBBC at all costs."

"Keep up-to-date on who went where in the off-season, who's installing a different kind of offense, who's injured."

"Avoid WRs on new teams unless they are around in late rounds. It usually takes a season for a QB and a WR to get on the same page."

"Teams with crappy defenses are usually good for WRs."

"Study the changes on a team's O-line."

"After solidifying RB, QB, and WRs, think about a defense; a top defense will outpoint a top-teir TE during the year."

"Know your league's lineup scoring and rules. For example, if your league only allows two QBs per team, and everyone else has already drafted their two QBs, there's no reason for you to take a QB before your last pick . . . so focus on other positions until then."

"Always wait until the last two rounds to draft a kicker."

"Even if you do not draft two stud RBs early, if you draft value (i.e., stud WRs, QBs, TEs), you can make trades to get the right team later."

"Don't rely upon anything your league-mates tell you. They don't care if you f*ck up."